Travels in the Interior of America in the Years 1809, 1810, and 1811

Travels in the Interior of America in the Years 1809, 1810, and 1811

By John Bradbury

Foreword by Donald Jackson

University of Nebraska Press
Lincoln and London

First Bison Book printing: 1986
Most recent printing indicated by the first digit below:
1   2   3   4   5   6   7   8   9   10

Library of Congress Cataloging-in-Publication Data
Bradbury, John, b. 1768.
   Travels in the interior of America in the years
1809, 1810, and 1811.
   "Bison book"—
Reprint. Originally published: 2nd ed. London:
Sherwood, Neely, and Jones, 1819. With new foreword.
   1. Mississippi River Valley—Description and travel.
2. Missouri River Valley—Description and travel.
3. Ohio River Valley—Description and travel.
4. Indians of North America—Northwestern States.
5. Botany—Missouri River Valley—History—19th century.
6. Osage language—Glossaries, vocabularies, etc.
7. United States—Description and travel—1783–1848.
8. Bradbury, John, b. 1768—Journeys—Middle West.
I. Title.
F353.B80   1986   977'.02   85-24615
ISBN 0-8032-6076-8 (pbk.)

This Bison Book edition reproduces the 1904 edition by Reuben
Gold Thwaites, published by the Arthur H. Clark Company as
Volume V of Early Western Travels, 1748–1846. The original map
has been omitted; a new foreword and a new map have been added.

CONTENTS

CONTENTS

FOREWORD
by Donald Jackson

On the early western frontier, it was difficult not to get involved in great events. A keen observer who had the ability to write well might readily become a kind of roving reporter although his original purpose in traveling may have been far different.

Perhaps he was a European nobleman like Maximilian, prince of Wied, with a passion to study Indian life and natural history in the Americas. Or an artist like George Catlin, who gave up a law practice in Pennsylvania and came west to make Indian portraits. More often, our amateur reporter was a scientist who, living at a time when every bend in the river might bring new species of plants and animals into view, attached himself to an expedition to collect specimens. The college student of today would call it a field trip.

John Bradbury's field trip brought him to St. Louis at a time when the great Lewis and Clark expedition had recently ended and the overland trek of the Astorians to the Pacific Northwest was just beginning. Traders had gone as far west as the eastern edges of the Rockies, and American farmers were raising corn and tobacco along the lower Missouri where only Indians and French traders had ventured a few short years earlier. Bradbury came there to study botany, and was the first trained botanist to work west of the Mississippi, but he is more important to us as a perceptive reporter.

Born in 1768 at Stalybridge, England, he had already become a notable botanist in his native country when he was sent to the United States by English scientific societies for a specific reason. He was to see if the supply of cotton from the United States could be increased. When he learned that New Orleans, where he had planned to go, was not a suitable area for raising cotton, he turned his attention to plant life on the western frontier. Apparently little came of his assignment to increase cotton production for export.

Although a colleague called him "old Bradbury," he was only about forty-one when he arrived from England, and was described as "swarthy, broad-shouldered, and of medium height, amiable yet stubborn in disposition."[1] He was the guest of ex-president Jefferson at Monticello for a week or so, spending every day in the woods and finding—even on Jefferson's land at Monticello—many plants hitherto unknown to science. Then he headed for St. Louis bearing a letter that Jefferson had addressed to Meriwether Lewis, recommending Bradbury for his botanical knowledge and his "correct conduct." What Jefferson hoped was that Lewis would seize the chance to use Bradbury as a consultant in putting together the scientific findings of the Lewis and Clark expedition. Trained men like Bradbury, as Jefferson well knew, would soon lessen the value of Lewis and Clark's findings through their own investigations.

Lewis was then governor of Upper Louisiana, while his old traveling companion William Clark was superintendent of Indian affairs west of the Mississippi. Unfortunately, by the time Bradbury arrived in St. Louis the nation was mourning the death of Meriwether Lewis—apparently by suicide. The problems in both his personal and public life had contributed to a melancholy that he could not overcome. An account of the Lewis and Clark adventure was thus further delayed, and full publication of their journals was not to occur for a century. Doubtless Bradbury talked plants with Clark and examined Lewis and Clark's collections, but there is no evidence that he gave any substantial assistance. He did become well acquainted with Clark, and wrote home that he found the man "more intelligent in Natural History than . . . might be expected."

Among the plant specimens that Lewis and Clark had brought down from the high plains, where the growing season was short, was Indian corn they had obtained from the sedentary and crop-growing Mandan and Arikara tribes. Bradbury raised specimens in his St. Louis garden—as Jefferson was doing in Virginia—and sent seeds off to Liverpool. Jefferson called it "quarantine" corn from the original meaning of the word, a period of forty days; he hoped the early corn would be useful for second plantings on his Virginia plantation when rains washed out the year's first sowing.

After canceling plans to examine the plant life of the Arkansas River, Bradbury decided to see the upper Missouri country. In the spring of 1811, he was invited to join the expedition of Wilson Price Hunt, a partner in the new Pacific Fur Company that had been formed by the well-known fur magnate John Jacob Astor. Astor's plan was to send one group of men up the Missouri and overland to the mouth of the Columbia while another group sailed around the tip of South America to combine their forces. The result was to be Astoria, a fur-trading post where the company could engage in trade with Europe, the Far East, and eastern seaports of the United States.

Hunt and his party were opposed by a rival group, the Missouri Fur Company, which was not going anywhere near the Pacific but had to compete with Hunt for employees and the good will of the Indians along the Missouri. This second expedition was led by Manuel Lisa, an aggressive French trader who was about Bradbury's age but seemed much older. He had already been up the Missouri and the Yellowstone as far as the mouth of the Big Horn, developing the fur industry. Bradbury was to have ample dealings with both parties, which found themselves moving up the river at the same time.

Bradbury was delighted to find in Hunt's entourage a fellow botanist, Thomas Nuttall, though he has little to say about him in his narrative and Nuttall — destined to become a more famous botanist than Bradbury — left no account of this trip. Also among the "guests" was Henry Marie Brackenridge, an author and traveler whose views of the trip as far upriver as the Mandans would become a book entitled *Journal of a Voyage up the Missouri*. Although Brackenridge would be riding in Lisa's keelboat, there would be plenty of opportunities for Bradbury to socialize with him.

The Astorians, as they would later become known, left St. Louis in mid-March 1811. The rivalry between Hunt and Lisa appeared early in the competition for the services of an interpreter. Pierre Dorion, son of the Pierre Dorion who had accompanied Lewis and

Clark, had been hired by Hunt. Manuel Lisa used an old legal ploy, seeking a judgment against him for a whiskey debt as a means of calling him home. Bradbury and Nuttall, who had not yet departed from St. Louis, hurried overland to intercept Hunt's brigade and warn him of the danger that he would lose his interpreter. Later they would both play a mediating role in conflicts between Lisa and Hunt.

Because Bradbury had been roaming the areas inland from St. Louis since coming west late in 1809, and had even made a previous trip up the river as far north as the Mandans, we can assume that his narrative is a composite of all his experiences. When he writes that the expedition stopped on the third day and visited with Daniel Boone, that renowned Kentuckian now residing on his last frontier, it may not have been Bradbury's first meeting with the old man. When he writes that on the next morning they were visited by John Colter and heard from his own lips the famous tale of how he outran the Blackfeet and saved his life in the Yellowstone country, we can imagine that to Bradbury the story was already well known. Yet his account became the first to spread the story widely and in detail. Later, Washington Irving would devote several pages to it in his *Astoria* (1836), and a small book entitled *John Colter: His Years in the Rockies* would be penned by Burton Harris as recently as 1952.

One of Lisa's employees was Toussaint Charbonneau, a half-blood interpreter who was accompanied by his wife, Sacagawea, more famous than her husband after the couple had returned with the Lewis and Clark expedition.

Hunt's four keelboats and Lisa's single one raced up the Missouri. Lisa hoped that the combined manpower of the two groups might enable them to pass through the country of the Teton Sioux unmolested. He also seemed to fear that Hunt, if he arrived first among the Sioux, would incite the Indians to attack the lagging vessel, for at least two leaders of the Hunt party, Ramsay Crooks and Robert McClellan, believed that Lisa had turned the Sioux against them during a trading expedition two years earlier.

By the time the Astorians had cleared the future site of Omaha, leaving behind the lower Missouri with its hazardous underwater obstructions, Lisa was only four days' travel below them. He sent Toussaint Charbonneau ahead to ask Hunt to wait. But Hunt, fearing that Lisa, if he got ahead, would agitate the hostile Indians, refused.

When Lisa's boat finally caught up, the flotilla of five vessels continued upstream together—but not in complete harmony. Lisa again tried to lure Dorion away from Hunt, and perhaps only the intervention of the neutral Bradbury and Brackenridge prevented a serious confrontation. Finally the rival leaders decided to keep the Missouri between them, Lisa staying close to one shore, Hunt to the other.

Historian Irving described the enthusiastic Bradbury as a man combining the hunter and sportsman with the naturalist. "He took his rifle or his fowling-piece with him . . . conformed to the hardy and rugged habits of the men around him, and of course gained favor in their eyes. He had a strong relish for incident and adventure, was curious in observing savage manners and savage life, and ready to join any hunting or other excursion."[2]

It was mid-July when the Astorians forsook the river at the Arikara villages, in what is now North Dakota, and began the first overland crossing to the Pacific since Lewis and Clark. Their decision not to follow the Lewis and Clark route along the Missouri but rather to take a more southerly way was in a sense the genesis of the Oregon Trail. For, having learned that the Missouri route was not the easiest or shortest to the Northwest, a party of returning Astorians the following year was to try an even more southerly one—across South Pass in Wyoming and down the North Platte and Platte rivers—marking out what was to become the standard road to Oregon a generation later.

Bradbury returned to St. Louis with a contingent of the Lisa party and left St. Louis late in the year, bound for New Orleans. His account of the great earthquake of December 1811, which occurred while he was on the lower Mississippi, is one of dozens that are available in travel accounts and newspaper reports of the time. The quake still ranks as the greatest ever recorded in North America, estimated to have been far stronger than the San

Francisco quake of 1906. Reelfoot Lake, in Tennessee, was formed by the series of tremors, and the townsite of New Madrid, Missouri (for which the quake has been named), was lowered several feet by the subsidence of the earth.

Even the most observant traveler will sometimes minimize an important event if the circumstances are not understood. In a single paragraph only (pp. 211–12), Bradbury tells of boarding "the steam boat from Pittsburg" as if he were discussing the regular run of a scheduled steamboat. He was, in fact, aboard the first steamboat ever to descend the Ohio and the Mississippi, thus opening more than a century of river commerce that would eventually extend up the Missouri to cities on the high plains. The *New Orleans,* 116 feet long and capable of hauling 440 tons, had been built in Pittsburgh at a cost of $38,000. It was a woodburning vessel, primitive by later standards but definitely a maker of transportation history. Besides the usual hazards of river navigation, such as underwater obstructions and shifting channels, it had survived the memorable earthquake and resulting floods. Lacking the horsepower to return up the Ohio, the *New Orleans* was consigned to run between Natchez and the Gulf. St. Louis residents were not to see their first steamboat until later in the decade.

The War of 1812 prevented Bradbury from returning home for several years. When he finally got to England, hoping to find there all the plant specimens he had sent from westen America, he discovered that botanist Frederick Pursh had studied and published the most important plants in his *Flora americae septentrionalis* of 1814. That event, to which Bradbury alludes only briefly, so discouraged him that he abandoned plant collecting forever. Susan McKelvey, a specialist in trans-Mississippi botanical exploration, explains that Bradbury's disappointment in being unable to publish a "flora" of his travels is more than made up for by the present volume, "perhaps a more generally useful book than any flora which he might have written!"[3]

This work is a reprint of Bradbury's journal as it appears in volume 5 of Reuben Gold Thwaites, ed., *Early Western Travels* (Cleveland: Arthur H. Clark, 1905), 30 vols. The Thwaites edition is a reprint of Bradbury's *Travels in the Interior of America in the Years 1809, 1810, and 1811,* 2d ed. (London, 1819). Editor Thwaites presented the original page numbers of the 1819 edition in brackets in the text, and made footnote references to other volumes in the series which are not applicable here.

For an eyewitness acount of the expedition that Bradbury accompanied, see Henry Marie Brackenridge, *Journal of a Voyage up the River Missouri, Performed in Eighteen Hundred and Eleven,* which is volume 6 in the *Early Western Travels* series. A secondhand account is presented by Irving in *Astoria,* cited above.

Notes

1. Susan Delano McKelvey, *Botanical Exploration of the Trans-Mississippi West, 1790–1880* (Jamaica Plain, Mass., 1955), 110. Her entire essay on Bradbury occupies pp. 107–49.

2. Washington Irving, *Astoria; or, Anecdotes of an Enterprise beyond the Rocky Mountains,* ed. Edgerly W. Todd (Norman, Okla., 1964), 171.

3. McKelvey, *Botanical Exploration,* 103.

PREFACE

Comparatively little is known of the life of John Bradbury, naturalist and traveller, beyond what is disclosed in the volume here reprinted. By birth he was a Scotchman; but he had lived long in England, and in 1809 was commissioned by the Botanical Society at Liverpool to make some researches into plant life in the United States. Arriving in this country during the summer of that year, he brought letters of introduction to Jefferson, and was invited to visit at Monticello. The following letter from Jefferson to General Meriwether Lewis, governor of Louisiana Territory at St. Louis,[1] proves the estimation in which Bradbury was held by that American savant and statesman:

MONTICELLO Aug. 16. '09

DEAR SIR:

This will be handed you . . . Mr Bradbury, an English botanist, who proposes to take S^t. Louis in his botanizing tour. he came recommended to me by mr Roscoe of Liverpool, so well known by his histories of Lorenzo of Medicis & Leo X. & who is president of the Botanical society of Liverpool. mr Bradbury comes out in their employ, & having kept him here about ten days, I have had an opportunity of knowing that besides being a botanist of the first order, he is a man of entire worth & correct conduct. as such I recommend him

---

[1] Miscellaneous Jefferson Papers, series 5, vol. 16, No. 7 K, in State Department, Washington, D. C.

to your notice, advice & patronage, while within your government or it's confines.   perhaps you can consult no abler hand on your Western botanical observations.[2]

Govr. Lewis.   Th^s. Jefferson

Acting upon Jefferson's advice, Bradbury decided to make St. Louis the centre for his explorations, instead of New Orleans, as originally intended.   He arrived at this then frontier town on the last day of 1809. After the necessary inquiries and preparations, the spring and summer of 1810 were spent in short excursions from St. Louis, not more than eighty or a hundred miles at a time.   In this manner he made an exhaustive study of the flora of that vicinity, and a considerable collection of living specimens; these he forwarded in the autumn to Liverpool, by way of New Orleans.

Bradbury had intended to remove to the Arkansas River, when, early the following year, he met at St. Louis the leaders of the overland Astorian expedition. Being invited to accompany them he gladly availed himself of the opportunity.   The major portion of his journal, therefore, is concerned with the tour from St. Louis to the Arikara villages, some eighteen hundred miles above the mouth of the Missouri.   From there, our author accompanied Ramsay Crooks to the fur-trading station among the Mandan, two hundred miles higher up the river.   On returning to the Ari-

<hr/>

[2] Lewis and Clark had not yet published the voluminous journals kept by them during their transcontinental expedition of 1804-06.   Jefferson was anxious that Lewis should get to press with these papers — hence this reference.   Later, upon Lewis's death, Clark arranged with Dr. Benjamin Smith Barton, of Philadelphia, to prepare the scientific data for publication; but Barton's death intervened, and these data were not published until 1904, edited by the present writer.

kara, he found the Astorians in active preparation for their journey across the continent by land.

Accompanying the party to the coast would not have assured him of a return passage by sea, or the transportation of his collections, so Bradbury decided to return down the river with his fellow traveller, Henry M. Brackenridge, who was to descend in one of the boats of a prominent fur-trader, Manuel Lisa. Embarking on July 17, their voyage down stream was so rapid that in less than two weeks they were again in St. Louis. The haste of the return voyage was a disappointment to Bradbury, who had hoped for delays sufficient to secure specimens of the plants of the later summer, or those that had evaded his notice on the slower outward journey.

The sequel to the hardships of the Missouri expedition was an attack of fever, which lasted nearly four months. At its conclusion, Bradbury embarked for New Orleans, and after a perilous voyage, in which he experienced the severe earthquake shocks which destroyed New Madrid (December, 1811), he arrived at the mouth of the Mississippi and set sail for New York. Before completing his preparations to return to England, the war between the two nations broke out, which led to his remaining nearly four years longer in the United States. It appears to have been after the conclusion of peace that he made that journey through the central Western States and to Illinois, the observations of which have been embodied in appendix v, ''Remarks on the States of Ohio, Kentucky, and Indiana, with the Illinois and Western Territory, and on the Emigrations to those Countries.''

Bradbury was in Liverpool when the first edition of his volume of travels was published. According to the editor's preface in the second edition (1819), the author had by that time returned to America and taken up his residence in St. Louis.

The volume was received with much favor both in England and America. Appearing after the animosity that had been aroused by the calumnies and caricatures of such travellers as Weld and Ashe, the just, kind, and judicious spirit of Bradbury's book poured oil upon troubled waters. The Edinburgh *Review* commented at some length (December, 1818) upon the first edition, describing it as worthy of attention.

The principal portion of the book deals with a region then beyond the pale of American settlement; hence it was to appendix v that Americans were obliged to turn for a favorable and appreciative estimate of the customs and institutions of the Western territory. Therein, after a brief summary of the vast resources of the region, our author proceeds to describe the conditions of settlement. He shows that the great Middle West was in that early day fast filling with immigrants from "almost every country of Europe;" that the "back-woodsman" was already passing — and, impatient with the trammels of settled society, was disposing of his "improvement" to the more tractable foreign immigrant, who welcomed the clearing in preference to the untamed forest. Passing to social conditions, Bradbury comments upon the spirit of co-operation and good neighborliness, by which every man aids his fellow in the larger operations of clearing and house-building, and makes this necessary aid an occasion for

merry-making, only expecting in return that his neigh-
bor will lend him a hand when a like opportunity offers.
He pictures the democratic manners of the West, as
the result of a sturdy, manly spirit, which feels no servility in honest labor. His remarks upon the hospitality of the people, and their moral character, compare
favorably with the sketches of the less sympathetic
Michauxs and Cuming. The article closes with some
practical advice to intending English emigrants.
Brief as this account of the Middle West is, its value
is considerable, not only for the spirit in which it is
couched, but for the light which it sheds upon conditions at the close of the War of 1812-15. Besides
noting the rush of immigration in 1816, Bradbury records
the beginnings of steam navigation, and the growth of
domestic manufactures. Incidentally, also, his lists of
prices show the great production of food stuffs, the
exclusively agricultural character of the population,
and the opportunity opened here for every man possessed of willing hands.

Aside from this brief picture of the Middle West, the
chief interest of Bradbury's *Travels* relates to the region
beyond the Mississippi. Since Lewis and Clark's
adventure (1804-06), no description of the Missouri
Valley had been given to the world.[3] Moreover, Bradbury accompanied an expedition whose daring purpose
and breadth of scope have made it one of the most
renowned in trans-Mississippi annals. Whoever would
trace the history of the overland Astorian expedition,

---

[3] Nicholas Biddle's paraphrase of Lewis and Clark's journals was published in February, 1814; Bradbury's *Travels* first appeared in 1817. But
the journal of Patrick Gass, one of Lewis and Clark's sergeants, had been
issued in 1807.

must depend upon this volume for information concerning the early part of the journey; while appendices
ii and iii briefly complete the account of the Astorians'
adventures as far as the Pacific. Washington Irving,
the classic, but not always accurate, historian of this
enterprise, acknowledges his indebtedness to our
author.

Brackenridge — see volume vi of our series — tells
us that Bradbury had come to America imbued with
that enthusiasm for the simple, untutored life of the
savage which was felt by so many cultivated Europeans
of his day. His illusions being quickly dispelled, there
appears no "Atala" upon his pages. Lover of truth
as he was, he portrayed the Indian as he found him,
in all his savagery and degradation. Next to Lewis
and Clark's journals we have no better ethnological
authority for the Western Indians of this period, than
Bradbury. His accurate descriptions of habitations,
methods of agriculture, implements and weapons,
games and dances, tribal affinities and hostilities, are
most interesting. In regard to natural history — the
minerals of the regions through which he passed, and
observations upon plants and animals — Bradbury's
book is the report of one trained for this species of
observation, and an enthusiast whose zeal is unflagging.

To the simple boatmen, the ways of our author were
inexplicable; a gentleman given to long rambling in
search of common shrubs and flowers might be an
eccentric, but when this peculiar being swam icy rivers
in March, braved the fatigues of long journeys on foot,
and the risk of captivity by hostile Indians, then amuse-
ment deepened into wonder. At times, this became

alarm and annoyance, for it was sometimes necessary to search for him before proceeding, and to guard him against the hostiles whom he was so ready to tempt. Nevertheless, the rivermen admired him for his unflinching endurance, his readiness to share all the vicissitudes of the expedition, and his good humor and kindness toward every member of the party. Even during the earthquakes upon the Mississippi, Bradbury's calm reasonableness secured his party's safety. It has been noted that in his description of the great danger to which his craft and all its passengers were once exposed in the fury of a tornado upon the Missouri, Bradbury was collected enough to note the species of shrub to which the boat was moored, and upon whose rooted tenacity the lives of all depended.

Another interesting feature of Bradbury's work is the conversations he had with the pioneers of the trans-Mississippi region. In the Femme Osage region he met the aged Boone; to Bradbury we owe much of our knowledge of John Colter's extraordinary adventures; the half-breeds and Indian chiefs with whom Lewis and Clark made us acquainted, appear again upon Bradbury's pages.

Taken as the record of a traveller of unusual intelligence, of a naturalist of rare enthusiasm, of a man with human qualities, Bradbury's *Travels in the Interior of America* is worthy of a twentieth-century presentation.

Valuable assistance in the annotation has been received from Louise Phelps Kellogg, Ph.D.

R. G. T.

MADISON, WIS., June, 1904.

TRAVELS

IN

THE INTERIOR OF AMERICA,

IN THE

YEARS 1809, 1810, AND 1811;

INCLUDING

A DESCRIPTION OF UPPER LOUISIANA,

TOGETHER WITH

THE STATES OF OHIO, KENTUCKY, INDIANA, AND TENNESSEE,

WITH THE

ILLINOIS AND WESTERN TERRITORIES,

AND CONTAINING

REMARKS AND OBSERVATIONS

USEFUL TO

PERSONS EMIGRATING TO THOSE COUNTRIES.

Second Edition.

BY JOHN BRADBURY, F.L.S. LONDON,

Corresponding Member of the Liverpool Philosophical Society, and Honorary Member of the Literary and Philosophical Societies, New York, United States, America.

LONDON: PUBLISHED BY SHERWOOD, NEELY, AND JONES.

1819.

PREFACE

WHEN I undertook to travel in Louisiana, it was intended that I should make New Orleans my principal place of residence, and also the place of deposit for the result of my researches. This intention I made known to Mr. Jefferson, during my stay at Monticello, when he immediately pointed out the want of judgment in forming that arrangement, as the whole of the country round New Orleans is alluvial soil, and therefore ill suited to such productions as were the objects of my pursuit. In consequence of his representations, I changed my intentions, and proceeded to St. Louis, one thousand four hundred miles above Orleans by the course of the Mississippi, where I employed myself, during the winter of 1810, in making such preparations as I deemed necessary for the preservation of what might be collected during the ensuing [vi] summer. In my subsequent journey up the Missouri, although every facility was afforded me that the nature of the expedition would allow, yet the necessity of conforming to the rules laid down to secure the safety of the party during the voyage, added to the known or supposed proximity of the hostile Indians, during a considerable part of our route, caused me to lose a great many opportunities, which, had my exertions been free, I should not have done. Besides these impediments, I lost the opportunity of collecting a great number of new plants on my return, through the breach of faith towards me by Mr. Lisa, who agreed that his boats should land me at different places; which promise he neither did, nor intended to, perform. For these reasons, I am persuaded that much yet remains to be done in that interesting country. When the whole of my collection was embarked on the Missouri, at the Aricara nation, it was extensive; but being then two thousand nine hundred miles from New Orleans, the losses by the way, and during my subsequent sickness at St. Louis, greatly diminished it. Immediately after my return to the United States, and before I could make any arrangement, either for my return to England, or for the publication of the plants I collected, the war broke out with this country:— I waited for its termination, and made some arrangements which caused a necessity for my stay some time longer.

[vii] I have made the above statement, because I think, that whoever undertakes a mission of the nature which I did, where the duty is to be performed in a wilderness, ought to give an account how he performed it, even in his own defence; as it often happens that men are found, who, from interested or malignant motives, will vilify his character. I had intended that this should have been accompanied by a description of the objects collected, that had not been before discovered; but on my return to England, I found that my design was frustrated, by my collection having been submitted to the inspection of a person of the name of Pursh, who has published the most interesting of my plants in an appendix to the *Flora Americæ Septentrionalis*.

As my chief object has been to convey information and to write the truth, I have not been particular in the choice of words; if, therefore, the style meets with criticism, I shall neither be surprised nor disappointed. A catalogue of some of the more rare plants in the neighbourhood of St. Louis, and on the Missouri, is added, together with their habitats. To many it will be of no value; but as it may be of some use to naturalists who may visit those parts hereafter, I have thought proper to insert it. In what relates to the country west of the Alleghanies, I have been brief, because a more dilated [viii] account would have swelled the work much beyond the limits I had prescribed to myself. A second visit to those parts, in which my movements shall be less circumscribed, may enable me to give a more finished picture. In what has been said on those countries, I disclaim any design to encourage emigration; and may be credited in the assertion, because I can have no possible interest in promoting it. I have told the truth, and I can see no reason why it should have been suppressed.

Liverpool, August 1, 1817.

SECOND EDITION

SHORTLY after the publication of the first Edition of this Work, Mr. Bradbury returned to America, and is now residing at St. Louis. The rapid sale of the first Edition, and its favourable reception by the Public, have induced the publication of a second, to which a Map of the United States has been added, carefully collated from the one published by Mr. Mellish.

Mr. Bywater's ingenious speculations on *animalculæ*, which were published in the first Edition, in a letter addressed by him to Mr. Bradbury, are omitted in the second, at the request of the author, who, on reconsidering the subject, wishes to make some alterations, that he does not feel himself at liberty to publish in Mr. Bradbury's Work, without previously consulting him.

Liverpool, 1819.

CONTENTS

TRAVELS IN THE INTERIOR OF AMERICA

On the 31st December, 1809, I arrived at St. Louis, in Upper Louisiana; intending to make that town or neighbourhood my principal place of residence, whilst employed in exploring the interior of Upper Louisiana and the Illinois Territory, for the purpose of discovering and collecting subjects in natural history, either new or valuable. During the ensuing spring and summer, I made frequent excursions alone into the wilderness, but not farther than eighty or a hundred miles into the interior. In the autumn of 1810 I dispatched for Orleans, in seven packages, the result of my researches; but had the mortification, soon after, to hear that the boat containing my collection had been driven ashore and damaged, on an island near St. Genevieve,[1] sixty miles below St. Louis. As soon as I received this information I went thither, but learned that the boat had been repaired, and had [18] proceeded on her voyage. On my return to St. Louis, I was informed that a party of men had arrived from Canada, with an intention to ascend the Missouri, on their way to the Pacific Ocean, by the same route that Lewis and Clarke had followed, by descending the Columbia River. I soon became acquainted with the principals of this party, in whom the manners and accomplishments of gentlemen were united with the hardihood and capa-

---

[1] For the history of Ste. Geneviève, see Cuming's *Tour*, vol. iv of our series, p. 266, note 174.— ED.

bili'.y of suffering, necessary to the backwoodsmen.
As they were apprised of the nature and object of my
mission, Mr. Wilson P. Hunt, the leader of the party,
in a very friendly and pressing manner invited me to
accompany them up the River Missouri, as far as might
be agreeable to my views.[2]   I had intended to remove
from St. Louis to Ozark, (or more properly Aux-arcs)
on the Arkansas, and to spend the remaining summer on
that river; but considering this opportunity for exploring the Missouri too valuable to be lost, I gladly
accepted the invitation, to which an acquaintance
with Messrs. Ramsey Crooks[3] and Donald M'Ken-

[2] The overland Astorian expedition which Bradbury was invited to
join, was led by Wilson Hunt, chief American partner of the Pacific Fur
Company.   A native of New Jersey, Hunt came to St. Louis about 1804,
entering a commercial business in connection with one Hankinson.   Detect-
ing the abilities and energy of the young merchant, Astor invited Hunt's
co-operation in the Astoria enterprise, and the latter dissolved his St. Louis
partnership.   After the adventures of this expedition, Hunt returned to St.
Louis, where in 1822 President Monroe appointed him postmaster, a position
he retained until his death or retirement in 1840.— ED.

[3] Ramsay Crooks was born at Greenock, Scotland, in 1787.   When
but sixteen years of age he entered the service of the North West Company,
and as early as 1806 was trading in Wisconsin, under the direction of Robert
Dickson.   Crooks then drifted to St. Louis (1807), and formed a fur-
trading partnership with Robert McClellan, their first enterprise being
balked by the hostility of the Teton on Missouri River.   Crooks's division
of the overland expedition to Astoria did not arrive at that place until May 11,
1812.   After the failure of the project of the Pacific Fur Company, Crooks
returned overland to St. Louis, arriving April 30, 1813.   The following
year saw him in Colonel Croghan's unsuccessful expedition against Mackinac,
attempting to protect Astor's interests at that post; and in 1815 Lockwood
met him on his way to reorganize the fur-trading interests at Mackinac
after its surrender to the United States — (*Wisconsin Historical Collections*,
ii, p. 101).   When the American Fur Company absorbed the South West
Company (1817), Crooks was made a partner and the Western manager
of the business.   His headquarters were in New York, but his journeys
to the West were frequent; for many years his advent at Mackinac was the
event of the fur-trading year.   In 1834, when Astor dissolved the American

zie,[4] also principals of the party, was no small inducement. As it would not be practicable to ascend the Missouri until the breaking up of the ice in spring, Mr. Hunt
concluded, that to avoid the expense of supporting his
party at St. Louis, it would be better to station them during the winter on some part of the Missouri, at a considerable [19] distance above its mouth, as, at any point
on that river above the settlements, five or six hunters
can easily provide for forty or fifty men. The party
therefore quitted St. Louis, and proceeded to the
mouth of the Naduet, which falls into the Missouri 450
miles from the Mississippi.[5]   In the beginning of March

Fur Company, Crooks bought out the Northern department, and continued
it under the same name, displaying executive ability of a high order. He
died in New York in 1859. Many of his letters to the Mackinac agents are
still preserved there, and others by the Wisconsin Historical Society; they
are valuable as sources for the history of the fur-trade during forty years.
Crooks was early interested in the Wisconsin Historical Society, and his
portrait is found in the museum of that institution.— ED.

[4] Donald McKenzie was a relative of the explorer Sir Alexander, and
had been in the North West Company before entering Astor's employ.
Being chosen to assist in the overland division of the enterprise, he felt
aggrieved that Hunt was made chief of the party, and his dissatisfaction
rendered him indifferent to the success of the project. He joined McDougal
in propositions for surrendering Astoria to the North West Company, and
upon the consummation thereof (1813) once more entered the North West
employ, returning via Canada to Fort William, where he arrived in July,
1814. Two years later he was again upon Columbia waters. After the
fusion of the Hudson's Bay and North West companies (1821), McKenzie
became chief factor of the former's post at Fort Garry on Red River (of
the North), and was for eight years governor of Assiniboia. In 1833 he
retired from the fur-trade, and settled at Mayville, New York, where he
died in 1851.— ED.

[5] The river is now called Nodaway. Coues, in his *History of the Lewis
and Clark Expedition* (New York, 1893), says that the word is an Indian
term for a kind of snake. It is marked on the map of the Missouri River
Commission as being five hundred and six miles above the mouth of the
river, and separates Andrew and Holt counties in Missouri.— ED.

Mr. Hunt returned to St. Louis in a boat with ten oars,[6] and on the morning of the 12th, having completed his arrangements, he again embarked for the Missouri. As the post was expected to arrive the morning following, I put my trunks on board the boat, and determined to wait until that time, and meet the party at St. Charles. I must here observe, that the post to St. Louis is dispatched from Louisville, in Kentucky, a distance of more than 300 miles, through a wilderness, and from various causes is often retarded for several weeks, as had been the case at that period. In the evening I was informed by a gentleman in St. Louis, that a writ for debt had been taken out against Dorion,[7] (whom Mr. Hunt had engaged as interpreter) by a person whose object was to defeat the intentions of the voyage. Knowing that the detention of Dorion would be of serious consequence to the party, I left St. Louis at two o'clock the following morning, in company with a young Englishman of the name of Nuttall,[8] determined

_____

[6] Irving, who had access to the records of the Pacific Fur Company, says in *Astoria* that Hunt left the Nodaway January 1 for St. Louis, where he arrived on the twentieth of the same month. In consideration of the business incident to the expedition, this would seem more probable than Bradbury's dates.— ED.

[7] Pierre Dorion (Durion) the elder was an early habitant of St. Louis, who having taken the oath of fidelity to the United States upon the conquest of Illinois by George Rogers Clark, requested permission to remove to Cahokia in 1780 (see original letter in Draper MSS., Wisconsin Historical Library, 50 J 34). Later he lived among the Yankton Sioux where was born the younger Dorion, son of a Sioux woman. Both of the Dorions were utilized as interpreters by Lewis and Clark. The younger performed important services for the Astorians, but was killed by an Indian on the Boise River, Idaho. His wife and two sons were living in Oregon as late as 1850.— ED.

[8] Thomas Nuttall was a Yorkshireman, who having emigrated to Philadelphia as a journeyman printer, attracted the notice of Dr. B. S. Barton,

to meet the boat previous to its arrival at St. Charles, which I effected; and Dorion was sent into the woods, [20] his squaw accompanying him. We arrived at St. Charles[9] about noon, and soon after Mr. Samuel Bridge, a gentleman from Manchester, then living at St. Louis, arrived also, with letters for me from Europe, the post having come in as was expected. We slept on board the boat, and in the morning of the 14th took our departure from St. Charles, the Canadians measuring the strokes of their oars by songs, which were generally responsive betwixt the oarsmen at the bow and those at the stern: sometimes the steersman sung, and was chorused by the men.[10] We soon met with Dor-

the well-known Philadelphia scientist. The latter persuaded Nuttall to devote himself to science, in whose interests he made extensive journeys into the interior of North America. From 1822-28 he was professor at Harvard, and curator of the botanical gardens. After a journey to the Columbia (1834-35), he returned to England, where he passed the remainder of his life on an estate near Liverpool, dying in 1859. For a more detailed sketch of Nuttall, see preface to his *Travels into the Arkansas Territory*, to be published as volume xiii of the present series.— ED.

[9] St. Charles was a small town on the north side, about twenty-one miles above the mouth of the Missouri. When Lewis and Clark embarked from here in 1804, they described it as stretching for nearly a mile along the bank, having one hundred houses and about four hundred and fifty population, "Chiefly French." See Thwaites, *Original Journals of Lewis and Clark Expedition* (New York, 1904), i, p. 18.— ED.

[10] A few verses of one of their most favourite songs is annexed; and to show its frivolity to those unacquainted with the language, an imitation in English is added.

I

Derriere chêz nous, il y ă un etang,
Ye, ye ment.
Trois canards s'en vont baignans,
Tous du lông de la rivière,
Legérément ma bergère,
Legèrement, ye ment.

ion, but [21] without his squaw, whom it was intended should accompany us. They had quarrelled, and he had [22] beaten her, in consequence of which she ran

II

Trois canards s'en vont baignans,
    Ye, ye ment.
Le fils du roi s'en va chassant,
Tous du lông de la rivière,
Legèrement ma bergère,
    Legèrement, ye ment.

III

Le fils du roi s'en va chassant,
    Ye, ye ment.
Avec son grand fusil d'argent,
Tous du lông de la rivière,
Legèrement, ma bergère,
    Legèrement, ye ment.— &c. &c.

I

Behind our house there is a pond,
    Fal lal de ra.
There came three ducks to swim thereon:
All along the river clear,
Lightly my shepherdess dear,
    Lightly, fal de ra.

II

There came three ducks to swim thereon,
    Fal lal de ra.
The prince to chase them he did run
All along the river clear,
Lightly my shepherdess dear,
    Lightly, fal de ra.

III

The prince to chase them he did run,
    Fal lal de ra.
And he had his great silver gun
All along the river clear,
Lightly my shepherdess dear,
    Lightly, fal de ra.— &c. &c.— BRADBURY.

away from him into the woods, with a child in her arms, and a large bundle on her back. A Canadian of the name of St. Paul was sent in search of her. The day was very rainy, and we proceeded only nine miles, to Bon Homme Island, where we encamped, and St. Paul arrived, but without the squaw. I observed in the broken banks of this island, a number of tuberous roots, which the Canadians call *pommes de terre.* They are eaten by them, and also by the Indians, and have much of the consistence and taste of the Jerusalem artichoke: they are the roots of *glycine apios.*

15th.— About two hours before day, we were hailed from the shore by Dorion's squaw, who had been rambling all night in search of us. She was informed, that we would cross over to her at daybreak, which we did, and took her on board. I walked the greater part of this day on the north side of the river, which is partly bounded by rocks of secondary lime-stone; at the foot of which I observed crystals of quartz and calcarious spar, or carbonate of lime. We encamped opposite the remains of the village of St. Andrew, which is now abandoned.[11]

16th.— We this day passed the Tavern Rocks, so called from a large cave therein, level with the [23] surface of the river.[12] These rocks are nearly three hundred feet high, and are of the same nature as those we passed

[11] St. Andrews was a small settlement laid off by John Henry in St. Louis County, early in the nineteenth century. It attained little note, and its site is now engulfed in the Missouri River.— ED.

[12] This cave is noted by all early travellers. The French traders had scrawled names upon its walls, and painted images thereupon, which the Indians regarded with superstitious awe. It appears to have taken its name from being a well-known lodging or camping place.— ED.

yesterday, but more abundantly filled with organic remains, consisting of *anomiæ* and *entrochii*. On the islands which we passed there is abundance of *equisetum hyemale*, called *rushes* by the settlers, by whom this plant is held in high estimation, on account of its affording winter food for their cattle. On the first settlement of Kentucky, the borders of the rivers were found to be thickly set with cane, (*arundinaria macrosperma* of Michaux) and it was one of the strongest inducements with the first settlers to fix on a spot if cane was abundant. On the Missouri, the rushes are equally valuable, affording to the first settler winter food for his cattle for several years, after which they perish, being destroyed if fed on during the winter. We this night arrived at Point L'Abaddie, where we encamped.[13]

17th.— Early this morning I walked along the river, and was much struck with the vast size to which the cotton wood tree[14] grows. Many of those which I observed this day exceed seven feet in diameter, and continue with a thickness very little diminished, to the height of 80 or 90 feet, where the limbs commence. After breakfast, we [24] crossed to the north side of the river, and in the afternoon landed at a French village, name Charette.[15] In the woods surrounding

---

[13] Point L'Abbadie was named for an early French settler, Sylvester L'Abbadie, who came to St. Louis in 1769 and married one of the Chouteau sisters. He became a prominent merchant in the city, dying in 1794.— ED.

[14] *Populus angulosa* of Michaux, called by the French Liard.— BRADBURY.

[15] La Charette (sometimes called St. Johns) was a French outpost in the Missouri Valley, founded probably as early as 1766. When Lewis and Clark passed here they described it in their journals as composed of seven small houses and as many poor families, the last establishment of whites upon the Missouri. The site of the town has long since been swept away

this place I observed a striking instance of the indolence of the inhabitants. The rushes in the neighbourhood had been already destroyed by the cattle, and from the neglect of the owners to provide winter food for their horses, they had been reduced to the necessity of gnawing the bark off the trees, some hundreds of which were stripped as far as these animals could reach. The cotton wood, elm, mulberry, and nettle trees (*celtis crassifolia*) suffered the most. On leaving Charette, Mr. Hunt pointed out to me an old man standing on the bank, who, he informed me, was Daniel Boone, the discoverer of Kentucky. As I had a letter of introduction to him, from his nephew Colonel Grant, I went ashore to speak to him, and requested that the boat might go on, as I intended to walk until evening. I remained for some time in conversation with him. He informed me, that he was eighty-four years of age; that he had spent a considerable portion of his time alone in the back woods, and had lately returned from his spring hunt, with nearly sixty beaver skins.[16] On

by the encroachments of the river. It was near the present Marthasville, Warren County.— ED.

[16] Daniel Boone migrated to Missouri in 1798, when it was still Spanish territory, and served for some years as syndic of the Femme Osage district, wherein his sons and several friends from Kentucky had settled. His son-in-law, Flanders Callaway, removed to the neighborhood of La Charette about 1800. Boone, in his later life, usually made his home with the Callaways. Bradbury was in error in regard to Boone's age, as the records show and he himself frequently stated that he was born in 1734. He was but eighty-six years old when he died in 1820. For further details of his later years, see Thwaites, *Daniel Boone* (New York, 1901). Israel Grant of Scott County, Kentucky, married Susan Bryan, a niece of Mrs. Boone. His son, Israel B., was a silversmith, who after emigrating to Missouri worked for some years at his trade in St. Louis, where Bradbury probably knew him. Later, Grant took up land in Callaway County, and became a local magistrate, serving twice in the state legislature. He was killed in 1835 by two of his slaves.— ED.

proceeding through the woods, I came to the river Charette, which falls into the Missouri about a mile above
the village, and was now much swelled by the late
rains.   As the boat had disappeared behind an island,
and was at too great a distance to [25] be hailed, I got
across by swimming, having tied my clothes together,
and inclosed them in my deer skin hunting coat, which
I pushed before me.   I overtook the boat in about three
hours, and we encamped at the mouth of a creek called
Bœuf, near the house of one Sullens.   I enquired of
Sullens for John Colter,[17] one of Lewis and Clarke's
party, whom General Clark had mentioned to me as
being able to point out the place on the Missouri where
the petrified skeleton of a fish, above forty feet long, had
been found.   Sullens informed me that Colter lived
about a mile from us, and sent his son to inform him of
our arrival; but we did not see him that evening.

18th.— At day-break Sullens came to our camp, and
informed us that Colter[18] would be with us in a [26] few

---

[17] John Colter (or Coalter) was of Virginian birth, but afterwards lived
at Maysville, Kentucky, where he joined the Lewis and Clark expedition
in the fall of 1803.   On the return journey, Colter was discharged at his
own request near Fort Mandan, whence he went back to the wilderness on
another trapping expedition.   In the spring of 1807, as he was returning
to civilization, he met the brigade of the Missouri Fur Company, and was
persuaded to accompany them to the waters of the Yellowstone.   In the
summer of that year he was the first white man to cross what is now the Yellowstone National Park.   It is supposed that the adventure here related
by Bradbury occurred in the spring of 1808, when Colter had been sent
on an embassy to the Blackfeet Indians.   The meeting described by Bradbury is our last positive knowledge of this intrepid explorer; but the *Missouri Gazette* (December 11, 1813) reports administration of the estate of a
"John Coulter deceased," who may have been the same man.— ED.

[18] This man came to St. Louis in May, 1810, in a small canoe, from the
head waters of the Missouri, a distance of three thousand miles, which he
traversed in thirty days.   I saw him on his arrival, and received from him

minutes.   Shortly after he arrived, and accompanied
us for some miles, but could not give me [27] the information I wished for.   He seemed to have a great

---

an account of his adventures after he had separated from Lewis and Clarke's
party: one of these, from its singularity, I shall relate.   On the arrival of the
party on the head waters of the Missouri, Colter, observing an appearance of
abundance of beaver being there, he got permission to remain and hunt
for some time, which he did in company with a man of the name of Dixon,
who had traversed the immense tract of country from St. Louis to the head
waters of the Missouri alone.   Soon after he separated from Dixon, and
trapped in company with a hunter named Potts; and aware of the hostility
of the Blackfeet Indians, one of whom had been killed by Lewis, they set
their traps at night, and took them up early in the morning, remaining concealed during the day.   They were examining their traps early one morning,
in a creek about six miles from that branch of the Missouri called Jefferson's
Fork, and were ascending in a canoe, when they suddenly heard a great
noise, resembling the trampling of animals; but they could not ascertain
the fact, as the high perpendicular banks on each side of the river impeded
their view.   Colter immediately pronounced it to be occasioned by Indians,
and advised an instant retreat; but was accused of cowardice by Potts, who
insisted that the noise was caused by buffaloes, and they proceeded on.   In
a few minutes afterwards their doubts were removed, by a party of Indians
making their appearance on both sides of the creek, to the amount of five
or six hundred, who beckoned them to come ashore.   As retreat was now
impossible, Colter turned the head of the canoe to the shore; and at the
moment of its touching, an Indian seized the rifle belonging to Potts; but
Colter, who is a remarkably strong man, immediately retook it, and handed
it to Potts, who remained in the canoe, and on receiving it pushed off into
the river.   He had scarcely quitted the shore when an arrow was shot at
him, and he cried out, *"Colter, I am wounded."*   Colter remonstrated with
him on the folly of attempting to escape, and urged him to come ashore.
Instead of complying, he instantly levelled his rifle at an Indian, and shot
him dead on the spot.   This conduct, situated as he was, may appear to
have been an act of madness; but it was doubtless the effect of sudden, but
sound reasoning; for if taken alive, he must have expected to be tortured to
death, according to their custom.   He was instantly pierced with arrows so
numerous, that, to use the language of Colter, *"he was made a riddle of."*
They now seized Colter, stripped him entirely naked, and began to consult
on the manner in which he should be put to death.   They were first inclined
to set him up as a mark to shoot at; but the chief interfered, and seizing him
by the shoulder, asked him if he could run fast?   Colter, who had been
some time amongst the Kee-kat-sa, or Crow Indians, had in a considerable
degree acquired the Blackfoot language, and was also well acquainted with

inclination to accompany the expedition; [28] but having been lately married, he reluctantly took leave of us.
I walked this day along the bluffs, [29] which were

Indian customs. He knew that he had now to run for his life, with the
dreadful odds of five or six hundred against him, and those armed Indians;
therefore cunningly replied that he was a very bad runner, although he was
considered by the hunters as remarkably swift. The chief now commanded
the party to remain stationary, and led Colter out on the prairie three or four
hundred yards, and released him, bidding him *to save himself if he could*.
At that instant the horrid war whoop sounded in the ears of poor Colter,
who, urged with the hope of preserving life, ran with a speed at which he
was himself surprised. He proceeded towards the Jefferson Fork, having
to traverse a plain six miles in breadth, abounding with the prickly pear,
on which he was every instant treading with his naked feet. He ran nearly
half way across the plain before he ventured to look over his shoulder, when
he perceived that the Indians were very much scattered, and that he had
gained ground to a considerable distance from the main body; but one
Indian, who carried a spear, was much before all the rest, and not more than
a hundred yards from him. A faint gleam of hope now cheered the heart
of Colter: he derived confidence from the belief that escape was within the
bounds of possibility; but that confidence was nearly being fatal to him, for
he exerted himself to such a degree, that the blood gushed from his nostrils,
and soon almost covered the fore part of his body. He had now arrived
within a mile of the river, when he distinctly heard the appalling sound of
footsteps behind him, and every instant expected to feel the spear of his
pursuer. Again he turned his head, and saw the savage not twenty yards
from him. Determined if possible to avoid the expected blow, he suddenly
stopped, turned round, and spread out his arms. The Indian, surprised
by the suddenness of the action, and perhaps at the bloody appearance of
Colter, also attempted to stop; but exhausted with running, he fell whilst
endeavouring to throw his spear, which stuck in the ground, and broke in
his hand. Colter instantly snatched up the pointed part, with which he
pinned him to the earth, and then continued his flight. The foremost of
the Indians, on arriving at the place, stopped till others came up to join
them, when they set up a hideous yell. Every moment of this time was improved by Colter, who, although fainting and exhausted, succeeded in gaining the skirting of the cotton wood trees, on the borders of the fork, through
which he ran, and plunged into the river. Fortunately for him, a little below
this place there was an island, against the upper point of which a raft of
drift timber had lodged. He dived under the raft, and after several efforts,
got his head above water amongst the trunks of trees, covered over with
smaller wood to the depth of several feet. Scarcely had he secured himself,
when the Indians arrived on the river, screeching and yelling, as Colter

beautifully adorned with *anemone hepatica.* We encamped near the lower end of Lutre (Otter) Island.[19]

The 19th commenced and continued rainy.— When
we had passed the lower settlements, we began to see
the river and its borders in a state of nature. The
rushes, *equisetum hyemale,* were so thick and tall, that
it was both painful and difficult to walk along, even at a
very slow pace.

20th.— The river on the south side, during this
day's travel, is mostly bounded by bluffs, or rocks, of
whitish limestone: their appearance is very picturesque;
the tops are crowned with cedar, and the ledges and
chinks are adorned with *mespilus Canadensis,* now in
flower. We encamped this night seven miles above
the mouth of Gasconade River.

21st.— The rain, which had been almost incessant
since our departure from St. Charles, had now ceased.

---

expressed it, ''like so many devils.'' They were frequently on the raft
during the day, and were seen through the chinks by Colter, who was congratulating himself on his escape, until the idea arose that they might set
the raft on fire. In horrible suspense he remained until night, when hearing
no more of the Indians, he dived from under the raft, and swam silently
down the river to a considerable distance, when he landed, and travelled
all night. Although happy in having escaped from the Indians, his situation was still dreadful: he was completely naked, under a burning sun; the
soles of his feet were entirely filled with the thorns of the prickly pear; he
was hungry, and had no means of killing game, although he saw abundance
around him, and was at least seven days journey from Lisa's Fort, on the
Bighorn branch of the Roche Jaune River. These were circumstances
under which almost any man but an American hunter would have despaired.
He arrived at the fort in seven days, having subsisted on a root much esteemed
by the Indians of the Missouri, now known by naturalists as *psoralea esculenta.*— BRADBURY.

[19] Loutre (or Otter) Island was first settled in 1809, by an English emigrant named Hale Talbott. Not far from this place occurred the Indian
ambuscade wherein Captain James Callaway, grandson of Daniel Boone,
was slain (1815).— ED.

[30] I went ashore, after breakfast, intending to walk along the bluffs, and was followed by Mr. Nuttall. We observed that the boat immediately passed over to the other side of the river, on account of its being more easy to ascend. As this sometimes happened several times in a day, we felt no concern about it, but proceeded on our researches. In the forenoon we came to a creek or river, much swelled by the late rains: I was now surprised to find that Mr. Nuttall could not swim. As we had no tomahawk, nor any means of constructing a raft, and were certain that the boat was before us, we looked for no alternative but to cross the creek by fording it. We therefore continued to ascend, and in about half an hour arrived at a place where a tree had fallen in on the opposite side of the river, which reached about half way across it. I stripped, and attempted to wade it, but found it impracticable. I then offered to take Nuttall on my back, and swim over with him; but he declined, and we continued our route. About a league further up, we found a raft of drift-wood, which had been stopped by a large tree that had fallen into the river; this we crossed and with some difficulty overtook the boat. We arrived at a French village, called Cote sans Dessein, about two miles below the mouth of Osage River.[20] After we had formed our camp, the interpreter went into the village, where he had some acquaintance. On his return, he informed us that [31] there was a war

---

[20] Côte sans Dessein was a French settlement begun about 1808, three years previous to this voyage. One of the most stubborn defenses during the War of 1812-15 occurred here, wherein Baptiste Louis Roi, with two men and two women, in a blockhouse fort kept a large number of savages at bay for some hours, and finally caused their retreat. The town was near the present Barkersville.— ED.

party of Indians in the neighbourhood, consisting of the Ayauwais, Potowatomies, Sioux, and Saukee nations, amounting to nearly three hundred warriors.[21] He had learned, that this party were going against the Osages; but having discovered that there was an Osage boy in the village, they were waiting to catch and scalp him. He also informed us, that we might expect to fall in with other war parties crossing the Missouri higher up. This was unpleasant news to us, as it is always desirable that white men should avoid meeting with Indian war parties: for if they are going to war, they are generally associated in larger parties than can subsist by hunting, from which they refrain, to prevent being discovered by their enemies, wherefore they are almost certain to levy contributions of provisions or ammunition on all they meet. When they return from war, the danger is still greater; for, if successful, they often commit wanton ravages; and if unsuccessful, the shame of returning to their nation without having performed any achievement, often induces them to attack those whom they would, in other circumstances, have peaceably passed. As we were sixteen men, well armed, we were determined to resist any act of aggression, in case of a rencontre with them.

22nd, 23rd, and 24th.— Almost incessant rain.

[21] Tribes living at this time about the borders of the present state of Iowa. The Sioux were probably the Yankton branch, with whom the other tribes mentioned were at peace, the rest of the great Sioux nation being their inveterate enemies. The Iowa (Ayauwais) were of Siouan stock, and had their chief village on the Des Moines River. The Potawatomi and Sauk were Algonquian tribes, formerly resident in Wisconsin, who at this time had their chief villages west of the Mississippi. The Sauk had amalgamated with the Foxes, and were usually spoken of as the "Sauks and Foxes." Indians of all these tribes still live on government reservations in Iowa, Kansas, and Indian Territory.— ED.

Our bread was now becoming very mouldy, not [32] having been properly baked. Mr. Hunt anxiously waited for a fine day to dry it, together with the rest of the baggage.

25th.— Met a boat with sixteen oars coming from Fort Osage to St. Louis, for supplies: news had arrived at the fort, that the Great Osages had lately killed an American at their village.[22]

26th.— It rained nearly the whole of this day: the flats near the river still continue to be so thickly covered with rushes, that it is almost impossible to travel over them.

27th.— The north bank of the river now assumes a most interesting appearance: it consists of a range of rocks, nearly perpendicular, from 150 to 300 feet high; they are composed of a very white limestone, and their summits are covered to the edge with cedar. The length of this range is about six miles, and at the upper end they assume a semi-circular form. These are called the Manitou Rocks, a name given to them by the Indians, who often apply this term *Manitou* to uncommon or singular productions of nature, which they highly venerate. On or near these Manitous, they chiefly deposit their offerings to the *Great Spirit* or *Father of Life*. This has caused some to believe that these Manitous are the objects that they worship; but this opinion is erroneous. The Indians believe that the [33] Great

---

[22] The Osage Indians were a large tribe of Siouan stock, dwelling chiefly on the river to which they gave their name. They were divided into three bands — the Great Osage, Little Osage, and Arkansas band (*i. e.*, those living on the river of that name). Lewis and Clark praised their physical appearance and advance in agriculture. They still have a population of about eighteen hundred in Indian Territory.— ED.

Spirit either inhabits, or frequently visits, these mani-
festations of his power; and that offerings deposited
there, will sooner attract his notice, and gain his aus-
pices, than in any other place. These offerings are
propitiatory, either for success in war or in hunting,
and consist of various articles, of which the feathers of
the war eagle (*falco melanœtos*) are in the greatest estimation. On these rocks several rude figures have
been drawn by the Indians with red paint: they are
chiefly in imitation of buffaloe, deer, &c. One of these,
according with their idea of the Great Spirit, is not unlike our common representation of the devil. We encamped this night a little above the mouth of the Bonne
Femme, a small river on the north side,[23] where the
tract of land called Boone's Lick settlement commences,
supposed to be the best land in Western America for
so great an area: it extends about 150 miles up the Missouri, and is near fifty miles in breadth.

28th.— I left the boats early, intending to walk to
the Lick settlements, which are the last on the river,
excepting those occupied by one or two families near
Fort Osage. After travelling eight or ten miles, I was
surprised in the woods by a severe thunder storm.
Not knowing whether I could reach the settlements
before night, I returned to meet the boat, and found
our two hunters, who [34] had sheltered themselves in
a hollow tree: they had killed a buck, on a part of which
we dined, and carried the remainder to the boat, and
soon after we arrived at the first house, belonging to a

---

[23] Lewis and Clark note these painted rocks, and describe one as having
the bust of a man and the horns of a stag. The Bonne Femme River is in
Howard County, Missouri.— ED.

planter named Hibband.[24] This evening we had a
most tremendous thunder storm; and about nine o'clock,
a tree, not more than fifty yards from our camp, was
shivered by lightning. Mr. Hunt, Mr. Nuttall, and
myself, who were sitting in the tent, sensibly felt the
action of the electric fluid.

29th.— As Mr. Hunt had some business with one of
the settlers, we walked to his house, where we heard
that war had already commenced between the Osages
and the confederate nations, and that the former had
killed seven of the Ayauways. This determined us to
continue our practice of sleeping on our arms, as we
had done since the 21st. We slept this night about a
league above the settlements.

30th.— We were now beyond all the settlements,
except those at Fort Osage, and Mr. Hunt resolved to
send the hunters out more frequently, as game might
now be expected in abundance. I accompanied them,
and we killed a buck and a doe. I found the country,
three or four miles from the river, very broken or stony.
The almost incessant rains had now raised the Missouri

---

[24] Boone's Lick was discovered early in the nineteenth century — possibly by Daniel Boone, upon one of his long hunting excursions — but took
its name from his sons, Daniel Morgan and Nathan, who came hither in
1807 to make salt. The next year some emigrants moved to the neighborhood, but Goverr or Meriwether Lewis sent them word of his inability to
protect so distant an outpost, whereupon they returned to the older settlements. The second colony came to this region in 1810. Although but a
year old at the time Bradbury passed, the settlement already contained
seventy-five families, and Boone's Lick road became one of the best-travelled
in the Missouri District. Brackenridge calls this "by far the best settlement on the Missouri," *Views of Louisiana* (Pittsburgh, 1814), p. 115.
The settler Bradbury calls Hibband was probably Hubbard, several of
that name being in 1812 at Fort Kincaid, about a mile north of where the
Missouri, Kansas & Texas Railway crosses the river.— ED.

to within a few [35] feet of its annual flood, which rendered the navigation very difficult.

31st.—The morning was rainy, and was succeeded by a strong north wind, which caused a sudden change in the temperature of the weather: the 30th had been warm, but this night the water, in a tin cup of a pint measure, that had been left full in the boat, was found to be nearly all solid ice on the morning of the first of April.

April 1st.— After breakfast I went ashore with the two hunters, Harrington and Mears, but soon separated from them in order to visit the bluffs. In the evening I descended into the valley, and on my way to find the boat, observed a skunk,[25] (*Viverra mephitis*) and being desirous of procuring the skin, fired at it, but with shot only, having that day [36] taken out my fowling-piece instead of my rifle. It appeared that I had either missed entirely, or only slightly wounded it, as it turned round instantly, and ran towards me. Being well aware of the consequence if overtaken, I fled, but was so closely pursued, that I was under the necessity of re-loading whilst in the act of running. At the next discharge I killed it; but as it had ejected its offensive liquor upon its tail, I could not touch it, but cut a slender vine, of which I made a noose, and dragged my prize

---

[25] This animal in its defence discharges a few drops of a liquid so fœtid, that the stench can scarcely be endured by any animal. Clothes on which the smallest particle has fallen, must be buried in the earth for at least a month before they can be worn. This liquor is highly inflammable, and is secreted in a gland beneath the tail, from which it is thrown with a force that will carry it to the distance of three or four yards. Only a very few of the American dogs can be induced to attack it, and those are so powerfully affected by the horrid stench, that they continue to howl for a considerable time afterwards, and instinctively relieve themselves by scratching holes in the earth, into which they put their nose.— BRADBURY.

to the boat. I found that the Canadians considered it as a delicacy, and were desirous of procuring it to eat: this enabled me to obtain the skin without having to perform the disgusting operation of taking it off myself. Soon after my arrival, Harrington came in, and brought the intelligence that they had killed a large bear about four miles off. He had left Mears engaged in skinning it, and came to request that one or two men might be sent to assist in fetching it in. As it was near night, Mr. Hunt determined to stop, and two of the Canadians were sent along with Harrington; I also accompanied them. Although our course lay through a very thick wood, Harrington led us with great precision towards the place, and when he supposed himself near it, he stopped, and we gave a shout. In a few seconds afterwards we heard the discharge of a rifle, and also a shout from Mears, who was within two hundred [37] yards of us. On joining him we were surprised to find that he had two bears. He informed us, that after the departure of Harrington he re-loaded his rifle, and laid it beside him whilst he was skinning and cutting up the bear: he had nearly completed this operation, when he heard a rustling, as if an animal was coming towards him. To defend himself, he seized his piece, and at the moment we shouted, a bear appeared in view. Not seeing Mears, he laid his fore paws on the trunk of a fallen tree, and turned his head to look back. Mears could not have wished for a better opportunity; he shot him through the head. The bears were very large, and as the night had set in before the latter was skinned and cut up, it was too late to send to the boat for assistance: I therefore offered to carry a part, provided they would allot to me the skins, as they were the only clean part of the spoil. This proposition was agreed to, and we set out. Before we had proceeded far, it became quite dark, which caused us to take a wrong direction, that led to a swamp. In addition to our difficulties, the underwood consisted chiefly of the prickly ash, (*zanthoxylon clava Hercules*) by which our faces and hands were continually scratched: there was also an abundance of small prickly vines entwined among the bushes, of a species of *smilax.* These were easily avoided during [38] day-light, but they were now almost every instant throwing some of us down. Whilst we were deliberating whether it would not be advisable to stop, make a fire, and remain there during the night, we heard the report of a gun, which we thought proceeded from the boat: we therefore steered our course in the direction of the sound. Shortly afterwards we perceived before us a light glimmering through the trees, and in less than half an hour we had a full view of it. Mr. Hunt, from our long delay, had become apprehensive of what had really happened, viz. that we had lost our way, and having observed near the camp a very large cotton-wood tree, which was dead, and evidently hollow, he caused a hole to be cut into the cavity near the root, and a quantity of dry weeds being put in, it was set on fire. The trunk was at least seventy or eighty feet in length before the broken limbs commenced; several of these projected eight or ten feet, and were also hollow. The flames, impelled by so long a column of rarefied air, issued from the top, and from the ends of the limbs, with a surprising force, and with a noise equal to that of a blast furnace. Although smarting with pain, weary, wet, and hungry, not having eaten any thing since morning, I sat down to enjoy the scene, and have seldom witnessed one more magnificent. On relating to the hunters this evening that I had [39] been pursued by a skunk, they laughed heartily, and said it was no uncommon thing, having been often in the same predicament themselves.

2nd.— We this day passed the scite of a village on the north-east side of the river, once belonging to the Missouri tribe. Four miles above it are the remains of Fort Orleans, formerly belonging to the French; it is 240 miles from the mouth of the Missouri.[26] We passed the mouth of La Grande Riviere, near which I first observed the appearance of prairie[27] on the allu-

[26] The Missouri Indians, from whom the river takes its name, were a prominent tribe of Siouan stock, who appear to have lived originally at the mouth of the river; but about the beginning of the eighteenth century they had moved up to this place, where their principal village was found by early French explorers. The Spaniards, alarmed by the alliance of these Indians with the French, sent an expedition (1720) against them, which was, however, betrayed into the hands of the savages and cut off to a man. The commandant in Illinois thereupon (1722) sent De Bourgemont to found an outpost upon the Missouri. This was the origin of Fort Orleans, whose site cannot now be definitely determined, owing to the changes of the river bed. Du Pratz, *Histoire de la Louisiane* (Paris, 1758), places it upon an island in the river. Lewis and Clark speak of all traces thereof being gone. The fort was abandoned in 1726. Later, the French had another post upon the Missouri, among the Kansas Indians. See note 37, *post*. W. B. Douglas, of St. Louis, thinks that Fort Orleans was just above the mouth of Wakenda Creek, in the present Carroll County, which is a little below the former mouth of the Grand River.— ED.

[27] Prairie is the term given to such tracts of land as are divested of timber. In travelling west from the Alleghanies they occur more frequently, and are of greater extent as we approach the Mississippi. When we proceed to the distance of two or three hundred miles west of that river, the whole country is of this description, which continues to the Rocky Mountains westward, and from the head waters of the Mississippi to near the Gulf of Mexico; an extent of territory which probably equals in area the whole empire of China.— BRADBURY.

vion of the river. Our hunters went out, but soon returned without attempting to kill any thing, having
heard some shots fired, which they discovered proceeded
from Indians in pursuit of elk. The navigation had
been very difficult for some days, on account of the
frequent occurrence of, what is termed by the boatmen,
embarras. They are formed by large trees falling into
the river, where it has undermined the banks. Some
of these trees remain still attached by their [40] roots
to the firm ground, and the drift-wood being collected
by the branches, a dam of the length of the tree is
formed, round the point of which the water runs with
such velocity, that in many instances it is impossible to
stem it. On account of these obstacles, we were frequently under the necessity of crossing the river. This
day the carcases of several drowned buffaloes passed
us.

3rd.— I walked the greatest part of the day, but
found it troublesome, being much annoyed by the
prickly ash. In the evening we had another severe
thunder storm.

4th.— The navigation became less difficult, as the
river had fallen four feet.

5th.—Went out with the hunters, who shot nothing
but a goose, (*anas Canadensis*) that was sitting on a
tree beside its nest, in which was the female. Observed for the first time that the rocks bordering the
river were sandstone. In these I found nodules of
iron ore imbedded.

6th.—Walked all day, and in the afternoon met the
hunters, who had found a bee tree,[28] and were [41] re-

---

[28] The term given in America to a hollow tree, containing a swarm of
bees.— BRADBURY.

turning to the boat for a bucket, and a hatchet to cut
it down. I accompanied them to the tree. It contained a great number of combs, and about three gallons of honey. The honey bees have been introduced
into this continent from Europe, but at what time I
have not been able to ascertain. Even if it be admitted
that they were brought over soon after the first settlement took place, their increase since appears astonishing, as bees are found in all parts of the United States;
and since they have entered upon the fine countries of
the Illinois and Upper Louisiana, their progress westward has been surprisingly rapid. It is generally known
in Upper Louisiana, that bees had not been found westward of the Mississippi prior to the year 1797.[29] They
are now found as high up the Missouri as the Maha
nation, having moved westward to the distance of 600
miles in fourteen years. Their extraordinary progress in these parts is probably owing to a portion of the
country being prairie, and yielding therefore a succession of flowers during the whole summer, which is
not the case in forests. Bees [42] have spread over this
continent in a degree, and with a celerity so nearly
corresponding with that of the Anglo-Americans, that
it has given rise to a belief, both amongst the Indians
and the Whites, that bees are their precursors, and that
to whatever part they go the white people will follow.
I am of opinion that they are right, as I think it as im-

---

[29] At that time the natural history of the bee was not very well known at
St. Louis. They relate there, that a French lady of that place having received a present of honey from Kaskaskias, was much delighted with it,
and being told it was produced by a kind of fly, she sent a negro with a small
box to Kaskaskias (60 miles) to get a pair of the flies, in order that she
might obtain the breed.— BRADBURY.

possible to stop the progress of the one as of the other. We encamped this night at the bottom of an island.

7th.— This morning I went upon the island, accompanied by one of the Frenchmen named Guardepée, to look for game. We were wholly unsuccessful in our pursuit, although the island is of considerable extent. On arriving at the upper end of it, we perceived a small island, of about two acres, covered with grass only, and separated from the large one by a narrow channel, the mouth of which was covered with drift timber. We passed over, and walked through the grass, and having given up all hopes of game, we were proceeding to the river to wait for the boat, when my companion, who was before me, suddenly stopped, fired, and jumped aside, crying out, *"Voila, O diable, tirez,"* at the same time pointing towards the grass a few steps before him. I looked, and saw a bear not five yards from us. I immediately fired, and we retired to a short distance to reload, but on our [43] return found the animal expiring. It was a female, with three small cubs in her bed, about two yards from where she was killed. She had heard us approach, and was advancing to defend them. I took one of the cubs in my arms. It seemed sensible of its misfortune, and cried at intervals. It was evident that whenever it uttered a cry, the convulsions of the dying mother increased, and I really felt regret that we had so suddenly cut the ties of so powerful an affection.[30] Whilst we breakfasted the bear was cut up,

[30] The great attachment which the she bear has for her young is well known to the American hunter. No danger can induce her to abandon them. Even when they are sufficiently grown to be able to climb a tree, her anxiety for their safety is but little diminished. At that time, if hunted and attacked by dogs, her first care is to make her young climb to a place of

and, with the young ones, taken on board. We encamped this night about twelve miles below Fort
Osage.[31]

8th.— About ten o'clock we came in sight of the fort,
about six miles distant. We had not been long in
sight before we saw the flag was hoisted, and at noon
we arrived, when we were saluted with a volley as we
passed on to the landing place, where we met Mr.
Crooks, who had come down from the [44] wintering
station at the mouth of the river Naduet to meet us.
There were also collected at the landing place about
200 Indians, men, women, and children, of the Petit
Osage nation, whose village was then about 300 yards
from the fort. We passed through them to pay our
respects to Lieutenant Brownson, who then com-

---

safety. If they show any reluctance, she beats them, and having succeeded,
turns fearlessly on her pursuers. Perhaps in animal economy maternal
affection is almost always commensurate with the helplessness of the young.
— BRADBURY.

[31] Lewis and Clark, on their outward journey in 1804, observed a bluff
of high land on the south side of the river (near the present town of Sibley
in Jackson County), as a site suitable for a fort, and laid down the place
upon their map as "Fort Point." When, in 1808, Clark was requested by
the secretary of war to choose a place for a trading factory and fort, he reverted
to this site, and sent out a detachment under Captain Clemson to begin the
post. Clark following, made a treaty thereat with the Osage, whereby they
surrendered land between the Arkansas and Missouri rivers, and the federal
government on its part promised to keep a garrison at Fort Osage (Fort
Clark) for their protection This treaty was later repudiated by the Osage
chiefs, but a similar one was signed (November 10, 1808) by Pierre Chouteau
on behalf of the United States. In 1813, after the outbreak of the war with
England, this post was evacuated; the garrison was restored in 1816, but
was thereafter only intermittently maintained. One trader reported (1822)
that it consisted of an officer and two soldiers, the latter of whom had deserted. The treaty with the Osage made by Clark in 1825, released the government from its obligation to maintain the post, and upon the erection of
Fort Leavenworth (1827) Fort Osage was permanently abandoned.— ED.

manded in the absence of Captain Clemson.[32] He
received us very politely, and insisted that we should
eat at his table during our stay. I had with me an
introductory letter to Dr. Murray, physician to the
garrison, whom I found disposed to give me every
information relative to the customs and manners of the
Osage nation, and from him also I received a vocabu-
lary of a considerable number of words in that
language.[33] He walked with me down to the boats,
where we found several squaws assembled, as Dr. Murray assured me, for the same purpose as females of a
certain class in the maritime towns of Europe crowd
round vessels lately arrived from a long voyage, and
it must be admitted with the same success. Towards
evening an old chief came down, and harangued the
Indians assembled about the boats, for the purpose of
inviting the warriors of the late expedition to a feast
prepared for them in the village. I was told it was
intended that the dance of the scalp should be performed, on the [45] occasion of the war party having
brought in seven scalps from the Ayauwais, a village
belonging to whom they had destroyed, and killed two
old men and five women and children. All the rest
had fled at their approach; but as rain came on the
dance was not performed. At evening Dr. Murray

[32] Captain Eli B. Clemson was a native of Pennsylvania, and was commissioned lieutenant of the 1st United States infantry in 1789, being pro-
moted to a captaincy in 1807. He served as major of the same regiment
during the War of 1812-15, and was made colonel of the 6th in 1814. After
the close of the war, he retired to private life, dying in 1845. Lieutenant
John Brownson enlisted in 1804, was three years later made lieutenant,
and a captain in 1814. After the second war with Great Britain, he retired
from the service.— ED.

[33] See Appendix, No. I.— BRADBURY.

proposed that we should walk into the village, which I
found to consist of about one hundred lodges of an
oblong form, the frame of timber, and the covering
mats, made of the leaves of flag, or *typha palustris*.   On
our return through the town, we called at the lodge
belonging to a chief named Waubuschon, with whom
Dr. Murray was particularly acquainted.   The floor
was covered with mats, on which they sat; but as I was
a stranger, I was offered a cushion.   A wooden bowl
was now handed round, containing square pieces of
cake, in taste resembling gingerbread.   On inquiry I
found it was made of the pulp of the persimon, (*dio-
spyros Virginiana*) mixed with pounded corn.   This
bread they called staninca.   Shortly afterwards some
young squaws came in, with whom the doctor (who understood the Osage language) began to joke, and in a
few minutes they seemed to have overcome all bash-
fulness, or even modesty.   Some of their expressions,
as interpreted to me, were of the most obscene nature.
The squaw of our host laughed heartily, and did all in
her power to promote this kind of conversation.   I expressed [46] my surprise to Dr. Murray, but was informed by him that similar conduct would have been
pursued at any other lodge in the village.   We left the
lodge of Waubuschon, and went to that of the chief.
On the roof the seven scalps were placed, tied to sticks
ornamented with racoons' tails.   We were shewn to
the upper end of the lodge, and sat down on the ground.
I learned that the chief was not present; that he was a
boy of six years of age, his name Young White Hair, and
that the tribe was now governed by a regent.   Immediately a warrior came in, and made a speech, frequently

pointing to the scalps on the roof, as they were visible through the hole by which the smoke escaped. I understood that he had distinguished himself in the late expedition against the Ayauways. After shaking hands with all round, we left the lodge, and in our return to the boat we met the squaw belonging to our interpreter, who being of the Ayauway nation, appeared to be much afraid of the Osages during our passage up the river, and it was thought with reason, as on our first interview with the commandant, it had been debated whether or not it would be prudent to send a file of men to conduct her from the boat to the fort during our stay. On inquiry we found that she had been invited up to the village by some of the Osages, and of course, according to Indian custom, would be as safe with them as in the fort.

[47] I inquired of Dr. Murray concerning a practice which I had heard prevailed among the Osages, of rising before day to lament their dead. He informed me that such was really the custom, and that the loss of a horse or a dog was as powerful a stimulus to their lamentations as that of a relative or friend; and he assured me, that if I should be awake before day the following morning, I might certainly hear them. Accordingly on the 9th I heard before day that the howling had commenced; and the better to escape observation, I wrapped a blanket round me, tied a black handkerchief on my head, and fastened on my belt, in which I stuck my tomahawk, and then walked into the village. The doors of the lodges were closed, but in the greater part of them the women were crying and howling in a tone that seemed to indicate excessive grief. On the

outside of the village I heard the men, who, Dr. Murray had informed me, always go out of the lodges to lament. I soon came within twenty paces of one, and could see him distinctly, as it was moonlight: he also saw me, and ceased, upon which I withdrew. I was more successful with another, whom I approached nearer unobserved. He rested his back against the stump of a tree, and continued for about twenty seconds to cry out in a loud and high tone of voice, when he suddenly lowered to a low muttering, mixed with sobs: in a few seconds he again raised to the [48] former pitch.[34] We breakfasted with the commandant, and afterwards walked out to view some improvements he had made in the fort. In our walk we observed what, on the first view, appeared to be two squaws carrying a tub of water, suspended on a pole. Mr. Crooks desired me to notice them, which I did, and remarked that one of them had more the appearance of a man than of a woman. He assured me that it was a man, and that there were several others in the village, who, like the one we saw, were condemned for life to associate with the squaws, to wear the same dress, and do the same drudgery. I now learned, that when the Osages go to war, they keep a watchful eye over the young men who are then making their first essay in arms, and such as appear to possess the necessary qualifications are admitted to the rank of warriors, or, according to their own idiom, *brave men.* But if any

---

[34] I have been informed, that when the Osages were in the habit of robbing the white settlers, it was customary with them, after they had entered the house, and before they proceeded to plunder, to blacken their faces, and cry. The reason they gave for this was, that they were sorry for the people whom they were going to rob.— BRADBURY.

exhibit evident proofs of cowardice, on the return of
the party they are compelled to assume the dress and
character of women, and their doom is fixed for life,
as no opportunity is afterwards afforded them to re-
trieve [49] their character.[35]   The men do not associate
with them, nor are they suffered to marry, or have any
intercourse with the women: they may be treated with
the greatest indignity by any warrior, as they are not
suffered to resent it.   I found, on inquiry, that the late
war party had not been conducted by any of the principal chiefs, a circumstance which often happens, as any
of the noted warriors may lead a party, provided he can
obtain adherents, and he finds no difficulty in procuring
the sanction of the chiefs; but in this case he must
travel without mockasons, or even leggings.   He goes
the foremost of the party, makes the fire at night, and
stands to keep watch whilst the party lie down to sleep,
nor can he lie down unless a warrior rises [50] and
takes his place.   This indulgence he must not require,
but may accept, if voluntarily offered.   In pursuing
the object of the expedition, his commands are absolute,

---

[35] It is customary amongst the Missouri Indians to register every exploit
in war, by making a notch for each on the handle of their tomahawks, and
they are estimated as being rich or poor in proportion to the number of
notches.   At their war dances, any warrior who chuses may recount his
exploits.   This is done by pointing to each notch, and describing the particular act that entitled him to it.   The Nodowessies, or Sioux, fix up a post
near the war fire, to represent the enemy of each warrior in succession whilst
he is recounting his deeds.   During his harangue, he strikes the post when
in the act of describing how he struck his enemy, and, like Alexander,
"fights his battles o'er again."   Mr. Crooks informed me, that the day
before our arrival at the fort, he saw an Osage beating and kicking another,
who suffered it patiently.   Mr. Crooks asked him why he did not defend
himself?   "Oh!" said he, shewing the handle of his tomahawk, "*I am too
poor; he is richer than I am.*"— BRADBURY.

and he is obeyed without a murmur. The Osages are
so tall and robust as almost to warrant the application
of the term gigantic: few of them appear to be under six
feet, and many are above it. Their shoulders and
visages are broad, which tend to strengthen the idea of
their being giants. On our return from viewing the
improvements in the fort, I was introduced to Mr.
Sibly, the Indian agent there, who is the son of Dr.
Sibly of Natchitoches.[36] He informed me that he
purposed shortly to attend the Petits Osages in their
annual journey for salt, and invited me to accompany
him, offering as an inducement, to procure two horses
from the Indians for my own use. Learning that the
place where the salt is procured is that which has occasioned the report of a salt mountain existing in Upper
Louisiana, I was very much inclined to accept his invitation; but finding Mr. Hunt unwilling to release me
from my promise to attend him, I declined it. I accompanied Mr. Sibly and Dr. Murray in the evening,
to see the dance of the scalp. The ceremony consisted
in carrying the scalps elevated on sticks through the
village, followed by the warriors who had composed
the war party, dressed in all their ornaments, and
painted as for war.

---

[36] George C. Sibley was born in Massachusetts in 1782, and reared in
North Carolina. His father, who had been a surgeon in the Revolution,
removed to Louisiana, and his account of Red River exploration was embodied (1806) by Jefferson in his message presenting Lewis and Clark's
expedition as far as the Mandan. George Sibley came to St. Louis as an
employé of the Indian department, and for several years was stationed at
Fort Osage as factor. He made various journeys of exploration, one of
which was published. In 1825 he was appointed one of three commissioners
to open a road to New Mexico. Upon his retirement from the public
service, he lived on his estate in St. Charles County, Missouri, where his
benefactions to education made him much esteemed.— ED.

[51] On the 10th we again embarked on the river, although it rained very hard. Our number was now augmented to twenty-six by the addition of Mr. Crooks and his party. We had not proceeded more than two miles, when our interpreter, Dorion, beat his squaw severely; and on Mr. Hunt inquiring the cause, he told him that she had taken a fancy to remain at the Osages in preference to proceeding with us, and because he had opposed it, she had continued sulky ever since. We were obliged to encamp early this day, as the rain became excessive.

11th, 12th, 13th, and 14th.— We had a fair wind, and employed our sail, wherefore I could not go ashore without danger of being left behind. During these days the bread was examined, and being found wholly unfit for use, it was thrown overboard.

15th.— We passed the scite of a village which formerly belonged to the Kansas Indians.[37] I had an opportunity of going ashore, and found the soil to have the appearance of the greatest fertility. On the

---

[37] Lewis and Clark mention this deserted village, saying that the Kansas Indians have (1804) withdrawn to the river which takes its name from them, because of the hostile attacks of the Sauk and Iowa; the latter, coming more in contact with traders, are better armed than the Kansas. This was an important site in the early history of the river. Here was built the second French fort, mentioned by Bougainville in his list of 1757 — in *Northern and Western Boundaries of Ontario* (Toronto, 1878), pp. 80-85. Later (1827), Colonel Leavenworth chose the place as adapted for a United States post. The Kansas Indians were an important branch of the Siouan stock, numbering at this time about thirteen hundred. They are now reduced to less than two hundred, and live beside the Osage on a reservation in Oklahoma. In the early history of white settlement, they were an annoying tribe, plundering traders and committing petty depredations. For a full account of their customs, etc., see James's account of Long's expedition (1819-20), which will be published as volumes xiv, xv, xvi, and xvii of our series.— ED.

sides of the hills I noticed abundance of the hop plant, (*humulus lupulus.*)

16th.— We began to notice more particularly the great number of drowned buffaloes that were floating on the river; vast numbers of them were also [52] thrown ashore, and upon the rafts, on the points of the islands.[38] The carcases had attracted an immense number of turkey buzzards, (*vultur aura*) and as the preceding night had been rainy, multitudes of them were sitting on the trees, with their backs towards the sun, and their wings spread out to dry, a common practice with these birds after rain.

17th.— Arrived at the wintering houses, near the Naduet River, and joined the rest of the party.

18th.— I proceeded to examine the neighbouring country, and soon discovered that pigeons (*columba migratoria*) were in the woods. I returned, and exchanged my rifle for a fowling-piece, and in a few hours shot two hundred and seventy-one, when I desisted. I had an opportunity this day of observing the manner in which they feed: it affords a most singular spectacle, and is also an example of the rigid discipline maintained by gregarious animals. This species of pigeon associates in prodigious flocks: one of these flocks, when on the ground, will cover an area of several acres in extent, and the birds are so close to each other that the ground can scarcely be seen. This phalanx moves through the woods with considerable celerity, picking up, as it passes along, every thing that will serve for food. It is evident that the

---

[38] It was at this point on the river that the hunters of Lewis and Clark's party met their first buffalo.— ED.

foremost [53] ranks must be the most successful, and nothing will remain for the hindermost. But that all may have an equal chance, the instant that any rank becomes the last, it rises, and flying over the whole flock, alights exactly ahead of the foremost. They succeed each other with so much rapidity, that there is a continued stream of them in the air; and a side view of them exhibits the appearance of the segment of a large circle, moving through the woods. I observed that they cease to look for food a considerable time before they become the last rank, but strictly adhere to their regulations, and never rise until there is none behind them.

19th.— On the bluffs[39] under which the wintering [54] house was placed, there is a considerable number of flat stones. On examining one, I found beneath it several snakes, in a half torpid state, arising probably from the cold state of the weather, and I found on further examination, that the number of snakes under these stones was astonishing. I selected this day eleven species, and killed a great number.

[39] As the term bluff may not be understood, an explanation will render the application more intelligible. The alluvion of the great rivers west of the Alleghannies is considerably lower than the surrounding country, and is of a breadth nearly in the ratio of the magnitude of the river; that of the Missouri is from two to six or eight miles in breadth, and is for the most part from a hundred and fifty to three hundred feet below the general level of the country. The ascent from this valley into the country is precipitous, and is called "the Bluff;" it may consist of rock or clay. Betwixt these bluffs the river runs in a very crooked channel, and is perpetually changing its bed, as the only permanent bounds are the bluffs. It may here be remarked, that a view of the vast channel bounded by these bluffs, connected with the idea that all which it contained has been carried away by the river, would induce us to believe that this globe has existed longer than *some people* imagine.— BRADBURY.

20th.— It was this day arranged, by the desire of Mr. Donald M'Kenzie, that I should travel in his boat, and preparations were made for our departure the succeeding morning. I was employed in continuing my researches, and had a narrow escape from a rattle-snake; it darted at me from the top of a small rock, at the base of which I was gathering plants. The noise of its rattle just gave me sufficient notice to withdraw my head.

21st.— We again embarked in four boats. Our party amounted to nearly sixty persons: forty were Canadian boatmen, such as are employed by the North West Company, and are termed in Canada *Engagés* or *Voyageurs*. Our boats were all furnished with masts and sails, and as the wind blew pretty strong from the south-east, we availed ourselves of it during the greater part of the day.

22d, 23d, 24th.— The wind continuing favourable, [55] we sailed almost the whole of these three days, and made considerable progress.

25th.— Went ashore with the hunters, and collected a new species of rattle-snake, and a bird of the genus *recurvirostra*. The hunters killed two elks, but they were so lean that we left them for the vultures: at all times their flesh is much inferior to that of deer.

26th.— The wind had changed to the north-west, and blew so strong, that we were obliged to stop during the whole day. When I found this measure determined on, I resolved to avail myself of the opportunity to quit the valley of the Missouri, and examine the surrounding country. After travelling about three miles, I ascended the bluffs, and found that the face of the country, soil,

&c. were entirely changed. As far as the eye could reach, not a single tree or shrub was visible. The whole of the stratum immediately below the vegetable mould, is a vast bed of exceedingly hard yellow clay. In the valleys, the land floods, during the rainy season, have worn channels so deep, and with the sides so precipitous, that a traveller is often under the necessity of proceeding a mile or two along one of these ravines before he can cross it. In the bottoms of several I observed evident indications of coal.

[56] 27th.— The night had been very cold, and before we had been long on the river, the sides of the boats and the oars were covered with ice, although we were not farther north than 40°. After breakfast, I went out with the hunters, and found my hopes of a change in the vegetation realized. The bluffs forming the bounds of the river are no longer in part rocks, but a continued chain of rounded knobs of stiff clay: under these is a fine bed of bituminous coal, rendered visible wherever the river has washed away the base. This day I collected several new species of plants.

28th.— We breakfasted on one of the islands formed by La Platte Riviere, the largest river that falls into the Missouri. It empties itself into three channels, except in the time of its annual flood, when the intervening land is overflowed; it is then about a mile in breadth. We noticed this day the skeleton or frame of a skin canoe, in which the river had been crossed by Indians: we saw also other indications of war parties having been recently in the neighbourhood, and observed in the night the reflection of immense fires, occasioned by burning the prairies. At this late season,

the fires are not made by the hunters to facilitate their
hunting, but by war parties; and more particularly
when returning unsuccessful, or after a defeat, to prevent their enemies from tracing their [57] steps. As
the ash discontinues to grow on the Missouri above
this place, it was thought expedient to lay in a stock of
oars and poles; and for that purpose, we stopped in the
forenoon, about a league above the mouth of Papillon
Creek, and I availed myself of this opportunity to visit
the bluffs four or five miles distant from us, on the
north-east side.[40] On approaching them I found an
extensive lake running along their base, across which I
waded, the water in no part reaching higher than my
breast. This lake had evidently been in former times
the course of the river: its surface was much covered
with aquatic plants, amongst which were *nelumbium
luteum* and *hydropeltis purpurea*: on the broad leaves
of the former a great number of water snakes were
basking, which on my approach darted into the water.
On gaining the summit of the bluffs, I was amply repaid
by the grandeur of the scene that suddenly opened to
my view, and also by the acquisition of a number of new
plants. On looking into the valley of the Missouri from
an elevation of about two hundred and fifty feet, the
view was magnificent: the bluffs can be seen for more
than thirty miles, stretching to the north-eastward in a
right line, their summits varied by an infinity of undulations. The flat valley of the river, about six or seven

---

[40] The Lewis and Clark expedition also camped here for several days,
and treated with the Indians. Papillion (butterfly) Creek is in Sarpy
County, Nebraska; a town of the same name upon its banks serves as county
seat.— ED.

miles in breadth, is partly prairie, but interspersed with clumps of the finest trees, through the intervals of which could be seen [58] the majestic but muddy Missouri. The scene towards the interior of the country was extremely singular: it presents to the view a countless number of little green hills, apparently sixty or eighty feet in perpendicular height, and so steep, that it was with much difficulty I could ascend them; some were so acutely pointed, that two people would have found it difficult to stand on the top at the same time. I wandered among these mountains in miniature until late in the afternoon, when I recrossed the lake, and arrived at the boats soon after sun-set.

29th.— Being informed that the oars and poles would not be finished before noon, Mr. M'Kenzie obliged me by sending his boat to carry me across the river. I found the bluffs to be of a nature similar to those on the north-east side. I met the boats in the afternoon, and we encamped about fourteen miles below the wintering house belonging to Mr. Crooks, who proposed to me that we should walk to it the following morning, along the bluffs; as the distance was much less by that route than by the course of the river.[41]

30th.— I set out with Mr. Crooks at sunrise, for the wintering house, and travelled nearly a mile on a low piece of ground, covered with long grass: at its termination we ascended a small elevation, [59] and entered on a plain of about eight miles in length, and from two

---

[41] For an account of Crooks's earlier trading venture and his wintering home on the Missouri, see Chittenden, *History of American Fur Trade in the Far West* (New York, 1902), i, pp. 159-162.— ED.

and a half to three miles in breadth. As the old grass
had been burned in the autumn, it was now covered
with the most beautiful verdure, intermixed with flowers. It was also adorned with clumps of trees, sufficient
for ornament, but too few to intercept the sight: in the
intervals we counted nine flocks of elk and deer feeding,
some of which we attempted to approach near enough
to fire at, but without success. On arriving at the
termination of the plain, our route lay along a series of
the most rugged clay bluffs: some of them were in part
washed away by the river, and exhibited perpendicular
faces at least a hundred feet in height. At noon we
arrived at the wintering house, and dined on dried
buffaloe. In the evening the boats came up.

May 1st.— This day was employed in embarking
some articles necessary for the voyage, together with
Indian goods, and in the evening Mr. Crooks informed
me that he intended to set out the next morning on
foot, for the Ottoes, a nation of Indians on the Platte
River, who owed him some beaver.[42] From the Ottoes
he purposed travelling to the Maha nation, about two
hundred miles above us on the Missouri, where he should
again meet the boats. I immediately offered to accom-

---

[42] The Oto Indians were once a powerful nation, an offshoot of the
Missouri family. Their former village stood upon the Missouri River not far
from the city of Omaha; but worn down by wars with their more powerful
neighbors, they had retreated to the south side of Platte River, about thirty
miles above its mouth, where they lived in a village along with the remnants
of the Missouri tribe. They had a good reputation among the traders, for
honesty in repaying credits. Lewis and Clark (1804) sent for their chiefs,
and made a treaty with them at old Council Bluffs, above Omaha, on the
west side of the river. They numbered at that time about five hundred.
Now there are three hundred and seventy of these Indians on an extensive
reservation in Oklahoma.— ED.

pany him; he seemed much pleased, and we proceeded to cast [60] bullets, and make other arrangements necessary for our journey.

2d.— At day-break we were preparing to depart, as also were the rest of the party, when an occurrence took place that delayed us until sunrise, and created a considerable degree of confusion. Amongst our hunters were two brothers of the name of Harrington, one of whom, Samuel Harrington, had been hunting on the Missouri for two years, and had joined the party in autumn: the other, William Harrington, had engaged at St. Louis, in the following March, and accompanied us from thence. The latter now avowed that he had engaged at the command of his mother, for the purpose of bringing back his brother, and they both declared their intention of abandoning the party immediately. As it had already been intimated to us at the Osage nation, that the Nodowessie, or Sioux Indians, intended to oppose our progress up the river, and as no great dependence was placed on our Canadians in case of an attack, the loss of two good riflemen was a matter of regret to us all. Mr. Hunt, although a gentleman of the mildest disposition, was extremely exasperated; and when it was found that all arguments and entreaties were unavailing, they were left, as it was then imagined, without a single bullet or a load of powder, four hundred [61] miles at least from any white man's house, and six hundred and fifty from the mouth of the river. As soon as the final issue of this affair was known, Mr. Crooks and myself set out for the Otto village, attended by two of the Canadians, one named Guardépée, the

other La Liberté.[43]   Our equipments were, a blanket, a
rifle, eighty bullets, a full powder horn, a knife, and
tomahawk, for each.   Besides these, I had a large in-
flexible port-folio, containing several quires of paper,
for the purpose of laying down specimens of plants;
we had also a small camp-kettle, and a little jerked
buffaloe meat.   In half an hour we left the valley of
the Missouri, and entered on the vast plain.   We took
our course S. S. E. which we held for some hours, and
travelled at a great rate, hoping to reach the Platte that
night, although estimated at forty-five miles from the
place of our departure.   A little before noon we saw
four large animals at a great distance, which we supposed to be elk, but on crossing their footsteps some
time afterwards, we found to our great satisfaction
that they were buffaloe.   In the afternoon we crossed
two branches of Papillon Creek, and an hour before
sun-set arrived at the Corne du Cerf River, a deep clear
stream, about eighty yards in breadth: it falls into the
Platte about twenty miles below.   As our Canadians
could not swim, it was necessary to construct a raft,
and we concluded to remain here for the [62] night.

---

[43] Gardepied (or Gariépy) was a common French Canadian name,
several half-breeds bearing it having been employed in the fur-trade.   Possibly this was Jean Baptiste Gardepied, who is recorded as being in the
Astorian expedition, and later playing a prominent part at Fort Union, on
the Yellowstone.   For his bravery, and the tragic manner of his death at
the hands of the Sioux, see Larpenteur, *Journal* (Coues, New York, 1898),
p. 215.

La Liberty was a French Canadian who started with Lewis and Clark,
and disappeared or deserted in this vicinity.   But it was a common name
among voyageurs, and we have found no proof that he was the same individual.— ED.

This arrangement was very agreeable to me, as I was much exhausted, which Mr. Crooks considered was, in a great measure, owing to my having drank water too copiously during the day. Although we had not eaten any thing from the time of our departure, I was unable to eat at supper, and lay down immediately.

3d.— We arose at day break. I found myself completely refreshed. Our raft being ready at sun-rise, we crossed the river, and in two hours arrived at the Platte, exactly opposite the Otto village. The river is here about eight hundred yards in breadth, but appears to be shallow, as its name indicates. The southern bank is wholly divested of timber, and as the village is situated on a declivity near the river, we could see the lodges very distinctly, but there was no appearance of Indians. We discharged our rifles, but the signal was not answered from the village: in about five minutes we heard the report of a gun down the river, and immediately proceeded towards the place. At the distance of half a mile, we arrived opposite to an island, on the point of which a white man was standing, who informed us that we could cross over to him by wading: we did not stop to take off our clothes, but went over immediately, the water reaching to our arm-pits. This man proved to be an American, of the name of Rogers, and [63] was employed as an interpreter by a Frenchman from St. Louis, who was also on the island with a few goods. They informed us that they had been concealed for some days on the island, having discovered a war party hovering round, belonging, as they supposed, to the Loup, or Wolf nation, who had come in order to sur-

prise the Ottoes.[44]   They had nothing to give us as
food, excepting some beaver flesh, which Rogers obtained by trapping on Corne du Cerf, or Elk Horn
River; as it was stale, and tasted fishy, I did not much
relish it, but there was no alternative but to eat it or
starve.   We remained all day concealed on the island,
and on the morning of the 4th, before daylight, Rogers
set out to look at his traps, on Elk Horn River, distant
to the eastward not more than five miles.   I accompanied him, and on crossing the channel of the Platte,
found that in the same place where the day before it
reached to our arm-pits, it did not now reach to our
waists, although the river had not fallen.   Such changes
in the bottom of this river, Rogers told me were very
frequent, as it is composed of a moving gravel, in which
our feet sank to a considerable depth.   We arrived at
the Elk Horn River about sun-rise, but found no
beaver in the traps.   After our return to the island, I
expressed a wish to visit the Otto village, which was in
sight; and Rogers, who had a canoe concealed in the
willows that surrounded the island, [64] landed me on
the other side of the river.   I found the village to consist of about fifty-four lodges, of a circular form, and
about forty feet in diameter, with a projecting part at
the entrance, of ten or twelve feet in length, in the form
of a porch.   At almost every lodge, the door or entrance
was closed after the manner which is customary with

―――――――

[44] The Loup (Wolf) Indians were a branch of the Pawnee tribe, usually
known as the Panimahas.   They claimed to have migrated across the Mississippi about the middle of the eighteenth century, in company with the
Arikara, to whom they were related.   Their language (Caddoan), however,
shows close affinity to that of the other Pawnee.   They dwelt upon the
Loup branch of Platte River, and were a fierce and numerous people.— ED.

Indians when they go on hunting parties, and take their squaws and children with them. It consists in putting a few sticks across, in a particular manner, which they so exactly note and remember, as to be able to discover the least change in their position. Although anxious to examine the internal structure of the lodges, I did not violate the injunction conveyed by this slight obstruction, and after searching some time, found a few that were left entirely open. On entering one, I found the length of the porch to be an inclined plane to the level of the floor, about two and a half or three feet below the surface of the ground: round the area of the lodge are placed from fifteen to eighteen posts, forked at the top, and about seven feet high from the floor. In the centre, a circular space of about eight feet in diameter is dug to the depth of two feet; four strong posts are placed in the form of a square, about twelve feet asunder, and at equal distances from this space: these posts are about twenty feet high, and cross pieces are laid on the tops. The rafters are laid from the forked [65] tops of the outside posts over these cross pieces, and reach nearly to the centre, where a small hole is left for the smoke to escape: across the rafters small pieces of timber are laid; over these, sticks and a covering of sods, and lastly earth. The fire is made in the middle of the central space, round the edges of which they sit, and the beds are fixed betwixt the outer posts. The door is placed at the immediate entrance into the lodge: it is made of a buffalo skin, stretched in a frame of wood, and is suspended from the top. On entering, it swings forward, and when let go, it falls to its former position. On my return to the island, Mr.

Crooks informed me that he had resolved to send Rogers to find the Ottoes, who were hunting about twenty miles from us, in order to collect his debts, or to procure horses for us, to facilitate our journey to the Maha nation.

5th.— In the morning early, Rogers set out on his expedition, and returned on the 6th, without having obtained any beaver or horses, excepting one horse belonging to Mr. Crooks. This night I procured from Rogers what information I could relative to the Otto nation, and was informed that the Missouris are incorporated with them; that they are their descendants, and speak the same language. They call themselves Waddoké-tăh-tăh, and can muster one hundred and thirty [66] or one hundred and forty warriors. They are now at war with the Loups or Wolf Indians, the Osages, and the Sioux. He said they furnish a considerable quantity of bear, deer, and beaver skins, and are very well disposed towards their traders, who may safely credit them. They do not claim the property of the land on which they live, nor any other tract. A very considerable part of the surrounding country formerly belonged to the Missouris, who were once the most powerful nation on the Missouri river, but have been reduced by war and the small pox to be dependent on the Ottoes, by whom they are treated as inferiors. Rogers had with him a squaw of the Maha nation, with her child, whom he wished to send with us to her father. To this Mr. Crooks consented, and early on the morning of the 7th we set out, putting the squaw and her child on the horse. Having crossed over from the island, we steered a due north course, and came to the Elk Horn River, after travelling about ten miles. Mr. Crooks immediately stripped, to examine if the river was fordable, and found that, excepting about twenty yards in the middle, we might wade it. I offered to carry the child, but the squaw refused, and after stripping herself, she gave me her clothes, put the child on her neck, and swam over, the little creature sticking to her hair. After assisting our Canadians across, we continued along [67] the bank, in expectation of arriving at the creek, distant about five miles, which comes in a direction from the north. We observed, that as our distance from the island increased, the reluctance of the squaw to proceed also increased, and soon after we had crossed the river, she began to cry, and declared she would go no farther. Mr. Crooks, who understood the language, remonstrated with her; but finding it in vain, he ordered Guardepée to take her back, and we encamped to wait his return.

8th.— About two o'clock in the morning Guardepée returned with the horse, and at day-light we set out. In about an hour we came to the creek,[45] and continued along its banks, and found ourselves in a short time on a most beautiful prairie, along which the creek flowed, without having a single tree on its border, or even a shrub, excepting a few widely scattered plum bushes. We shot this day two prairie hens, (*tetrao umbellus*) on which we supped, having dined on some jerked buffalo, brought by Rogers from the Ottoes. We slept on the border of the creek, but not so comfortably as usual,

---

[45] This was Bell Creek, which, coming directly from the north, heads a short distance from Blackbird Creek.— Ed.

as the dew was so copious, that before morning our blankets were wet through.

9th.— We continued to pursue our course along the creek, but with great trouble, as our mockassons, [68] being of untanned skins, became so soft as to render it difficult to keep them on our feet. We shot a prairie hen, and prepared to breakfast, having first relieved the horse from the baggage, and turned him out to graze. Whilst we were collecting some dry stalks of plants to boil our kettle, a herd of elk, nineteen in number, appeared marching towards the creek, and Guardepée immediately ran to put himself in such a position that he might fire at them, when the horse took fright, broke his tie, and gallopped off. Guardepée fired, but only wounded one so slightly that it ran off with the rest, and escaped. The horse took the direct route back towards the Ottoes, and was followed by Mr. Crooks and Guardepée; but in vain: they gave up the chase, finding it impossible to recover him. After we had breakfasted, we threw the saddle and every thing belonging to the horse into the creek; each man took his share of the baggage, and we again set out, and travelled without stopping until evening, when we arrived at the head of the creek, and came to what is called a dividing ridge.[46] We passed over it, and came to the head of a creek, running in a N. E. direction. This we supposed to be Blackbird Creek, which falls into the Missouri, near the monument of a famous chief of the [69] Mahas, named Blackbird. At the distance of about two miles, we saw a small clump of trees on

---

[46] A term given to any elevation that separates the head waters of one creek from those of another.— BRADBURY.

the border of the creek, and resolved to remain there during the night, hoping to find fuel to boil a small portion of jerked buffalo, being all we had left. Whilst the supper was preparing, I walked back to an eminence, to collect some interesting plants, having noticed them in passing. I had not been long employed in that way, when I saw a distant flash of lightning in the south, and soon after others in quick succession. As these and other appearances indicated the approach of a violent storm, I hastened back to recommend precautions for the security of our arms and ammunition. Having boiled our meat, which amounted to a few morsels each, we secured our powder horns and some tow in our camp kettle, which we inverted, and discharged our rifles. Excepting the sound of distant thunder, which was continual, an awful silence prevailed, and the cloud which had already spread over one half of the visible horizon, was fast shutting out the little remains of day-light. As the trees afforded us no fuel, and in a few minutes would become no shelter, but might endanger our safety, I recommended that we should go to the open prairie, which we did, and lay down in our blankets: I put my plants under me. For several hours the thunder, lightning, and rain were incessant, and such rain as I have seldom witnessed. [70] In half an hour after the storm commenced, we had nothing more to fear from it, excepting the cold occasioned by the torrents that fell on us. At the approach of morning the rain ceased: we saw a few stars, and with joy noticed the first appearances of day. We arose, and wrung the water out of our blankets, and finding ourselves very much benumbed, we walked about to restore the circulation: when it was sufficiently light, we put our rifles in order, which was attended with considerable difficulty, as our hands were almost without sensation. Having arranged our arms, we set out, but were extremely uncomfortable, as our clothes, being made of dressed skins, stuck so close to our bodies as to make our march very unpleasant. We proceeded at a brisk pace to warm ourselves, and in about two hours came to a small ridge, which we ascended, and when near the top, Guardepée preceded us, to examine if any game was in sight. He gave the signal for us to remain quiet and soon afterwards fired at two buffalo cows, with their calves. One of the cows he wounded, and they ran off with so much speed, that the calves could not keep up with them. Perceiving this, I immediately pursued the calves, one of which I killed. The rest of the party followed the cows for a short distance, but finding the inutility of it, they soon returned: and notwithstanding my remonstrances, Guardepée killed the other calf. As we had eaten [71] but little the day before, we were very glad of this supply, and taking what we thought proper, proceeded on our journey. We soon began to perceive that the face of the country was changing in its appearance. From the Elk Horn River, our course had hitherto been over a most beautiful prairie, with scarcely a tree or shrub, but covered with grass and flowers: we now began to observe a more broken country to the eastward, and some scattered bushes in the valleys. From an eminence, we soon after perceived a hill, that had a heap of stones on the summit: Mr. Crooks assured me that this was the monu-

ment of Blackbird,[47] the famous [72] Maha chief, and
that it was one of the bluffs of the Missouri: we judged
it was about fifteen miles N. E. of us. Satisfied that
we were now near the boats, and having arrived at
some small timber, where we could procure fuel, we
dined on our veal; and although without bread or salt
it was to us a luxury, as we had long been unaccustomed

---

[47] This chief, called by the French, Oiseau Noir, ruled over the Mahas
with a sway the most despotic. He had managed in such a manner as to
inspire them with the belief that he was possessed of supernatural powers: in
council no chief durst oppose him — in war it was death to disobey. It is
related of him at St. Louis, that a trader from that town arrived at the
Mahas with an assortment of Indian goods: he applied to Blackbird for
liberty to trade, who ordered that he should first bring all his goods into
his lodge, which order was obeyed. Blackbird commanded that all the
packages should be opened in his presence, and from them he selected what
goods he thought proper, amounting to nearly the fourth part of the whole:
he caused them to be placed in a part of the lodge distinct from the rest,
and addressed the trader to this effect: — "Now, my son, the goods which
I have chosen are mine, and those in your possession are your own. Don't
cry, my son; my people shall trade with you for your goods *at your own
price.*" He then spoke to his herald, who ascended to the top of the lodge,
and commanded, in the name of the chief, that the Mahas should bring
all their beaver, bear, otter, muskrat, and other skins to his lodge, and not
on any account to dispute the terms of exchange with the trader, who declared, on his return to St. Louis, that it was the most profitable voyage he
had ever made. Mr. Tellier, a gentleman of respectability, who resided
near St. Louis, and who had been formerly Indian agent there, informed
me that Blackbird obtained this influence over his nation by the means of
arsenic, a quantity of that article having been sold to him by a trader, who
instructed him in the use of it. If afterwards any of his nation dared to
oppose him in his arbitrary measures, he *prophesied* their death within a
certain period, and took good care that his predictions should be verified.
He died about the time that Louisiana was added to the United States;
having previously made choice of a cave for his sepulchre, on the top of a
hill near the Missouri, about eighteen miles below the Maha village. By
his order his body was placed on the back of his favourite horse, which was
driven into the cave, the mouth of which was then closed up with stones. A
large heap was afterwards raised on the summit of the hill.— BRADBURY.

to those articles. We halted about three hours before
sunset, at about five miles from the monument of Blackbird,[48] to which place Mr. Crooks despatched Guardepée to look for a letter, as Mr. Hunt had promised
to leave one there on passing [73] the place. At night
he returned, but without a letter, and we concluded
that the boats had not yet arrived.

11th.— We set off early, and soon fell in with the
trace from the Maha village to the monument:[49] along
this we travelled, and about ten o'clock arrived at the
town, where we met one of the Canadians belonging
to the boats. He informed us that they arrived the
day before, and were stationed about four miles from

_____

[48] Much has been written of this Omaha chieftain, notably Irving's
description in *Astoria*, which sums up most of the traditions. Catlin, the
painter of Indians, attempted an apology for Blackbird's sinister reputation.
He also painted a picture of his burial hill, and carried off the chief's skull,
which is now in the National Museum — see Smithsonian *Report*, 1885,
ii, p. 263. The mound was for many years a well-known landmark upon
the river, but is now scarcely noticeable. The bluff is upon the Omaha
Indian reservation about seventy-five miles above the city of Omaha.— ED.

[49] The Omaha Indians (usually called Mahas) had formerly lived on
the Mississippi. They retain a definite tradition of their migrations, which
are traced by Dorsey, ''Omaha Sociology,'' in Bureau of Ethnology *Report*,
1881-82. They had formerly been one of the most powerful tribes of
Siouan stock, numbering from three to four thousand but were decimated
by small-pox. Lewis and Clark found less than six hundred of them.
They now have about twice that population, and live upon a reservation
in Nebraska just below the village where they then dwelt. The Omaha
have been much discussed and experimented with, showing an unusual
adaptability for education. The Presbyterians maintained a mission
school among them for many years. See *The Middle Five* (Boston, 1900),
by Francis La Flesche, son of one of their chiefs. In 1883-84 lands were
allotted to them in severalty, under the direction of Miss Alice Fletcher, who
has also made studies of their customs and music. They are to-day among
the most civilized and progressive of our Indian tribes, living in satisfactory
houses, devoting themselves to agriculture, and deriving good incomes from
their leased lands.— ED.

the village. As we were in want of food, we did not
stop, but proceeded to the boats, where we found a considerable number of Indians assembled to trade. They
gave jerked buffalo meat, tallow, corn, and marrow;
and in return they received tobacco in carottes, vermillion, blue beads, &c. There, also, we found Mr.
James Aird, an old and respectable trader, with whom
I had become acquainted at St. Louis.[50] He informed
me that he should go to the United States in a few days;
I therefore availed myself of this opportunity to forward letters, and was employed in writing until the 12th
at noon. Immediately after, I set out on an excursion
to the bluffs, and in my way passed through the village,
where the great number of children playing about the
lodges, entirely naked, drew my attention. I soon
attracted their notice also, and they began to collect
around me. Some of the [74] boldest ventured to
touch my hand, after which they ran back a few paces,
but soon again resumed their courage. When about
fifty or sixty had assembled, I came to where three
young squaws were repairing one of the stages erected
for the purpose of exposing the buffalo skins to dry,
whilst they are in preparation. The squaws, seeing
the children run after me, spoke to them in a com-
manding tone, when they instantly stopped, and not
one followed me afterwards. I doubt much if such a

---

[50] James Aird was a Scotchman who embarked in the fur-trade at Mackinac, and became one of the earliest settlers of Prairie du Chien. During
the War of 1812-15 he adhered to the British interests, and at its close continued his trading upon the upper waters of the Mississippi, until his death
in 1819. Lewis and Clark met him ascending the Missouri, upon their
return journey in 1806. He was a man of integrity, and much respected
throughout the Northwest. See *Wisconsin Historical Collections*, ix,
index.— ED.

crowd of children, in any European city, would have obeyed with such promptness, had such a phenomenon appeared among them, as they must have considered me. On arriving at the summit of the bluffs, I had a fine view of the town below. It had a singular appearance. The frame work of the lodges consists of ten or twelve long poles, placed in the periphery of a circle of about sixteen feet in diameter, and are inclined towards each other, so as to cross at a little more than half their length from the bottom; and the tops diverging with the same angle, exhibit the appearance of one cone inverted on the apex of another. The lower cone is covered with dressed buffalo skins, sewed together, and fancifully painted; some with an undulating red or yellow band, of ten or twelve inches in breadth, surrounding the lodge at half its height; in others, rude figures of horses, buffaloe or deer were painted; others again with attempts [75] at the human face, in a circle, as the moon is sometimes painted; these were not less than four feet in diameter. I judged there were not fewer than eighty lodges. I did not remain long on the summit of the bluffs, as I perceived, from the heaps of earth, some of these recent, that it was the burial ground, and I knew the veneration they have for the graves of their ancestors. I proceeded along the bluffs, and was very successful in my researches, but had not been long employed, when I saw an old Indian galloping towards me. He came up and shook hands with me, and pointing to the plants I had collected, said, "*Bon pour manger?*" to which I replied, "*Ne pas bon.*" He then said, "*Bon pour medicine?*" I replied "*Oui.*" He again shook hands and rode away, leaving me somewhat surprised at being addressed in French by an Indian. On my return through the village, I was stopped by a group of squaws, who invited me *very kindly* into their lodges, calling me wakendaga, or as it is pronounced, wa-ken-da-ga (physician.) I declined accepting their invitation, showing them that the sun was near setting, and that it would be night before I could reach the boats. They then invited me to stay all night: this also I declined, but suffered them to examine my plants, for all of which I found they had names. On my way to the boats, I met a number of Indians returning to the village, all of whom shook [76] hands with me. Two of them informed me that they had seen me at St. Louis, and at the same time gave me satisfactory proofs of it.[51] I did not reach the boats until it was dark.

13th.— In the forenoon of this day, Mr. Hunt was waited upon by two chiefs, who were contending for the sanction of the government of the United States, to determine their claim to kingly power. Mr. Hunt declined interfering, not being vested with the powers

---

[51] The Indians are remarkable for strength of memory in this particular. They will remember a man whom they have only transiently seen, for a great number of years, and perhaps never during their lives forget him. I had no recollection of these Indians, but they pointed down the river to St. Louis: afterwards they took up the corner of the buffalo robe, held it before their faces, and turned it over as a man does a newspaper in reading it. This action will be explained by relating that I frequented the printing-office of Mr. Joseph Charless, when at St. Louis, to read the papers from the United States, when it often happened that the Indians at that place on business came into the office and sat down. Mr. Charless, out of pleasantry, would hand to each a newspaper, which, out of respect for the custom of the whites, they examined with as much attention as if they could read it, turning it over at the same time that they saw me turn that with which I was engaged.— BRAD-BURY.

to act. The names of these two chiefs were the Big Elk[52] and the White Cow, the former of whom ultimately succeeded, and has since signalized himself by a fine specimen of Indian eloquence, at the funeral of a Sioux chief, in the [77] Missouri territory.[53] The Mahas seem very friendly to the whites, and cultivate corn, beans, melons, squashes, and a small species of tobacco (*nicotiana rustica.*) In 1802 they were visited by the small-pox, which made dreadful havoc, and destroyed at least two thirds of the whole nation. At present they muster nearly two hundred warriors, and from the great number of children, I judge that they are again increasing. In stature they are much inferior to the Osages, although I noticed several whom I thought would reach to six feet. Their hunting ground is from their village to *L'Eau qui Court*, and along that river.[54]

14th.— This day three Sioux Indians arrived, of the Yanktoon Ahna tribe,[55] who reported that several na-

---

[52] Big Elk, or Om-pah-ton-ga, became one of the greatest and most respected of the chiefs of the Omaha. See his portrait by Catlin, in Smithsonian *Report*, 1885, ii, p. 72. He died about 1846, and his burial place was long a landmark of the Omaha tribe.— ED.

[53] See Appendix, No. II.— BRADBURY.

[54] The French called the Niobrara River, L'eau qui court — the rapidly-running water. It is now the boundary between Nebraska and South Dakota.— ED.

[55] The Sioux Indians (properly Dakota) are the largest branch of the great Siouan famil   The Yankton are mentioned by Lewis and Clark as the first and most peaceably-inclined tribe of Dakota. They inhabited the territory north and east of the Missouri, roving upon the Vermillion, James, and Big Sioux rivers. They still number about three thousand, three-fifths of whom are upon reservations in South Dakota, the remainder being at Fort Peck agency in Montana. The term *ahna* was equivalent to tribe or people.— ED.

tions of the Sioux were assembling higher up the river, with an intention to oppose our progress. This news was concealed as much as possible from the *voyageurs*, and we prepared for our departure on the following morning.

15th.— We embarked early, and passed Floyd's Bluffs, so named from a person of the name of Floyd (one of Messrs. Lewis and Clarke's party) having been buried there.[56] In the course of this day, I was informed by Mr. M'Kenzie, that in the night of the [78] 7th instant, during our journey to the Ottoes, eleven Sioux Indians, who *had given or devoted their clothes to the medicine*,[57] ran into the camp with their tomahawks in their hands, and were instantly surrounded and taken prisoners. The leader, finding the party on their guard, and much stronger probably than he expected, immediately cried out to his followers in their language, ''My children, do not hurt the white people.'' As the party were fully apprized of the murderous intentions of these miscreants, the general voice was for putting them to death; but Mr. Hunt would not consent to it, and ordered that they should be conveyed over the river in one of the boats, at the same time informing

[56] Floyd's Bluff, upon which stands the grave of Sergeant Charles Floyd, was for many years a well-known landmark to Missouri travellers. It is just below the present Sioux City, Iowa, and here in 1895 the Floyd Monument Association erected a shaft to mark his resting place. For his life and journal, see Thwaites, *Original Journals of Lewis and Clark Expedition.*— ED.

[57] When a party on a war excursion are entirely foiled in their object, a dread of the scoffs which may be expected from their tribe, renders them furious; and it often happens in such cases, that they throw away their clothes, or devote them to the Great Spirit, with an intention to do some desperate act. Any white man, or any party of whites, whom they meet and can overcome, is almost certain to be sacrificed in this case.— BRADBURY.

them, that if they were again caught by the party, every man should be sacrificed. From a coincidence of time and circumstances, it appeared almost certain that it was this party that had crossed the Missouri, near the mouth of the river Platte, in the canoe of which we saw the skeleton on the 28th of April; and that it was also this party that was discovered by Rogers [79] hovering about the Otto village, as the Sioux are at war with the Ottoes: it therefore appeared that Mr. Crooks and myself had run a greater risk than we were sensible of at the time.

16th, 17th, and 18th.— We had a fair wind, and made considerable progress up the river; few opportunities were therefore afforded for walking. I regretted this circumstance, as the bluffs had a very interesting appearance. During a short excursion, I was enabled to ascertain that the lower part of the bluffs was impregnated with sulphur, mixed with sulphate of iron and selenite crystals.

19th.— About nine o'clock we observed three buffalo cows and a calf swimming across the river. Two of them and the calf were killed; but we found them to be so poor that we only preserved the calf.

20th.— We were stopped all day by a strong head wind. I availed myself of this circumstance, and was very successful in my researches. We found that the river was rising rapidly; it rose during this day more than three feet: we therefore concluded that this was the commencement of the annual flood of the Missouri, occasioned by the melting of the snow on the Rocky Mountains.

[80] 21st.—The river continued to rise, and the cur-

rent to increase in rapidity: the navigation was therefore rendered very difficult. I walked the greatest part of the day, chiefly on the bluffs, and found the summits for the most part covered with gravel, containing tumblers of feldspar, granite, and some porphyry.

22d.— In the morning our hunters killed three buffaloe and two elks on an island; and as we were now arriving at the country of our enemies, the Sioux, it was determined that they should in a great measure confine themselves to the islands, in their search for game. We dined at the commencement of a beautiful prairie; afterwards I went to the bluffs, and proceeded along them till near evening. On regaining the bank of the river, I walked down to meet the boats, but did not find them until a considerable time after it was dark, as they had stopped early in the afternoon, having met with a canoe, in which were two hunters of the names of Jones and Carson, who had been two years near the head of the Missouri.[58] These men agreed to join the party, and were considered as a valuable acquisition; any accession of strength being now desirable. This day, for the first time, I was much annoyed by the abundance of the prickly pear. Against the thorns of this plant I found that [81] mockasons are but a slight defence. I observed two species, *cactus opuntia* and *mamillaris*.

23d.— When on the bluffs yesterday, I observed in

---

[58] Ben Jones and Alexander Carson had probably been of the party of forty expert riflemen who escorted back to his home (1809), the Mandan chief who three years before had accompanied Lewis and Clark on a visit to the East. Carson later settled on the Willamette, Oregon, and was killed by the Indians at a place which still bears his name — Alec's Butte, in the North Yamhill country.— ED.

the river an extensive bend, and determined to travel across the neck.[59]   I therefore did not embark with the boats, but filled my shot pouch with parched corn, and set out, but not without being reminded by Mr. Hunt that we were now in an enemy's country.   In about two hours I had entirely passed the range of hills forming the boundary of the Missouri; and as I had before experienced, I found the soil and face of the country to improve very much as we proceed from the river.   The hills here are only gentle swellings, and, together with the intervening valleys, were covered with the most beautiful verdure.   At a small distance from my route I noticed a space, of several acres in extent, of a more vivid green than the surrounding prairie, and on my nearer approach it had the appearance of a rabbit burrow.   From the previous descriptions given by the hunters, I immediately conceived it to be, what it proved, a colony of the prairie dog.[60]   The little animals had taken the alarm before I reached their settlement, and were sitting singly on the small hillocks of earth at the [82] mouth of their holes.   They were very clamorous uttering a cry which had some resemblance to a shrill barking.   I fired at several, but at the instant of the flash, they darted with surprising quickness into their holes, before the shot could reach them.   I soon found the impossibility of procuring one with shot only, as unless they are instantaneously killed, they are cer-

---

[59] This bend would appear to be the one above Bon Homme Island, with the town of Springfield, South Dakota, on its upper side.— ED.

[60] A species of *sciurus* or squirrel, not described in the Syst. Natura.— BRADBURY.

tain to get into their holes, from the edges of which they never wander if a man is in sight.[61] I continued to travel through this charming country till near the middle of the afternoon, when I again came to the bluffs of the Missouri, where, amongst a number of new plants, I found a fine species of *ribes*, or currant. As it was now time to look for the boats, I went to the river and proceeded down the bank, in the expectation of meeting them. I had probably travelled about two miles, when suddenly I felt a hand laid upon my shoulder, and turning round, saw a naked Indian with his bow bent, and the arrow pointed towards me. As I had no expectation of meeting any Indians excepting the Sioux, and as with them the idea of danger was associated, I took my gun from my shoulder, and by a kind of spontaneous movement put my hand towards the lock, when I perceived that the Indian drew his bow still farther. I now found myself completely in his power; but recollecting that if an enemy, he would have shot me before I saw him, I held out my hand, which he [83] took, and afterwards laid his hand on my breast, and in the Osage language said *"Moi-he ton-ga de-ah,"* literally in English, *"*Big Knife you?"[62] which I luckily understood and answered, *"Hoya,"* (Yes) and laying my hand on his breast, said, *"No-do-wessie de-ah,"* (Sioux you.) He replied, *"Hon-koska ponca we ah,"* (No, Poncar me.) He then

---

[61] The prairie-dog (*cynomys ludovicianus*) was unknown to science until described by Lewis and Clark. It was first named *Arctomys ludoviciana* in 1815, and afterwards (1820) made a separate genus.— ED.

[62] The Americans are called "the Big Knives" by the Indians of the Missouri.— BRADBURY.

pointed up the river, and I saw two other Indians running towards us, and not more than fifty yards distant.
They soon came up, and all the three laid hold of me,
pointing over the bluffs, and making signs that I should
go with them. I resisted and pushed off their hands.
As the river had overflowed where we stood, I pointed
to a sand-hill a small distance from us, to which we
went and sat down. I amused them with my pocket
compass for some time, when they again seized me, and
I still resisted, and took out a small microscope. This
amused them for some time longer, when on a sudden
one of them leaped up and gave the war whoop. I laid
hold of my gun, with an intention to defend myself,
but was instantly relieved from apprehension by his
pointing down the river, and I perceived the mast of
one of the boats appear over the willows. The Indians
seemed very much inclined to run away, but I invited
them to accompany me to [84] the boats, and shewed
them by signs that I would give them something to
drink, which they complied with, but soon after disappeared. We travelled very late this evening, and encamped above the mouth of a small creek. It appeared
that the three Indians went to inform their nation,[63] as
in the morning a number of them came to our camp
and also a white man, with a letter to Mr. Hunt from
Mr. Lisa, one of the Missouri Fur Company, for whom

---

[63] The Ponca are closely allied with the Omaha, in whose company they
are supposed to have migrated to the Missouri, and settled near the Niobrara
River. They had shared the same fate of being, by small-pox and attacks
of Sioux, reduced from a powerful to an insignificant tribe. Being usually
friendly to the whites, a trading house was maintained among them for
many years. In 1877 they were removed to Indian Territory, and have
since been allotted lands in severalty. They now number about seven hundred.— ED.

he was agent.[64]   Mr. Lisa had arrived at the Mahas some days after we left, and had dispatched this man by land.   It appeared he had been apprised of the hostile intentions of the Sioux, and the purport of the letter was to prevail on Mr. Hunt to wait for him, that they might, for mutual safety, travel together on that part of the river which those blood thirsty savages frequent.   It was judged expedient to trade with the Indians for some jerked buffalo meat, and more than 1000 lbs. was obtained for as much tobacco as cost two dollars.   About noon we set out, and at the distance of a league passed the mouth of the river called L'Eau qui Court, or Rapid River.

25th.— It was discovered early this morning, that two men who had engaged at the Mahas, and had received equipments to a considerable value, had deserted in the night.   As it was known that one of them could not swim, and we had passed a [85] large creek about a league below, our party went in pursuit of them, but without success.

---

[64] Manuel Lisa was one of the most remarkable figures in the early history of the Missouri fur-trade.   Born of Spanish parents in New Orleans, in 1772, he came to St. Louis probably about 1790.   By the beginning of the nineteenth century his energy, address, and ability had secured him a large place in the fur-trading fraternity.   About 1800, he obtained a permit for monopolizing the trade upon Osage River.   Upon the return of Lewis and Clark (1806), he organized the Missouri Fur Company, and the following year reached the Three Forks of the Missouri in person, building a fort there.   Almost every year thereafter he made an expedition up the river, until his death in 1820.   During the War of 1812-15, his influence with the Indians was exerted on behalf of the United States government, and was powerful in protecting the Western settlements.   His success as a trader aroused bitter jealousy and hostility among his competitors; he has been called "a fur-trading Cortez," but it is difficult to prove that his methods were more cruel or more treacherous than those of his rivals.   See Chittenden, *American Fur Trade*, pp. 125-136.— ED.

26th.— Whilst at breakfast on a beautiful part of the river, we observed two canoes descending on the opposite side. In one, by the help of our glasses, we ascertained there were two white men, and in the other only one. A gun was discharged, when they discovered us, and crossed over. We found them to be three men belonging to Kentucky, whose names were Robinson, Hauberk, and Reesoner. They had been several years hunting on and beyond the Rocky Mountains, until they *imagined* they were tired of the hunting life; and having families and good plantations in Kentucky, were returning to them; but on seeing us, families, plantations, and all vanished; they agreed to join us, and turned their canoes adrift. We were glad of this addition to our number, as the Poncars had confirmed all that we had heard respecting the hostile disposition of the Nodowessies, or Sioux, towards us, with the additional information, that five nations or tribes had already assembled, with a determination to cut us off. Robinson was sixty-six years of age, and was one of the first settlers in Kentucky. He had been in several engagements with the Indians there, who really made it to the first settlers, what its name imports, ''The Bloody Ground.''   In one of these engagements he was [86] scalped, and has since been obliged to wear a handkerchief on his head to protect the part.[65]

---

[65] The career of these three Kentuckians — John Hoback, Jacob Rezner (Rizner, Regnier, etc.), and Edward Robinson — is typical of that of many pioneer hunters to whom the charms of the wilderness proved irresistible and fatal. Having accompanied the Astorians overland to Snake River, they were detached on a hunting expedition (October 10, 1811), without having reached Astoria. The next summer the returning party met them in the wilderness, destitute and starving, having been robbed by Arapaho. With fresh supplies, they determined to continue hunting, and according

The wind being fair, we this day made considerable progress, and had many fine views of the bluffs, along which, from the L'Eau qui Court, we observed excellent roads made by the buffaloes. These roads I had frequent opportunities of examining, and am of opinion that no engineer could have laid them out more judiciously.

27th.— The weather continues fine, as it has been for the last fortnight, and is delightful. For some days past it has been very warm, and the carcases of drowned buffaloes on the islands and shores of the river become extremely offensive. We had a fine breeze from the S. E. and made all the sail the extreme cowardice of our Canadians would permit, in order to reach Little Cedar Island,[66] as it was intended that we should stop there to procure new masts, some of our old ones being defective.[67] Late in the evening we accomplished our purpose to the joy of our voyageurs, who frequently in the course of the day, when the boats heeled, cried out in agony, *''O mon Dieu! abattez le goile.''* As we had now in our party five men who had traversed the Rocky Mountains in various directions, [87] the best possible route in which to cross them became a subject of anxious enquiry. They all agreed that the route followed

to the story of Dorion's squaw were murdered, together with that interpreter, during the winter of 1813. A river in Wyoming still bears the name of Hoback.— ED.

[66] One thousand and seventy-five miles from the mouth of the Missouri. — BRADBURY.

[67] There are several islands upon the Missouri named Cedar. The one to which Bradbury here refers, is that opposite the present town of Chamberlain, South Dakota, which was formerly the site of Fort Recovery, a Missouri Fur Company's post built in 1822. An earlier post in this vicinity was burned (1810), whence the name of the later fort.— ED.

by Lewis and Clarke was very far from being the best, and that to the southward, where the head waters of the Platte and Roche Jaune rivers rise, they had discovered a route much less difficult.[68]   This information induced Mr. Hunt to change his plan, which had originally been to ascend the Missouri to the Roche Jaune river, one thousand eight hundred and eighty miles from the mouth, and at that place to commence his journey by land.   It was now concluded that it would be more adviseable to abandon the Missouri at the Aricara Town, four hundred and fifty miles lower down the river.

28th.— We arose at day-break, and the men soon found trees suitable for masts.   Whilst they were preparing them, I employed myself in examining this delightful spot.   The island is about three quarters of a mile in length, and five hundred yards in width.   The middle part is covered with the finest cedar, round which there is a border from sixty to eighty yards in width, in which were innumerable clumps of rose and currant bushes, mixed with grape vines, all in flower, and extremely fragrant.   The currant is a new and elegant species, and is described [88] by Pursh[69] as *ribes aureum*.   Betwixt the clumps and amongst the cedars,

[68] Roche Jaune (Yellow Rock) was the French name for Yellowstone River, which Chittenden, in *Yellowstone Park* (Cincinnati, 1903, 4th ed.), thinks was a translation by French traders of an Indian word having the same significance.   It took its name from the Grand Cañon of the river, where yellow is the predominant tint.   Lewis and Clark made permanent the name Yellowstone, although British explorers had occasionally used it before them.— ED.

[69] This man has been suffered to examine the collection of specimens which I sent to Liverpool, and to describe almost the whole, thereby depriving me both of the credit and profit of what was justly due to me.— BRADBURY.

the buffaloes, elks, and antelopes had made paths, which
were covered with grass and flowers. I have never
seen a place, however embellished by art, equal to this
in beauty. In a few hours the masts were completed,
and we proceeded on our voyage with a fine breeze in
our favour. Since our departure from L'Eau qui Court
I noticed that the bluffs had gradually continued to
change in appearance. The quantity of alluvion on
the border of the river decreased as we proceeded, and
has now entirely vanished. The bluffs continue in a
regular declivity from their summits to the edge of the
river, and the narrowness of the valley indicates a
country formed of such hard materials as to oppose
considerable resistance to the abrasion of the river. On
these bluffs, and at about half the distance from the
summit to the river, I began to notice a number of places
of a deep brown colour, apparently divested of vegetation. They occurred on both sides of the river, with an
exact correspondence in altitude and breadth, and exhibited the appearance of two interrupted lines running as far as the bluffs could be seen. As we were now
in an enemy's country, it [89] was with reluctance Mr.
Hunt suffered me to land a little before dinner, when I
proceeded to examine one of these spots. I found it
almost entirely covered with iron ore, of that species
called by Kirwan *compact iron stone*; in Waller Syst. 2,
p. 144, *hæmatitis solidus*. Its specific gravity is 3.482.
The oxidation of the ore had so changed the earth, that
it resembled Spanish brown, and nothing grew on it
but a few scattered shrubs of a species of *artemisia*,
apparently a non-descript. I hastened to the boats, in
which we kept our sails up the rest of the day, the bodies

of ore becoming longer and more frequent as we proceeded. We travelled eighteen miles, and encamped one
hour after sunset.

29th.— Some arrangements being necessary, the
boats did not set out so early as usual, and daylight
opened to our view one of the most interesting prospects I had ever seen. We had encamped at the commencement of a stretch of the river, about fifteen miles
in length, as we judged, and nearly in a right line. The
bluffs on both sides formed, as before, a gentle slope to
the river, and not a single tree was visible. The body
of iron ore had now become continuous on both sides
of the river, and exhibited the appearance of two dark
brown stripes, about one hundred yards in breadth,
and fifteen miles long. The exact conformity of the
two lines, and the contrast of colour produced [90] by
the vivid green which bounded them, formed a coup
d'oeil which I have never seen paralleled. I lamented
much that the wind was fair, but availed myself of the
short delay, and hastened up the bluff to the vein of ore,
where, although the soil was so strongly impregnated
with iron as to resemble rust, I observed a number of
large white flowers on the ground, belonging to a new
species of *œnothera*, having neither stem nor scape, the
flower sitting immediately on the root. On a signal
being given from the boats, I was obliged to return, and
had no further opportunity to examine this enormous
body of ore, without doubt sufficient to supply the whole
of North America with iron for thousands of years: and
if we combine in the same view the abundance of coal
on the Missouri, it warrants a presumption that in some
future age it will become an object of vast national importance.

30th.— We set out this morning with a favourable wind, which continued during the whole of the day; and the course of the river being less crooked than usual, we made thirty miles, and slept on an island.

31st.— Before breakfast this morning we discovered two Indians on a bluff on the north-east side of the river: we stopped opposite to them to breakfast, during which they frequently harangued [91] us in a loud tone of voice. After we had breakfasted, Mr. Hunt crossed the river to speak to them, and took with him Dorion, the interpreter. We noticed, that when he landed, one of the Indians went away, but immediately after re-appeared on horseback, and went at full speed over the bluffs. Mr. Hunt informed us on his return, that these Indians belonged to the Sioux nations; that three tribes were encamped about a league from us, and had two hundred and eighty lodges. They were the Yangtons Ahnah, the Tetons Bois Brulé, and the Tetons Min-na-kine-azzo. The Indian informed Mr. Hunt that they had been waiting for us eleven days, with a decided intention of opposing our progress, as they would suffer no one to trade with the Ricaras, Mandans, and Minaterees, being at war with those nations. It is usual to reckon two warriors to each lodge; we therefore found that we had to oppose near six hundred savages, with the character of whom we were well acquainted;[70] [92] and it had also been stated by the

---

[70] In the statistical account of the Missouri, by Lewis, read before Congress in February, 1806, the character of these Indians is thus described:— "These are the vilest miscreants of the savage race, and must ever remain the pirates of the Missouri, until such measures are pursued by our government as will make them feel a dependence on its will for their supply of merchandize. Unless these people are reduced to order by coercive measures, I am ready to pronounce that the citizens of the United States can

Indian that they were in daily expectation of being joined
by two other tribes, Tetons Okandandas and Tetons
Sahone.[71] We proceeded up the river, and passed
along an island, which for about half an hour inter-
cepted our view of the northeast side of the river.   On
reaching the upper point we had a view of the bluffs,
and saw the Indians pouring down in great numbers,
some on horseback, and others on foot.   They soon

never enjoy, but partially, the advantages which the Missouri presents.
Relying on a regular supply of merchandize through the channel of the river
St. Peter's, they view with contempt the merchants of the Missouri, whom
they never fail to plunder when in their power.   Persuasion or advice with
them is viewed as supplication, and only tends to inspire them with contempt
for those who offer either.   The tameness with which the traders of the
Missouri have heretofore submitted to their rapacity, has tended not a little
to inspire them with a poor opinion of the white persons who visit them
through that channel.   A prevalent idea, and one which they make the rule
of their conduct, is, that the more harshly they behave towards the traders,
the greater the quantity of merchandize they will bring them, and that they
will obtain the articles they wish on better terms.   They have endeavoured
to inspire the Aricaras with similar sentiments, but happily without effect.''
— BRADBURY.

[71] Bradbury here follows the nomenclature of Lewis and Clark as given
in their *Statistical View* (London, 1807), which differs from their original
manuscripts; see *Original Journals of Lewis and Clark Expedition*,
appendix.   At present the Teton are classified in seven bands; see Bureau
of Ethnology *Report*, 1893-94, pp. 153-158.   The Teton were an important
branch of the Dakota, numbering at the time of Bradbury's journey about
five thousand, inhabiting the territory of the upper Missouri and the neighborhood of the Black Hills.   They were exceedingly troublesome to traders
in all the days of the Missouri traffic, and could only be overawed by show
of force.   Their alliance with British traders from the Red River region
rendered them independent of the Americans and hostile to their plans;
the Teton outbreak in the War of 1812-15 being with difficulty restrained.
Their opposition to trading parties passing up the river arose partly from
enmity with the Indians above, whom they did not wish to have furnished
with fire-arms, and partly from a desire to act as middle-men, hoping to
reap profit in the trade.   Justly known as the "pirates of the Missouri,"
the Teton have always been difficult to control; they had their full share
in the Sioux wars of 1862, 1876, and 1890.   They are now living upon
reservations chiefly in South Dakota, with one band in Montana.— ED.

took possession of a point a little above us, and ranged themselves along the bank of the river. By the help of our glasses, we could perceive that they were all armed and painted for war. Their arms consisted chiefly of bows and arrows, but a few had short carbines: they were also provided with round shields. We had an ample sufficiency of arms for the whole party, which [93] now consisted of sixty men; and besides our small arms, we had a swivel and two howitzers. Any attempt to avoid the Indians would have been abortive, as a boat, in ascending the Missouri, can only effect it by going along the edges of the river, it being wholly impossible to stem the middle current; and as the banks are in many places high and perpendicular, we must inevitably be frequently in their power, as they might several times in the course of a day shower a volley of arrows upon us, and retire unseen. Our alternative, therefore, was, as we supposed, either to fight them or return. The former was immediately decided on, and we landed nearly opposite to the main body. Our first care was to put all the arms in complete order: afterwards the swivel and the howitzers were loaded with powder only, and fired to impress them with an idea that we were well prepared. They were then heavily loaded, and with as many bullets as it was supposed they would bear, after which we crossed the river. When we arrived within about one hundred yards of them, the boats were stationed, and all seized their arms. The Indians now seemed to be in confusion, and when we rose up to fire, they spread their buffaloe robes before them, and moved them from side to side. Our interpreter called out, and desired us not to fire, as the action indicated, on their part, a wish to avoid an

engagement, and to [94] come to a parley.   We accordingly desisted, and saw about fourteen of the chiefs
separate themselves from the crowd who were on the
summit of the bank, and descend to the edge of the
river, where they sat down on the sand, forming themselves into a portion of a circle, in the centre of which
we could see preparations making to kindle a fire,
evidently with a design to smoke the calumet with us,
and signs were made, inviting us to land.   Mr. Hunt
requested that Messrs. Crooks, M'Kenzie, Miller, and
M'Clellan[72] would attend him in his boat, and I accom-

---

[72] These were the partners in the enterprise.   For Hunt, Crooks, and
McKenzie, see notes 2-4, *ante*.

Joseph Miller was a well-educated man, of a good family in Baltimore,
who joined the United States army in 1799, having by 1802 become lieutenant of the 1st infantry.   His fiery temper, however, could not brook
military discipline, and upon being refused a furlough he resigned (1805).
Thereupon he drifted to St. Louis, and began an individual career of fur-
trading, hunting, and trapping.   In 1809 he was a member of the Crooks-
McClellan party, and with them joined the Astorians.   Becoming, in the
autumn of this same year, disgusted with the ill-success of the enterprise,
he abandoned the expedition at Fort Henry, on Snake River, in spite of the
remonstrances of the rest of the party.   Stuart met Miller on his overland
return journey (1813), and the latter acted for some time as guide.   After his
return to St. Louis with this division, nothing more is known of his career.

Robert McClellan possessed great strength, agility, and daring, and
before entering the fur-trade had had much experience in Indian fighting.
He had been one of Wayne's chief scouts in the latter's campaigns against
the Northwest Indians.   For an account of these exploits, see Roosevelt,
Winning of the West, iv, pp. 80-82.   Lewis and Clark upon their return
(1806), met him on a trading journey to the Omaha.   The following year
he formed a partnership with Ramsay Crooks, and built a wintering-house
near old Council Bluffs.   McClellan's hostility to Manuel Lisa arose from
his belief that the latter had played him false upon an expedition up the
river in 1809.   McClellan reached Astoria in January, 1812; in July of the
same year he determined to return to St. Louis with Stuart's party.   After
wandering nine months in the wilderness, they finally arrived at their destination April 30, 1813.   See appendix iii, *post*.   McClellan died three years
later, as is proved by a published notice for administering his estate.— ED.

panied Mr. M'Kenzie. The object was to consider
whether it was advisable to put so much confidence in
so ferocious and faithless a set, as to accept the invitation. It did not require much deliberation, as we found
ourselves under the necessity of either fighting or treating with them; it was therefore determined to hazard
the experiment of going ashore. The party who remained in the boats were ordered to continue in readiness to fire on the Indians instantly, in case of treachery,
and Messrs. Hunt, M'Kenzie, Crooks, Miller, and
M'Clellan, with the interpreter and myself, went ashore.
We found the chiefs sitting where they had first placed
themselves, as motionless as statues; and without any
hesitation or delay, we sat down on the sand in such a
manner as to complete the circle. When we were all
seated, the pipe was [95] brought by an Indian, who
seemed to act as priest on this occasion: he stepped
within the circle, and lighted the pipe. The head was
made of a red stone, known by mineralogists under the
term of *killas*, and is often found to accompany copper
ore: it is procured on the river St. Peter's, one of the
principal branches of the Mississippi.[73] The stem of
the pipe was at least six feet in length, and highly deco-
rated with tufts of horse hair, dyed red. After the pipe
was lighted, he held it up towards the sun, and afterwards pointed it towards the sky in different directions.

[73] The red pipestone used by the Indians for their calumets was found at
Pipestone quarry, in a county of that name in southwestern Minnesota.
This was first visited and described by George Catlin in 1836, and in his
honor the stone is now known as "catlinite." It is not confined, however,
to this one locality, but is also found in Dakota, Wisconsin, and Iowa.
See *American Naturalist*, July, 1883, for a good description of this material
and the pipes made therefrom.— Ed.

He then handed it to the great chief, who smoked a few whiffs, and taking the head of the pipe in his hand, commenced by applying the other end to the lips of Mr. Hunt, and afterwards did the same to every one in the circle. When this ceremony was ended, Mr. Hunt rose, and made a speech in French, which was translated as he proceeded into the Sioux language, by Dorion. The purport of the speech was to state, that the object of our voyage up the Missouri was not to trade; that several of our brothers had gone to the great salt lake in the west, whom we had not seen for eleven moons; that we had come from the great salt lake in the east, on our way to see our brothers, for whom we had been *crying* ever since they left us; and our lives were now become so miserable for the want of our brothers, that we would rather die than not go to [96] them, and would kill every man that should oppose our passage: that we had heard of their design to prevent our passage up the river, but we did not wish to believe it, as we were determined to persist, and were, as they might see, well prepared to effect our purpose; but as a proof of our pacific intentions, we had brought them a present of tobacco and corn. About fifteen carrottes of tobacco, and as many bags of corn, were now brought from the boat, and laid in a heap near the great chief, who then rose and began a speech, which was repeated in French by Dorion. He commenced by stating that they were at war with the Ricaras, Mandans, and Gros Ventres or Minaterees, and that it would be an injury to them if these nations were furnished with arms and ammunition; but as they found we were only going to our brothers, they would not attempt to stop us: that he also had brothers at a considerable distance northward, whom he had not seen for a great many moons, and for whom he also had been *crying*. He professed himself satisfied with our present, and advised us to encamp on the other side of the river, for fear his *young men* should be troublesome. When the speech was ended, we all rose, shook hands, and returned to the boats. During the conference, I had an opportunity of noticing these Indians, a great number of whom were assembled on the bank above us, and observed that [97] they are in stature considerably below the Osages, Mahas, and Poncars, and much less robust. They are also more deficient in clothing and ornaments, a considerable number being entirely naked, but all armed. Several of our party were acquainted with these tribes, and represent them much as described by Lewis. Although the squaws are very ill treated by all Indians, it is said they are treated much worse by the Sioux than any other tribe, whence it follows that mothers frequently destroy their female children, alleging as a reason, that it is better they should die than continue a life so miserable as that to which they are doomed. Amongst the Sioux women, it is also said, suicide is not unfrequent, and the mode which they adopt to put an end to their existence, is, by hanging themselves. They are of opinion that suicide is displeasing to the *Father of Life*, and believe it will be punished in the *land of spirits* by their ghosts being doomed for ever to drag the tree on which they hung themselves: for this reason they always suspend themselves to as small a tree as can possibly sustain their weight. In the course of the afternoon we met a chief who belonged to a party of Teton Okandandas, which consisted, he said, of thirty lodges. He requested to have a passage in the boats for the remainder of the day. It was granted to him, and he remained with us during the night.

[98] June 1.— This morning the old chief was conveyed over the river, and landed on the opposite side, as he said he expected to meet his people, but we did not see him again. In the afternoon we entered upon the Great Bend, or, as the French call it, the Grand Detour, and encamped about five miles above the lower entrance. This bend is said to be twenty-one miles in circuit by the course of the river, and only nineteen hundred yards across the neck.[74]

2d.— In the morning early we discovered two Indians standing on the bluffs, who upon discovering us, spread their buffalo robes to denote that they were amicably inclined towards us. We crossed over the river, and when we approached them, they extended their arms in a horizontal position. This action, I was informed, was an appeal to our clemency. When we landed they showed evident symptoms of alarm. This was soon accounted for by Messrs. Crooks, M'Clellan, and Miller, who informed us that they knew these fellows, and that they were chiefs of the Sahonies and Okanandans, who the year preceding had behaved extremely ill, by plundering and otherwise maltreating them, in such a manner as to render it necessary for their safety to escape down the river in the night, and

---

[74] Lewis and Clark estimated the circuit of the Great Bend as being thirty miles, and the distance across the neck two thousand yards. According to the Missouri River Commission's map, the bend is now about twenty-five miles around. It is in South Dakota, between the Crow Creek and Lower Brulé Indian reservations.— ED.

abandon the trade with [99] the upper Indians for that
year, which had been a great loss to them. They
seemed very apprehensive that Mr. Crooks would now
resent their conduct; but after we had smoked with
them they became more tranquil. During the smoking, Mr. Hunt asked them why they killed white men,
as he heard that they had killed three during the last
summer? They replied, because the white men kill
us: that man (pointing to Carson) killed one of our
brothers last summer. This was true. Carson, who
was at that time among the Ricaras, fired across the
Missouri at a war party of Sioux, and it was by a very
extraordinary chance he killed one of them, as the river
is full half a mile in breadth, and in retaliation the Sioux
killed three white men. I observed that, as before, in
smoking the pipe they did not make use of tobacco, but
the bark of *cornus sanguinea*, or red dog wood, mixed
with the leaves of *rhus glabrum*, or smooth sumach.
This mixture they call kinnikineck. After we had
smoked, they spoke of the poverty of their tribes, and
concluded by saying they expected a present. A few
carrottes of tobacco and bags of corn were laid at their
feet, with which they appeared satisfied. As these were
the last of the Sioux tribes we expected to meet, I now
determined to walk all day, and was much pleased that
the restraint imposed on me by the proximity of these
vagabonds was [100] removed. I therefore proceeded
up the bluffs nearly abreast of the boats. In about a
quarter of an hour afterwards two other Indians rode
hastily past me, and overtook the boats. I observed
that they had a short conference with Mr. Hunt, when
they turned their horses about, and again rode past me,

seemingly in a rage. Mr. Hunt called to me, and requested that I would come on board instantly, when he
informed me that these fellows were also chiefs, and
had seen our presents, with which they were much dis-
satisfied, and in consequence had followed the boats to
extort more. In reply to their insolent demands, Mr.
Hunt informed them that "he had given all he intended
to give, and would give no more," adding, "that he
was much displeased by their importunity, and if they
or any of their nation again followed us with similar
demands, he would consider them as enemies, and treat
them as such." As we were not exactly acquainted
with the strength of these two tribes, and expected
that, in consequence of the disappointment in their
rapacious demands, they would attack us, it was arranged that the large boat should ascend on the N. E.
side of the river, and the three small boats on the S. W.
as the bluffs on either side of the river can be seen much
better from the opposite side; and it was agreed that
the signal on seeing Indians [101] should be two shots
fired in quick succession. As we had not much apprehension of being attacked on the S. W. side, I went
ashore after dinner, and continued along the river
nearly on a line with the boats, and about four o'clock
heard the signal given of Indians being seen. I instantly ran towards the boats, and arrived as they were
preparing to quit the shore to aid Mr. Hunt and his
party in the large boat, who were then apparently in
the most imminent danger. They had passed betwixt
a large sand bar and the shore, and it was evident to
us that at that juncture they found the water too shallow at the upper end, and were under the necessity of

turning back. The sand bar prevented the possibility
of putting out into the river, and we saw with horror
that at least a hundred Indians had arrived on the bank
at the lower end of the bar: we could also perceive
that they were a war party, as they were painted with
black and white stripes, and all had shields.[75] We had
every reason to conclude that these were the Teton
Okandandas and the Teton Sahonies, and our anxiety
for the safety [102] of Mr. Hunt and the party in the
large boat was indescribable when we saw large bodies of
Indians every moment arrive at the point near which he
must unavoidably pass, before we could possibly give
him any assistance: but our anxiety was changed to
surprise on seeing the boat pass within a short distance
of them unmolested; soon after which the Indians ran
along the bank to the upper end of the sand bar, threw
down their arms, their shields, and their buffalo robes,
and plunged into the river in crowds to meet us; and
before we could reach the sand bar, they were round our
boats, holding up their hands in such numbers, that it
became tiresome to shake hands with so many. We
now found that this was a war party, consisting of
Aricaras, Mandans, and Minetarees, or Gros Ventres,[76]

[75] It may be observed here, that all the Indians who inhabit the prairie
use shields in war; but to those who inhabit a woody region they are wholly
unknown: as in action, excepting in close fight, each man conceals himself
behind a tree. The shields made use of are circular, and are nearly thirty
inches in diameter. They are covered with three or four folds of buffalo
skin, dried hard in the sun, and are proof against arrows, but not against a
bullet.— BRADBURY.

[76] These three tribes, although of different stocks, had become closely
associated with one another by the exigencies of war and the propinquity of
their villages. They still live on the same reservation — Fort Berthold, in
North Dakota.

The Arikara are a Caddoan tribe, and appear in the seventeenth cen-

who were coming against the Sioux, and having discovered us, had determined for the present to abandon the enterprise, expecting that on our arrival at the Aricara Town they should obtain a supply of fire arms and ammunition, which would give them a superiority over their enemies. During the ceremony of shaking hands we were joined by the large boat, and it was agreed that we should encamp at the first con-

tury to have broken away from their kinsfolk the Pawnee, and advanced northward into the Sioux country. They lived below the Cheyenne River until late in the eighteenth century, when they moved still farther north to be near the Mandan. Lewis and Clark found them at war with the latter tribe, however, but effected a peace between their chiefs. The Arikara carried on an extensive commerce in horses, and their alliance was much sought by the traders, to whom, however, they often proved treacherous. Lewis and Clark note that they abstained from spirituous liquors. They now number about four hundred.

The Mandan were one of the most famous of the Western tribes, because of their strategic position at the most northerly point of the Missouri River, not far from the British fur-trading region of the Assiniboine and Saskatchewan rivers. They were visited by the French in the first half of the eighteenth century, Chevalier de la Vérendrye setting out thence to explore the Rocky Mountains. (See Thwaites, *Rocky Mountain Exploration*, New York, 1903.) Lewis and Clark wintered among the Mandan (1804-05), and found them in two villages not far from the site of Bismarck, North Dakota. They then numbered about two thousand, but had been much more numerous, for remains of nine abandoned villages were noted by the explorers. The Mandan are of Siouan origin, but more sedentary than most of their tribes; they fortified their villages and were occupied with agriculture. In 1837 a severe scourge of small-pox reduced their numbers to less than a hundred, whereupon they amalgamated with the Arikara. There are now about two hundred and fifty Mandan.

The Minitaree (called by the French Grosventres) are of the Hidatsa family, allied with the Crows. They numbered two thousand five hundred at the time of Lewis and Clark, and having long lived with the Mandan had adopted many of their customs, but not their language. They were usually friendly to traders. There are now about four hundred of this tribe.

Allotments in severalty have been made to many members of these three tribes, while a good proportion of them have houses and profitably practice agriculture.— ED.

venient place. We soon found one that was suitable,
and the Indians fixed their camp about one hundred
yards from ours. I now ascertained that the party consisted of nearly three hundred warriors. As we [103]
had plenty of provisions, a supply was given to the Indians, who prepared their supper, after which the
chiefs and principal warriors came to our tents. In Mr.
M'Kenzie's tent there were seven of them, none of
whom appeared to me to be lower than five feet ten
inches, and some were more than six feet. Most of them
had very good countenances, differing from the heavy
face of the Osage, and the keen visage of the Sioux.
One of them who had an aquiline nose, had a scarified
line running along each arm, which met on his stomach.
This our interpreter informed us was done to show
his grief for the death of his father. Whilst I was endeavouring to converse with him, an Indian boy came
into the tent, and handed water round to the chiefs in a
gourd shell tied to the end of a stick. He spoke to the
boy, who went out, but soon returned with a new pair of
ornamented mockasons, and handed them to the warrior, who it then appeared had observed that mine were
dirty and much worn, as he took them off my feet, and
put on the new pair, which he tied himself. Observing
that he had a short carbine and powder flask, I begged to
look at the latter, and finding it only contained a very
small quantity of powder, I immediately filled it from
my own flask. He was greatly pleased with the acquisition of so much powder, and informed me that he was
a Ricara, and should meet me at their town, where we
should be brothers. We [104] were interrupted by
one of the chiefs crying ''How,'' which signifies among

the Indians, ''Come on,'' or ''let us begin.'' This
occasioned silence, and he began to strike on one hand
with a war club which he held in the other. It had a
globular head, on one side of which was fixed the blade
of a knife, five or six inches in length. The head was
hollow, and contained small bits of metal, which made
a jingling noise as he struck it in quick time. The
singing now commenced, and continued at intervals
until past midnight. The song is very rude, and it
does not appear that they combine the expression of
ideas and music, the whole of their singing consisting
in the repetition of the word *ha* six or seven times in one
tone, after which they rise or fall a third, fourth, or
fifth, and the same in quick time. I observed that
their voices were in perfect unison, and although, according to our ideas of music, there was neither harmony nor melody, yet the effect was pleasing, as there
was evidently system, all the changes of tone being as
exactly conformable in point of time, as if only one
voice had been heard. Whenever their performance
ceased, the termination was extremely abrupt, by pro-
nouncing the word *how* in a quick and elevated tone.[77]

On the morning of the 3d, the chiefs declared to Mr.
Hunt their intention of immediately returning [105] to
their nation, where they expected to arrive in three days,
although they had been sixteen days in coming out.
They also demanded some arms and ammunition.
This demand, being conformable to the custom of war
parties, had been foreseen, but was not complied with,

---

[77] See on this subject, Fletcher, ''Indian Songs,'' in *Century Magazine*,
xxv, p. 421; and a more detailed article, ''Study of Omaha Indian Music,''
in Peabody Museum *Archæological and Ethnological Papers*, i, no. 5.— ED.

Mr. Hunt informing them, that when we arrived at their nation, we should furnish abundance. After we had left them, the chief overtook us on horseback, and said that his people were not satisfied to go home without some proof of their having seen the white men. Mr. Hunt could not now resist, and gave him a cask of powder, a bag of balls, and three dozen of knives, with which he was much pleased. Whilst the articles were delivering to him, an Indian came running up, and informed us that there was a boat in sight, coming up the river. We immediately concluded that it was the boat belonging to Manuel Lisa, and after proceeding five or six miles, we waited for it. I was much pleased on the boat's joining us, to find that Mr. Henry Brackenridge was along with Mr. Lisa; I became acquainted with him at St. Louis, and found him a very amiable and interesting young man. Mr. Lisa had made the greatest possible exertions to overtake us, being well apprised of the hostile disposition of the Sioux. He had met a boat, which, it appeared, had passed us in the night, and the people informed him that they had been fired upon by the [106] Indians. As the conjunct party now consisted of ninety men, and we were approaching the nations that were at war with the Sioux, our fears almost subsided; for myself, I was much gratified on finding the restraints removed which had so long circumscribed my motions. In the early part of this day the wind was fair, but after we had proceeded some miles, it changed to north-east, and blew so strong, that we could not stem the torrent, which was increased by the rising of the river. I went to the bluffs, which in this part are of considerable elevation, but rise in a

gentle slope from the river: near the summit is a stratum
of deep brown-coloured earth, from two to three hundred feet in breadth, on the declivity of the hill.   This
earth appears mostly to consist of decomposed iron ore,
and is evidently a continuation of that seen near Little
Cedar Island, although distant from it near a hundred
miles in a right line.   I observed, that uniformly the
flat tops of the hills were almost covered with masses
of stone, chiefly *breccia*.   There was something so singularly constant in this appearance, that I was tempted
to attend to a particular examination, and became convinced that these groupes of stone were the *passive*
cause of the hills.   If the group was of an oblong form,
the hill was a *ridge*; if it was nearly circular, the hill
was a *cone*.   It would be difficult to describe the sensa-
tions occasioned by a view at once of these hills [107]
and the valley of the Missouri.   The mind is irre-
sistibly impressed with the belief that the whole surface
of the surrounding country was once *at least* on a level
with the tops of these hills; and that all below has been
carried away by the erosion of water, from which it
has been protected in the parts where these stones were
collected.[78]   I remarked this day, that the wolves were
more numerous and more daring than in any former
part of our voyage.   Within the last week we frequently
saw a few every day, but now, some of them were almost
constantly in sight, and so fearless, as frequently to
stand at no great distance to gaze.   For the present,
they were protected by their worthlessness, their skins

---

[78] An enquiry into the length of time which it has required to produce
this effect, might be a matter of great interest to the *Chinese* philosophers.—
BRADBURY.

being out of season. It appears that in a natural state, the wolf is a *diurnal* animal; but in the neighbourhood of condensed and stationary population its habits change, and it becomes *nocturnal*.[79]   On my route this day I saw numerous colonies of the prairie dog; and from the frequency of the occurrence, I noticed that my approach to their [108] burrows was announced by the screams of a species of curlew.   I shot one, and ascertained it to be a variety of *scolopax arquata*; and perceived, after I noticed the fact, that the alarm was invariably given.   On my return to the boats, I found that some of the leaders of our party were extremely apprehensive of treachery on the part of Mr. Lisa, who being now no longer in fear of the Sioux, they suspected had an intention of quitting us shortly, and of doing us an injury with the Aricaras.   Independent of this feeling, it had required all the address of Mr. Hunt to prevent Mr. M'Clellan or Mr. Crooks from calling him to account for instigating the Sioux to treat them ill the preceding year.   Besides, it was believed by all, that although apparently friendly, he was anxiously desirous that the expedition should fail.   Lisa had twenty oars, and made much greater expedition than we could; it was evident, therefore, that he had it in his power to leave us, and it was determined to watch his conduct narrowly.

4th.— The boats did not make much way, and I walked chiefly on and beyond the bluffs, which I found

---

[79] During the autumn, whilst the Indians are employed in killing game for their winter's stock, the wolves associate in flocks, and follow them at a distance to feed on the refuse of the carcasses; and will often sit within view, waiting until the Indians have taken what they chuse, and abandoned the rest.— BRADBURY.

of the same description as those observed yesterday,
and on still farther examination, became more confirmed
in my opinion regarding the origin of the hills.   On
the summit of one I found some fragments of bones in
a petrified state, apparently [109] belonging to the
buffalo.   I had for some time past noticed on the declivities circular spaces of about six or seven feet in diameter, wholly divested of every kind of vegetation, and
covered with small gravel.   The frequent occurrence
of these this day attracted my more particular attention, and I found that they were caused by a large
species of black ant, hundreds of which were running in
every direction within the area with astonishing ac-
tivity.   On finding a large beetle, I put it in the centre
of one of these areas, when it was instantly seized by
those nearest to it.   For a short time the ants were
dragged along with ease; but by some unknown and
surprising faculty the intelligence was immediately
spread throughout the whole space: the ants ran from
every direction towards the centre, and in a few seconds
the poor beetle became completely covered, and escape
was impossible.

5th.— We had not proceeded more than four miles
before a very heavy rain commenced, and we were compelled to stop and fix up the tents.   I went as usual to
the bluffs, and on my return to secure some interesting
specimens of plants, found that Lisa had encamped
about one hundred yards above us.   After I had dried
my clothes, I again visited the bluffs in company with
Mr. Brackenridge.   We discovered on the bank of a
small creek the remains of an Indian encampment,
which had [110] apparently been occupied by a con-

siderable number, and for some time, as there was a great quantity of bones spread on the ground, and the marks where the wigwams stood were numerous. We agreed that the situation was judiciously chosen to prevent surprise. On ascending the hills, and looking over the summit, we observed near us a small herd of buffaloes, consisting of two cows and three bulls. We immediately drew back, and taking advantage of a ravine, approached within thirty or forty yards, and fired. We wounded one of the cows, which Mr. Brackenridge pursued. Several other herds of buffaloes were in view, and some antelopes or cabri. I found the hills all capped with stones, and was still more confirmed in my opinion respecting their formation by observing some large detached blocks, each lying on a small pyramid of clay. After Mr. Brackenridge joined me, we saw a large hare, *lepus variabilis*, the first I had noticed, and also a number of wolves in several directions, and returning through an extensive colony of prairie dogs, we regained the boats. Immediately on my return to our camp, a circumstance happened that for some time threatened to produce tragical consequences. We learned that, during our absence, Mr. Lisa had invited Dorion, our interpreter, to his boat, where he had given him some whiskey, and took that opportunity of avowing his intention to take him away from [111] Mr. Hunt, in consequence of a debt due by Dorion to the Missouri Fur Company, for whom Lisa was agent. Dorion had often spoken to us of this debt, and in terms of great indignation at the manner in which it had been incurred, alleging that he had been charged the most exorbitant prices for articles had at Fort

Mandan, and in particular ten dollars per quart for whiskey. Some harsh words having passed betwixt him and Lisa, he returned to our camp. On the instant of my arrival, Mr. Lisa came to borrow a *cordeau*, or towing-line, from Mr. Hunt, and being perceived by Dorion, he instantly sprang out of his tent, and struck him. Lisa flew into the most violent rage, crying out, *"O mon Dieu! ou est mon couteau!"* and ran precipitately to his boat. As it was expected he would return armed, Dorion got a pair of pistols, and took his ground, the party ranging themselves in order to witness the event. Soon after Mr. Lisa appeared without pistols; but it was observed that he had his knife in his girdle. As Dorion had disclosed what had passed in Lisa's boat, Messrs. Crooks and M'Clellan were each very eager to take up the quarrel, but were restrained by Mr. Hunt, until an expression from Lisa, conveying an imputation upon himself, made him equally desirous of fighting. He told Lisa that the matter should be settled by themselves, and desired him to fetch his pistols. I followed Lisa to his boat, [112] accompanied by Mr. Brackenridge, and we with difficulty prevented a meeting, which, in the present temper of the parties, would certainly have been a bloody one.

The river had risen considerably during the night, and we were now convinced that the floods we had before encountered, and which were of short duration, were only partial, and caused by the rising of the tributary streams that have their sources in the lower regions. The periodical flood is occasioned by the melting of the snows on the Rocky Mountains, and the plains at their feet. The boats ascended with difficulty, which gave opportunities for walking the whole of the day. In the early part, we passed the remains of an old Aricara village. The scite was indicated by an embankment, on which there had been pallisadoes, as the remains were still visible. Within the area, the vestiges of the lodges were very apparent, and great quantities of bones and fragments of earthenware were scattered in every part. The wolves are still numerous, and are mostly of a light grey colour, with a few black hairs intermixed on the hind part of the back: they are seen singly, and although not timid, show no disposition to attack. Happening to come on one this day suddenly and unperceived, I shot him. He was large, and appeared to be old, as his teeth were much worn. [113] The country beyond the bluffs continues still very fine, but cut up in many places by deep ravines, occasioned by torrents during heavy rains. The sides of these ravines uniformly exhibited an under stratum of hard yellow clay, of an indeterminate depth.

7th.— Went out early on the S. W. side, with some of the hunters, and on reaching the summit of the bluffs, observed, in a westwardly direction, a range of high hills, apparently at the distance of thirty or forty miles. These, I was informed by the hunters, bounded the Chien or Chayenne River. Two buffaloes were killed, and one cabri, or antelope. The hunter who killed the last assured me that he had allured it by putting a handkerchief at the end of his ramrod, and lying down, continued to wave it, whilst he remained concealed. The animal, it seems, after a long contest betwixt curiosity and fear, approached near enough to become a sacrifice to the former.

8th.— Since the affair of the 5th, our party have had no intercourse with that of Mr. Lisa, as he kept at a distance from us, and mostly on the opposite side of the river. This deprived me of the society of my friend Brackenridge. I regretted this circumstance, and purposed to join him this morning, but was prevented by our stopping [114] on an island to breakfast, where our hunters killed two buffaloe and two elks. Of the former we had for some days past seen a great number of herds, consisting of from fifty to a hundred in each. On expressing my surprise at seeing so many, the hunters assured me, that so far from its being extraordinary, they had been in the expectation of seeing them in much greater numbers. Some of the hunters, who had been six or eight years about the head of the Missouri, said they had seen them during their annual migrations from north to south in autumn, and to the northward in spring; and agreed in stating, that at these times they assemble in vast herds, and march in regular order. Some asserted that they had been able to distinguish where the herds were even when beyond the bounds of the visible horizon, by the vapour which arose from their bodies. Others stated that they had seen herds extending many miles in length. It appeared also to be a well known fact among them, that in these periodical migrations, they are much less fearful of the hunter. I must observe of the hunters, that any accounts which I heard from them, and afterwards had an opportunity to prove, I found to be correct;[80] and when

---

[80] During our voyage, I often associated with the hunters, to collect information from their united testimony, concerning the nature and habits of animals, with which no men are so well acquainted. This knowledge is

the great [115] extent of this plain, and its fertility in grass are considered, we cannot but admit that the number of animals it is capable of containing must be immense. [116] In the forenoon we passed the mouth of Chayenne River, where it is four hundred yards in width. It is described by the hunters as being a very

---

absolutely necessary to them, that they may be able to circumvent or surprise those which are the objects of chase, and to avoid such as are dangerous; and likewise to prevent being surprised by them. They can imitate the cry or note of any animal found in the American Wilds, so exactly, as to deceive the animals themselves. I shall here state a few of what I certainly believe to be facts; some I know to be so, and of others I have seen strong presumptive proofs. The opinion of the hunters, respecting the sagacity of the beaver, goes much beyond the statements of any author whom I have read. They state that an old beaver, who has escaped from a trap, can scarcely ever afterwards be caught, as travelling in situations where traps are usually placed, he carries a stick in his mouth, with which he probes the sides of the river, that the stick may be caught in the trap, and thus saves himself.

They say also of this animal, that the young are educated by the old ones. It is well known that in constructing their dams, the first step the beaver takes, is to cut down a tree that shall fall across the stream intended to be dammed up. The hunters in the early part of our voyage informed me, that they had often found trees near the edge of a creek, in part cut through and abandoned; and always observed that those trees would not have fallen across the creek, and that by comparing the marks left by the teeth on those trees, with others, they found them much smaller; and therefore not only concluded that they were made by young beavers, but that the old ones, perceiving their error, had caused them to desist. They promised to show me proofs of this, and during our voyage I saw several, and in no instance would the trees, thus abandoned, have fallen across the creek.

I have myself witnessed an instance of a doe, when pursued, although not many seconds out of sight, so effectually hide her fawn, that we could not find it although assisted by a dog. I mentioned this fact to the hunters, who assured me that no dog, nor perhaps any beast of prey, can follow a fawn by the scent, and showed me in a full grown deer, a gland and a tuft of red hair, situated a little above the hind part of the fore foot, which had a very strong smell of musk. This tuft they call the *scent*, and believe that the route of the animal is betrayed by the effluvia proceeding from it. This tuft is mercifully withheld until the animal has acquired strength. What a benevolent arrangement! — BRADBURY.

fine river, and navigable for several hundred miles.[81]
We encamped this night in a beautiful grove, ornamented with a number of rose and currant bushes, entwined
with grape vines, now in bloom.

9th.— Mr. M'Clellan, with two of our men, and
three belonging to Lisa, were despatched to the Aricaras,
to apprise them of our coming, and to see how far it
was practicable to procure horses for the journey by
land.   Soon after we set out, we saw a great number of
buffaloe on both sides of the river, over which several
herds were swimming.   Notwithstanding all the efforts
made by these poor animals, the rapidity of the current
brought numbers of them within a few yards of our
boats, and three were killed.   We might have obtained
a [117] great many more, but for once we did not kill
because it was in our power to do so; but several were
killed from Lisa's boat.   In the evening Mr. Lisa
encamped a little above us, and we were informed
by his party, that about sun-set they had seen six
Indians.

10th.— A fine breeze sprang up early in the day,
and we proceeded rapidly.   About noon Mr. M'Clellan
and his party appeared on the bank of the river, having
found that they could not reach the Aricara nation
before the boats.   About the middle of the afternoon,
we met a canoe with three Indians.   They had come
from the Aricaras, where intelligence of our approach
had been brought by the war party that met us on the
1st.   They had made a great parade of the presents
which they received from us, and of the exploit which

---

[81] The Cheyenne River takes its rise in the Black Hills, and flows eastward into the Missouri, draining the central part of western South Dakota.
It takes its name from the Indians of that designation, who lived upon its
upper waters at the time of Lewis and Clark's expedition.— ED.

they had achieved in discovering the white men coming. They reported that the Mandans, who were of the party, had urged an attack on Mr. Hunt's boat, when it was in the situation already described, which they (the Aricaras) had prevented. They also stated, that the Minetarees, or Gros Ventres Indians, had killed two white men on the river above the Missouri Fur Company's fort. We encamped three miles above the mouth of the river *Cer-wer-cer-na*, after travelling thirty-five miles.[82]

[118] 11th.— We hoped this day to arrive at the Aricaras, but did not derive so much benefit from the wind as we expected; and after passing the river *Ma-ra-pa*, encamped about six miles below the town, near an island on which they were formerly settled.[83]

12th.— During this night we had a severe thunder storm, accompanied by torrents of rain, so that our beds were completely wet. We set out early, and about half way to the town, met a canoe with two chiefs, and an interpreter, who is a Frenchman, and has lived with this tribe more than twenty years. He married a squaw, and has several children.[84] The chiefs were

[82] Sergeant Gass of the Lewis and Clark expedition gives this form for the river which Clark calls in his journal, Sur-war-carna or Park River. This is the Arikara name for the present Moreau River, named for a French Canadian who traded in this region and was stabbed by a Cheyenne squaw. Moreau River rises in the northwestern part of South Dakota, and flows through the Cheyenne River Indian reservation into the Missouri. It is also known as Owl River.— Ed.

[83] The Arikara villages were situated on the west bank of the Missouri, above Grand River, on the South Dakota portion of Standing Rock reservation, about opposite the present town of Campbell. Marapa (Maropa) River is now known as Rampart or Owl Creek.— Ed.

[84] The interpreter was probably Joseph Gravelines, who had been serviceable to Lewis and Clark, and had accompanied the Arikara chief to Washington in 1805.— Ed.

good looking men: one of them is called the head chief,
or king, and is named by the French *Le Gauche*, being
left-handed; the other is the war chief, and called the *Big
Man*. The interpreter informed us that the chiefs had
come to a resolution to oppose our farther progress up
the river, unless a boat was left to trade with them.
Mr. Hunt explained to the chiefs the object of his voyage, and that he would willingly trade for horses.
About ten o'clock we landed on the north side, opposite
the town, or rather towns, as there are two distinct
bands, and their villages are about eighty yards apart.
Our first care was to spread out the beds and baggage
to dry. Whilst [119] the men were occupied in this
business, the chief informed us, from the other side of
the river, that he would be ready to meet us in council
when we should chuse to come over. As the river is
here at least eight or nine hundred yards in breadth, it
may appear surprising that he could make himself
understood at so great a distance; but to those who
have heard the Indian languages spoken, and who are
acquainted with the Indians, it will appear very credi-
ble. In all the Indian languages which I have heard,
every syllable of the compound words is accented; as,
for instance, the primitive name of this nation, *Starrahe*
they pronounce *Stăr-ră-hĕ*. In addition to this con-
struction of their languages, the Indians have remarkably loud voices. The leaders of our two parties had
not yet spoken to each other since the affair of the 5th;
nor had any communication, except through the medium of Mr. Brackenridge or myself. It was evident
that Lisa was still suspected; and M'Clellan, in particular, carefully watched his motions, determined to

shoot him if he attempted to cross the river before us, to attend the council of the Indians, contrary to what had been previously agreed upon with Mr. Brackenridge on his behalf. Soon after noon Mr. Hunt manned the large boat, and with Messrs. M'Kenzie and M'Clellan, went over the river; Lisa also attended in his barge. Mr. Brackenridge and myself were of the party. [120] On landing, amongst a crowd of Indians, we were conducted to the council lodge by some chiefs who met us; where we sat down on buffaloe skins prepared for us, and spread on the ground. I noticed that this lodge was constructed in a manner similar to those already described, belonging to the Ottoes. An old Indian lighted the pipe, and handed it to the chief; after which he squatted himself on his hams, near the entrance of the lodge. Although there were nearly twenty present, I learned from Dorion, (near whom I had placed myself) that several of the chiefs were not yet assembled. After we had smoked for a short time, *Le Gauche*, the chief, spoke to the old Indian at the door, who went out of the lodge: he soon after appeared on the top, and was visible to us through the hole left for the smoke. What the chief dictated to him from within, he bawled out aloud, with the lungs of a stentor. I understood that his object was to summon the chiefs to council, and it was promptly obeyed, as in ten minutes all were assembled. I learned that although we had smoked, the council pipe had not yet been lighted: this was now done by the same old Indian, who it seems was both priest and herald. *Le Gauche* made the customary appeal to the Great Spirit, by puffing the smoke in different directions

towards heaven and earth; after which the pipe was
applied to the lips of each assembled, the chief still
holding [121] it. He then opened the council by a
short speech: in the first place he spoke of their poverty,
but said that they were very glad to see us, and would
be still more glad to trade with us. Lisa replied, and
expressed his intention to trade, if they did not rate
their buffaloe and beaver too highly. He then mentioned Mr. Hunt and his party as his friends, and said
he should join them in resenting and repelling any
injury or insult. Mr. Hunt declared that the object
of his journey was not to trade, but to see our brothers,
at the great salt lake in the west; for that undertaking
he should now want horses, as he purposed to go thence
by land, and that he had plenty of goods to exchange,
if they would spare the horses. Mr. Lisa and Mr.
Hunt accompanied their speeches by suitable presents
of tobacco. *Le Gauche* spoke, and expressed the satisfaction of his people at our coming, and their attachment to the white men. In respect to the trade with
Mr. Lisa, he wished for more time to fix the price of
dried buffaloe skins, (usually called buffaloe robes)
being an article they had most of: his present idea of
the price was thirty loads of powder and ball for each
robe. Respecting Mr. Hunt's proposition, he was
certain they could not spare the number of horses that
he understood he wanted; and that he did not think
they ought to sell any horses. *Les Yeux Gris*, another
chief, replied to the latter part of his [122] speech, by
stating that they might easily spare Mr. Hunt a considerable number of horses, as they could readily re-

place them by stealing or by smoking.[85]   These arguments governed the opinions of the chiefs, and it was
determined to open a trade for horses, when they were
satisfied with the price Mr. Hunt purposed to give.
The council now broke up, and Messrs. Hunt, M'Kenzie, M'Clellan, Dorion, and myself were conducted
to the lodge of one of their chiefs, where there was a
feast of sweet corn, prepared by boiling, and mixing
it with buffaloe grease.   Accustomed as I now was to
the privation of bread and salt, I thought it very palatable.   *Sweet corn* is corn gathered before it is ripe, and
dried in the sun: it is called by the Americans *green
corn*, or *corn in the milk*.   I quitted the feast, in order
to examine the town, which I found to be fortified all
round with a ditch, and with pickets or pallisadoes, of
about nine feet high.   The lodges are placed [123] without any regard to regularity, which renders it difficult
to count them, but there appears to be from a hundred
and fifty to a hundred and sixty of them.   They are
constructed in the same manner as those of the Ottoes,
with the additional convenience of a railing on the
eaves: behind this railing they sit at their ease and smoke.
There is scarcely any declivity in the scite of the town;
and as little regard is paid to cleanliness, it is very dirty

---

[85] It was not difficult to comprehend that horses might be obtained by
stealing, but how they could be procured by smoking I did not then understand.   On the first opportunity, I enquired from Mr. Crooks, who is remarkably well acquainted with Indian customs: from him I learned, that
it is a practice with tribes in amity to apply to each other in cases of necessity.
When one tribe is deficient in any article of which the other has abundance,
they send a deputation, who smoke with them, and inform them of their
wants.   It would be a breach of Indian courtesy to send them away without
the expected supply.— BRADBURY.

in wet weather. I spent the remainder of the day in
examining the bluffs, to ascertain what new plants
might be collected in the neighbourhood; having now,
for the first time in the course of our voyage, an opportunity to preserve living specimens. During this time
the rest of the boats crossed over the river, and a camp
was formed about two hundred yards below the town.
Lisa's party was nearer to it than our's.

13th.— The morning being rainy, no business was
done in the village until the afternoon, when Mr. Hunt
exhibited the kind and quantity of goods he purposed
to give for each horse. These were placed in the lodge
of *Le Gauche*, for general inspection, and proved to be
satisfactory. This day I employed myself in forming
a place for the reception of living specimens, a little
distance below our camp, and near the river, for the
convenience of water.

[124] 14th.— I understood that Lisa and the chiefs
had agreed that the price of a buffalo robe should be
twenty balls, and twenty loads of powder. He removed a part of his goods to the lodge of *Le Gauche*,
and Mr. Hunt began to trade at the lodge of the *Big
Man*. The trade for horses soon commenced: the
species of goods most in demand were carbines, powder,
ball, tomahawks, knives, &c. as another expedition
against the Sioux was meditated. During this traffic,
I walked with Mr. Brackenridge to the upper village,
which is separated from the lower one by a small
stream. In our walk through the town, I was accosted
by the *Medicine Man*, or doctor, who was standing at
the entrance of a lodge into which we went. It appeared that one of his patients, a boy, was within, for

whom he was preparing some medicine. He made me understand that he had seen me collecting plants, and that he knew me to be a *Medicine Man*. He frequently shook hands with us, and took down his medicine bag, made of deer skin, to show me its contents. As I supposed this bag contained the whole *materia medica* of the nation, I examined it with some attention. There was a considerable quantity'of the down of reedmace, (*typha palustris*) which I understood was used in cases of burns or scalds: there was also a quantity of a species of *artemisia*, common on the prairies, and known to the hunters by the name of [125] *hyssop*; but the ingredient which was in the greatest abundance, was a species of wall-flower: in character it agrees with *cheiranthus erysimoides*: besides these, I found two new species of *astragalus*, and some roots of *rudbeckia purpurea*. After examining the contents of the bag, I assured the doctor it was all very good, and we again shook hands with him, and went into several other lodges, where we were very hospitably received. Although they sit on the ground round the fire, buffalo robes were always spread for us, and the pipe was invariably brought out, whilst the squaw prepared something for us to eat: this consisted of dried buffalo meat, mixed with pounded corn, warmed on the fire in an earthen vessel of their own manufacture. Some offered us sweet corn, mixed with beans (*phaseolus*.) The squaws were particularly attentive to us, and took every opportunity to examine such parts of our dress as were manufactured, and not of skins. After our return, I went to the trading house, and found that the trade for horses went on very briskly. The instant a horse was bought, his tail was cropped, to render him more easily distinguished from those belonging to the Indians, which are in all respects as nature formed them. On my return to our camp, I found the warrior there with whom I had become acquainted on the 1st instant. He insisted so much on my going to his lodge, that I went with him; where [126] he spread a very finely painted buffalo robe for me to sit on, and shewed me by signs that it was now mine. In return I gave him a pair of silver bracelets, with ornaments for the ears and hair, having brought a considerable quantity of those articles from St. Louis. With these he was so much pleased, that he requested me to sleep at his lodge during our stay, and informed me that his sister should be my bed-fellow. This offer I declined, alleging as an excuse, that I had voluntarily engaged to assist in keeping guard round our camp. I found, on my return, that the principals of our party were engaged in a very serious consultation on our present situation. All our fresh provisions were exhausted, and of the dried buffaloe bought from the Poncars, not more remained than was thought necessary to reserve for the journey by land: of Indian corn we had left only a few bags, which it was thought expedient to parch, grind, and mix with sugar, in order to apply it to the same object. It had been this day ascertained that the Aricaras could not spare us any provisions, as the excessive rains had penetrated into their *caches*,[86] and spoiled the whole

---

[86] The nations on the Missouri, always liable to be surprised and plundered by the *Teton* villains, annually conceal a quantity of corn, beans, &c. after harvest, in holes in the ground, which are artfully covered up. These hoards are called by the French *caches*, from the verb *cacher*, to hide.—BRADBURY.

of their reserved stock, so [127] that they expected to
be in want themselves before the harvest would come
in.   In addition to our difficulties, a rumour had been
spread this afternoon, and it was believed, that the
Sioux had followed us, and were now in the neighbourhood, to the amount of four or five hundred.   Whether
this was true or not, the consequences were the same
to us, as our hunters could not, with any degree of
prudence, be suffered to go out; nor indeed were they
willing.   In this dilemma, no means could be thought
of for the removal of our difficulties, but to purchase
from the Indians some of their spare dogs, particularly
those employed in dragging their sledges, and this
measure was resolved on.   It may here be remarked,
that horses and dogs are the only animals which the
Indians domesticate: of the latter they have two varie-
ties: one of these they employ in hunting; the other
appears to be of a stupid and lazy nature, always remaining about the village, and employed as above
mentioned.

15th.—In conformity with the measure determined
upon last evening, a number of dogs were purchased
this morning, brought to the camp, and shot for breakfast.   I went out to collect, accompanied by Mr.
Brackenridge, and proceeded farther into the interior
than I had before done.   I was rewarded by finding
several new species of plants, and by an additional confirmation of the geological [128] formations, as the
hills situated at a distance from the river have uniformly flat summits, covered with fragments of rock,
mixed with smaller stones and gravel.   On our return,
when about three miles from the camp, we saw Indians
pouring out from the village, some on horseback, others

on foot, and all at full speed.   They went in a direction
to our right, towards some hills, five or six miles distant
down the river.   A young Indian, soon after, in passing
us at some distance, changed his course, and came up
to me.   He spoke with great earnestness, frequently
pointing to the hills, on the tops of which I observed
some horsemen apparently meeting each other, and
after passing, turn back, and continue gallopping.   I
at length comprehended that enemies were near, and
that seeing me only armed with a pistol, he wished me
to hasten to the camp.   When we came nearer the
town, I observed that the tops of the lodges were
crowded with women, children, and old men, all looking
earnestly towards the hills, and considerable numbers
were still running past our camp.   I now enquired the
cause of the tumult, and found that a signal had been
given, indicating the appearance of a war party of the
Sioux.   The noise and confusion were such as I have
not often witnessed: the war whoop was heard in every
direction, and even the old men in the village were
busily employed in animating the warriors.   Some aged
Nestors tottered [129] along with the crowd, raising
their shrill voices to encourage the young and vigorous
to exert themselves in repelling the foe.   If any enemy
really appeared, they had immediately fled on being
discovered; a thing not at all unlikely, as it is conformable to their customs, and in this instance the
more probable, as the Sioux would naturally expect
that our party would join their adversaries.   At all
events, the party soon returned in as much disorder
as they went out.   I observed, that amongst the warriors of this and the other nations, several had foxes'

tails attached to the heels of their mockasons, and I am informed by Captain Winter, who resided some time at Michillimakinac, that the same custom prevails among the tribes in Upper Canada, and that this honour is only permitted to such warriors as have killed an enemy on his own ground.

16th.—I went into the village, and found that the chiefs were assembled to hear from the warriors an account of what had passed the preceding day. As they were not *in the habit of printing newspapers*, the news was carried through the village by heralds, who attend at the door of the council-lodge, and from time to time go through the village to give information. On my return to the camp, I found that Mr. Hunt and Mr. Lisa were negociating respecting the boats belonging to our party, [130] which were no longer of any use to us. Mr. Hunt was willing to exchange them with Mr. Lisa for horses, who had a considerable number of them at the Fort belonging to the Missouri Fur Company, about two hundred miles higher up the river.[87] Mr. Hunt, some days previous to this, presented to me the smallest boat, which was a barge built at Michillimakinac; and three American hunters, whom we found at the Aricara nation, agreed to assist me in navigating it down the river, when I should be disposed to return. The three other boats, and some Indian goods, were finally exchanged with Mr. Lisa. In consequence of this arrangement, I found that a party were to be dispatched in a few days to the Fort

---

[87] Chittenden, *American Fur Trade*, locates this post ten or twelve miles above the mouth of Big Knife River, near Emanuel Rock and Creek. It was abandoned during the War of 1812-15.— ED.

for the horses, and I resolved to accompany them, if permitted. After an excursion to collect plants, I walked into the village in the evening, and found that a party had arrived, who had been on an expedition to steal horses, in which they were successful. This event, and the return of the war party, caused an unusual bustle: the tops of the lodges were crowded with men, women, and children. Several of the old men harangued them in a loud voice. The subject I understood to be an exhortation to behave well towards the white people, and stating the advantages they derived by an intercourse with them. Notwithstanding all this tumult, some of the women continued their employment in dressing [131] buffaloe skins, which are stretched on frames, and placed on stages, erected both for this purpose, and to dry or jerk the flesh of animals cut into thin slices.

17th.—It was arranged that Mr. Crooks should go to the Company's Fort for the horses; and as more than thirty had been bought from the Aricaras, the men who were to accompany him began to select from amongst them such as they thought the best able to perform the journey. Notwithstanding I had resolved to accompany them, I neglected taking the same precaution, which occasioned me afterwards much vexation. I had already expressed my wish to undertake the journey, and although Mr. Hunt had not absolutely refused to permit me, yet he tried by arguments to dissuade me from it, in representing the danger which the party ran of being cut off by the Sioux, the fatigue of riding on an Indian saddle, &c. I therefore did not for the present press the subject, and spoke of it only to Mr. Crooks, who, knowing my determination, was much pleased with it. After devoting the greatest part of the day to the increasing of my collection, I went into the village, and found that some Indians had arrived from the Chayenne nation, where they had been sent to inform the Aricaras of their intention to visit them in fifteen days. One of these Indians was covered with a buffalo [132] robe, curiously ornamented with figures worked with split quills, stained red and yellow, intermixed with much taste, and the border of the robe entirely hung round with the hoofs of young fawns, which at every movement made a noise much resembling that of the rattlesnake when that animal is irritated. I understood that this robe had been purchased from the Arapahoes, or Big Bead Indians, a remote tribe, who frequent the Rocky Mountains. I wished much to purchase the robe, and offered him such articles in exchange as I thought most likely to induce him to part with it; but he refused. The day following it was purchased by Mr. M'Clellan, who gave it to me for silver ornaments and other articles, which amounted to about ten dollars. As these Indians could not speak the Aricara language, they had need of an interpreter, whose place was supplied by one of the Aricaras that could speak their language. They were tall and well proportioned men, but of a darker complexion than the Aricaras. This nation has no fixed place of residence, but resort chiefly about the Black Hills, near the head of Chayenne River, having been driven by the Sioux from their former place of residence, near the Red River of Lake Winnipic. Their number is now inconsiderable, as

they scarcely muster one hundred warriors.[88]   On my
return to the camp, I found it crowded with Indians
and squaws, as it had been for the two preceding
evenings. [133] Travellers who have been acquainted
with savages, have remarked that they are either very
liberal of their women to strangers, or extremely jealous.
In this species of liberality no nation can exceed the
Aricaras, who flocked down every evening with their
wives, sisters, and daughters, anxious to meet with a
market for them. The Canadians were very good
customers, and Mr. Hunt was kept in full employ
during the evening, in delivering out to them blue beads
and vermillion, the articles in use for this kind of traffic.
This evening I judged that there were not fewer than
eighty squaws, and I observed several instances wherein
the squaw was consulted by her husband as to the
quantum sufficit of price; a mark of consideration
which, from some knowledge of Indians, and the estimation in which their women are held, I had not expected.

18th.— Went early to the bluffs to the south-west-

---

[88] The Cheyenne tribe was an outlying branch of the Algonquian stock
which had become separated from the parent race and pushed into the
country of the Sioux. Although few in numbers they are good fighters and
have given the United States much trouble. The first treaty was made
with them in 1825, after which they continued friendly until about the time
of the War of Secession. At the close of that war, Hancock and Custer
entered upon a long campaign against them. The Cheyenne participated
in the Custer massacre in 1876. In 1885, there was another outbreak,
whereupon Sheridan took the field in person. The Southern Cheyenne,
with the Arapaho, are at present in Oklahoma, and number about twenty-
eight hundred; they have received allotments in severalty, and made some
progress toward civilization. The Northern Cheyenne, numbering about
fourteen hundred, are still chiefly ''blanket Indians,'' upon the Tongue
River reservation in Montana.— ED.

ward of the town, on one of which I observed fourteen buffalo skulls placed in a row. The cavities of the eyes and the nostrils were filled with a species of *artemisia* common on the prairies, which appears to be a non-descript. On my return, I told our interpreter to inquire into the reason of this, and learned that it was an honour conferred by the Indians on the buffaloes which they had killed, in order to appease their spirits, and prevent [134] them from apprising the living buffaloes of the danger they run in approaching the neighbourhood. After my return, I walked into the village with Mr. Donald M'Kenzie, who wore a green surtout. This attracted very much the attention of the squaws, and from the surprise they shewed, I believe it is a colour with which they were unacquainted. They were so anxious to obtain a part of it, that several offered him *favours* as an equivalent for a piece which they marked out. This occasioned much mirth be-twixt us, and on my part a pretended alarm lest his coat should become a *spencer*. We amused ourselves sometime by watching a party who were engaged in play. A place was neatly formed, resembling a skittle alley, about nine feet in breadth and ninety feet long: a ring of wood, about five inches in diameter, was trundled along from one end, and when it had run some distance, two Indians, who stood ready, threw after it, in a sliding manner, each a piece of wood, about three feet long and four inches in breadth, made smooth on one edge, and kept from turning by a cross piece pass-ing through it, and bent backwards so as to resemble a cross bow. The standers by kept an account of the game, and he whose piece, in a given number of throws, more frequently came nearest the ring after it had fallen, won the game.

[135] 19th.— We breakfasted early, having killed the dogs the night before, and ten horses were brought into the camp for the party appointed to go to the Fort, beyond the Mandans, to escort the horses agreed for with Mr. Lisa, and I now declared to Mr. Hunt that, unless he absolutely refused me the privilege, I was determined to accompany them. With his accustomed kindness he consented, and a man was dispatched to catch a horse for me on the prairie. As the party had cast their bullets, and made every other preparation the preceding night, we were all ready, when the man returned with a very bad horse. He was small, and apparently weak; but being unwilling to delay the party, I fixed my saddle, and we set out, having previously agreed with one of the men to take care of my plants in my absence. We had for our guide a person of the name of Jones, who was acquainted with the whole of the country betwixt the Mandans and Aricaras; and after passing the villages, kept as much as possible in the ravines and valleys, to avoid being seen by the Sioux Indians, who we had reason to think were still lurking about the country; as we knew that if they discovered us, they would, almost to a certainty, cut us off. There being no provisions to spare in the camp, except a little dog's flesh, we took nothing with us to eat, nor made the least attempt to look for game, as our safety perhaps depended on the celerity and [136] silence of our march. We continued at a smart trot until near eight o'clock in the evening, having only stopped once to give the horses an opportunity to feed. Our

course lay nearly north, and we kept the river in sight the whole of the day, being sometimes very near it, and at other times five or six miles distant. We encamped on the border of a creek, not more than a mile from the Missouri, on the open prairie. We found this place so much infested with mosquitoes, that scarcely any of us slept. In the latter part of the day I discovered the insufficiency of my horse, as it was with difficulty I could keep up with the rest. The reflections on my situation, combined with the pain occasioned by mosquitoes, kept me from closing my eyes; in addition to this, I had already painfully experienced the effects of an Indian saddle, which I shall describe. It consists of six pieces of wood: two of these are strong forked sticks, one of which is formed to fix on the shoulders of the horse; the other is adapted to the lower part of the back: they are connected by four flat pieces, each about four inches in breadth: two of these are so placed as to lie on each side of the backbone of the horse, which rises above them; the two others are fastened to the extremities of the forked sticks, and the whole is firmly tied by thongs. Two strong slips of buffalo hide are doubled over each of the upper connecting pieces, for the purpose of holding [137] the stirrup, which is formed of a stick about two feet long, and cut half way through in two places, so as to divide it into three equal parts: at these places it is bent, and when the two ends are strongly tied, it forms an equilateral triangle. The conjunct end of the foremost forked stick rises to the height of eight or ten inches above the back of the horse, and serves to fasten on it the coiled end of the long slip of dried skin intended to serve as a bridle: this slip is also made use of to fasten the horse at night, to allow him sufficient space wherein to graze, and is mostly fifty or sixty feet long. Under the saddle is laid a square piece of buffalo skin, dressed with the hair upon it, and doubled four-fold, and on the saddle the rider fixes his blanket.

20th.—We were on horseback on the first appearance of day, and immediately abandoned the river, passed over the bluffs, and struck into the interior of the country. Besides my rifle and other equipments, similar to those of the rest of the party, I had a portfolio for securing specimens of plants. I had contrived already to collect some interesting specimens, by frequently alighting to pluck them, and put them into my hat. For these opportunities, and to ease my horse, I ran many miles alongside of him. Notwithstanding this, about noon he seemed inclined to give up, and I proposed to Mr. [138] Crooks that I should turn back: this he would by no means agree to, but prevailed on the lightest man in company to exchange horses with me for the rest of the day. Soon after noon, we observed some deer grazing at a distance; we therefore halted in a small valley, suffered the horses to graze, and dispatched one of the men to look after the deer, who soon returned, having killed one. As we had not eaten any thing from the morning of the preceding day, this news was very acceptable, and some were sent to fetch the meat, whilst others gathered dry buffaloe dung to boil our kettle. This opportunity afforded me the pleasure of adding to my little collection, besides securing in my portfolio what I had before gathered. It is perhaps needless to observe that the

men were not slow in bringing the meat, nor that we
were equally expeditious in our cooking. We were so
confident of finding game, that we did not take any
part of the remains of our feast, but proceeded, in the
hope of being able to reach Cannon-ball River,[89] intending to encamp on its banks. In the course of the
afternoon we perceived innumerable herds of buffaloe;
and had we wished to hunt, we might have killed
[139] great numbers; but we avoided them as much
as possible, for fear of disturbing them, as it might
have been the means of enabling some lurking war
party to discover us. It is well known to the hunters
and the Indians, that a herd of buffaloe, when fright-
ened, will often run ten, fifteen, or even twenty miles
before they stop. About five o'clock we perceived
before us the valley of Cannon-ball River, bounded
on each side by a range of small hills, visible as far as
the eye can reach; and as they appear to diminish
regularly, in the proportion of their distance, they
produce a singular and pleasing effect. In the evening, as we considered the danger from the Sioux much
decreased, we ventured to kill a buffalo: each man
cut what he thought proper, and the remainder was
left for the wolves, who doubtless picked the bones
before the morning. On descending into the valley of
the river, some deer were observed, feeding near the
bank, whilst others were lying down near them. Some
of our men stole cautiously round a grove, and shot

[89] Cannon-ball River derives its name from the singularly round form
of the stones which are found in its bed. These are of all sizes, from one
to twelve inches in diameter, or sometimes more: they are of a brownish
sand-stone, and before they were rounded by attrition, must have been
formed in cubes.— BRADBURY.

two of the poor animals, although we had no great
occasion for them. The Cannon-ball River was muddy
at this time; but whether it is constantly so or not, I
could not learn. It is here about one hundred and
sixty yards wide, but so shallow that we crossed it
without swimming, but not without wetting some of
the blankets on our saddles. We encamped on a very
fine prairie, near [140] the river, affording grass in
abundance, nearly a yard high, in which we stationed
our horses. The alluvion of the river is about a mile
in breadth from bluff to bluff, and is very beautiful,
being prairie, interspersed with groves of trees, and
ornamented with beautiful plants, now in flower.
Amongst others which I did not observe before, I
found a species of flax, resembling that which is cultivated: I think it is the species known as *linum perenne*.
I rambled until it was quite dark, and found my way
to the camp by observing the fire.

21st.— We arose before day. Each man cooked his
own breakfast, cutting what suited him from the venison,
and fixing it on a stick set in the ground, which inclined
over the fire. At break of day we were on horseback,
and soon after ascended the bluffs, and proceeded on
our route. I noticed a sensible change in the face of
the country after we had left the river. We now found
some of the more elevated places covered with small
stones, and divested of herbage, and throughout the
soil was of less depth, and the grass shorter and more
scanty. About ten o'clock we again found the country
to assume the same fertile appearance as on the preceding day, and saw herds of buffaloe in every direction: before mid-day two were killed, but very little

was taken, except the marrow-bones: each man who chose to take one, hung it to his [141] saddle. In the course of this forenoon we observed three rattlesnakes, of an entirely new and undescribed species: one of them I killed, and carried in my shot-pouch, and during the time we stopped to feed our horses, I secured the skin.[90]   We passed very close to several herds of buffaloe during the afternoon, near which we always observed a number of wolves lurking.   I perceived that those herds which had wolves in their vicinity, were almost wholly females with their calves; but noticed also, that there were a few bulls with them, and that these were always stationed on the outside of the herd, inclosing the cows with their calves within.   We came suddenly on one of these herds, containing, as we judged, from six to eight hundred buffaloes: they immediately gallopped off.   One of our party rode after them, and overtook a calf which could not keep pace with the rest: he instantly dismounted, caught it by the hind leg, and plunged his knife into its body.   We took what we wanted, and rode on.   This afternoon I noticed a singularly formed hill on our right, in the direction of the Missouri, apparently about ten miles from us.   It is of an oblong shape, nearly perpendicular at the ends, and level at the top, so as to resemble a regular building: near the centre there rises a pic, very steep, which seems to be elevated at least one hundred feet above the hill on which it stands.   We rode this day almost without intermission, and [142]

---

[90] Lewis and Clark describe the Western rattlesnake (*Crotalus confluentus*) as differing from that of the Atlantic states; not by its colors, but by their form and arrangement.— ED.

late in the evening arrived at *Rivière de Cœur*, or
Heart River, and encamped on its banks, or, more
properly, lay down in our blankets.[91]   I found that
my horse did not get worse, although he showed a
great disposition to lag behind; a certain proof of his
being very much tired, as the Indian horses, when on
a journey, have an aversion to be separated from their
companions.

22nd.— Although the distance from this place to the
Missouri Fur Company's Fort was estimated at about
sixty miles, we determined if possible to reach it this
day, and were, as usual, on horseback at day-break,
having previously breakfasted on veal.   I observed the
preceding days a sufficient number of buffaloes to
induce me to credit the hunters in their reports of the
vast numbers they had seen; but this day afforded me
ample confirmation.   Scarcely had we ascended the
bluffs of Heart River, when we discerned herds in
every direction; and had we been disposed to devote
the day to hunting, we might have killed a great number,
as the country north of Heart River is not so uniform
in its surface as that we had passed.   It consists of
ridges, of small elevation, separated by narrow valleys.
This renders it much more favourable for hunting, and
although we did not materially deviate from our course,
five were killed before noon.   Mr. Crooks joined me in
remonstrating against this [143] waste; but it is impossible to restrain the hunters, as they scarcely ever lose
an opportunity of killing, if it offers, even although not

---

[91] Heart River, called by Lewis and Clark Ches-che-tar, flows into the
Missouri nearly opposite Bismarck, North Dakota.   There had formerly
been a large Mandan village at its mouth, near the present railway town
of Mandan, seat of Morton County.— ED.

in want of food. About two o'clock we arrived on the summit of a ridge more elevated than any we had yet passed. From thence we saw before us a beautiful plain, as we judged, about four miles across, in the direction of our course, and of similar dimension from east to west. It was bounded on all sides by long ridges, similar to that which we had ascended. The scene exhibited in this valley was sufficiently interesting to excite even in our Canadians a wish to stop a few minutes and contemplate it. The whole of the plain was perfectly level, and, like the rest of the country, without a single shrub. It was covered with the finest verdure, and in every part herds of buffaloe were feeding. I counted seventeen herds; but the aggregate number of the animals it was difficult even to guess at: some thought upwards of ten thousand. We descended into the plain, and each having two marrow bones hung to his saddle, we resolved to dine wherever we could first find water. In descending into the plain, we came upon a small herd feeding in a valley. One buffalo was shot by our party before we could possibly restrain them. At about half the distance across the plain we reached a small pond, where we halted, and having collected a sufficient quantity of dry buffaloe's-dung, we made a fire, in which we disposed [144] our bones, and although the water was stagnant, we made free use of it. During our stay here a very large herd of buffaloe continued to feed within a quarter of a mile of us. Some of them I observed gazing at us; but as they were to the windward, they had not the power of discovering what we were by the sense of smelling. I found, on inquiry from some of our party

who were well acquainted with the habits of these
animals, that they seem to rely chiefly on that sense
for their safety. Around this herd we counted fifteen
wolves, several of which stood for some minutes looking
at us, without exhibiting any signs of fear: and as we
did not think them worth shooting, we left them unmolested. On gaining the summit of the ridge forming
the northern boundary of the plain, we noticed a chain
of hills on our right hand, at the distance of about six
miles. Jones, our guide, assured us they were the
bluffs of the Missouri, and although we might not
arrive at the Fort that night, yet he was certain of our
being able to go to the Mandan village. About four
o'clock we fell into a trace that Jones said was one
of the roads which the Mandans usually followed when
they went out to hunt. We resolved to keep along it,
as we found it led towards the bluffs, at which we
arrived in about an hour, and passed through a narrow
valley, bounded on each side by some small rocks of
secondary limestone. On [145] turning an angle in
the valley, we came suddenly in view of the Missouri,
at no great distance from us. The sight of the river
caused much joy in our party; but no one had so much
occasion as myself to be pleased with it, as it was with
the greatest difficulty I could keep up with the party,
my horse being so tired, that Dorion and others of the
party occasionally rode after me, to beat him forward.
The trace turned up a long and very fine plain, betwixt
the bluffs and the river. The plain continued to increase in breadth as we advanced, and had on it a
sufficiency of clumps of cotton woods, so interspersed as
to prevent our seeing its upper termination. We had
not been on this plain more than half an hour, when we

suddenly saw an Indian on horseback, gallopping down the bluffs at full speed, and in a few minutes he was out of sight, having proceeded nearly in the same direction we were pursuing. We considered this as a certain proof that we were not far from the Mandan town, and shortly after, on turning round the point of a large grove, we came in full view of it. We could perceive that the Indian had already given notice of our approach, as the tops of the lodges were crowded with people; and as we advanced, we saw crowds coming from the town to meet us. From the time the first of the Indians met us till we arrived in the town, we were continually employed in shaking hands, as every one was eager to [146] perform that ceremony with the whole party, and several made us understand that they had seen us before, having been of the war party which we had met at the Great Bend. They conducted us to the lodge of She-he-kè, the chief, where we alighted. He met us at the door, and after shaking hands with us, said, to my great surprise in English, ''Come in house.'' I was again surprised, on entering the lodge, to see a fine dunghill cock. On inquiry I found that She-he-kè had brought it with him from the United States, at the time he accompanied Messrs. Lewis and Clarke, where also he learnt his English.[92] It appeared that immediately on the centinel announcing our ap-

---

[92] She-he-kè (Shahaka), also called Big White (Le Gros Blanc), was chief of the lower village of Mandan. Upon the earnest solicitation of Lewis and Clark he descended the Missouri with them to visit President Jefferson (1806). In 1807 Sergeant Pryor was detailed to escort Big White to his home. The detachment of soldiers was attacked among the Arikara, and forced to retreat. See report of Pryor published in *Annals of Iowa*, January, 1895. It was not until 1809 that the Mandan was finally returned to his village under the care of a brigade of the Missouri Fur Company. See note 58, *ante*; also Chittenden, *American Fur Trade*, chaps. 4-6.— ED.

proach, the squaw had *set on the pot*. The victuals
being ready before we had done smoking, and Mr.
Crooks expressing a determination to proceed to the
Missouri Fur Company's Fort this evening, we soon
finished our meal, which consisted of jerked flesh of
buffaloe and pounded corn. The sun was setting when
we mounted, and several of our horses appeared much
jaded, but mine in particular. I therefore proposed
to remain at the Mandans; but the party, and in particular Mr. Crooks, wished me to go on. With some
reluctance I consented, and we pushed on our horses,
in order to reach Knife River before it was quite dark,
which by much exertion we effected, and arrived opposite to the third village of the Minetaree, or Gros
Ventres [147] Indians, as the night was closing in. On
hallooing, some Indians came down to the bank on the
other side of the river, and immediately ran back to
the village. In a few minutes we saw them returning
along with six squaws, each of whom had a skin canoe
on her back, and a paddle in her hand. Whilst we
unsaddled our horses they crossed the river in their
canoes, and the Indians swam over, and all shook
hands with us. The squaws put our saddles in their
canoes, where we also placed ourselves, and left the
Indians to drive our horses over the river, which they
managed with much address, by placing themselves in
such a way as to keep them in a compact body. This
river is not rapid, but it has the appearance of being
deep, and is about eighty yards wide at this place.
After saddling our horses, and giving the squaws three
balls and three loads of powder for each man, being
the price of ferriage, we passed through the village,

having seven miles still to travel in order to reach the Fort. We could not now make our horses exceed a walk. On the hill above the town I imperfectly distinguished something that had the appearance of cavalry, which Jones told me were the stages whereon the Indians deposit the bodies of their dead. About eleven o'clock we reached the Fort, after having travelled this day more than eighteen hours, with very little intermission. We were received in a very friendly manner by Mr. [148] Reuben Lewis, brother to Captain Lewis, who travelled to the Pacific Ocean:[93] the mosquitoes were much less friendly, and were in such numbers, and so troublesome, that notwithstanding our excessive fatigue, it was next to impossible to sleep.

23rd.— We went early to look at the horses. The greater part were lying down, and appeared to have scarcely moved from the place where they had been left the preceding night, seeming to prefer rest to food. In consequence of their jaded state, Mr. Crooks resolved to remain at the Fort four or five days, that they might recruit themselves. On our return to breakfast, we found that the Fort was but ill supplied with pro-

---

[93] Reuben, the only brother of Meriwether Lewis, was born in Albemarle County, Virginia, February 14, 1777. He accompanied his brother to the West, upon the latter's journey to assume his office as governor of Missouri Territory, and entered (1809) into the partnership that formed the Missouri Fur Company. Reuben Lewis was still absent among the Mandan at the time of his brother's death (October, 1809), not returning to St. Louis until the spring of 1812. After visiting the place of Meriwether's death, he was made Indian agent, and in 1819 Nuttall met him among the Cherokee on Arkansas River. See volume xiii of our series. Later he went back to Virginia, and settled on the family plantation, not far from Charlottesville, where he married (1822) Mildred Dabney. His home, where he died in 1844, was known as ''Valley Point.''— ED.

visions, having little of any thing but jerked meat; but
as that, or any other accommodation the place afforded,
was accompanied by kindness and the most polite
attention from Mr. Lewis, we were much pleased with
our reception.   The bluffs here have a very romantic
appearance, and I was preparing to examine them
after breakfast, when some squaws came in belonging
to the uppermost village of the Minetarees, with a
quantity of roots to sell.   Being informed that they
were dug on the prairie, my curiosity was excited, and
on tasting found them very palatable, even in a raw state.
They were of the shape of an egg: some of them were
nearly as large as those of a goose; others were smaller.
Mr. Lewis [149] obligingly caused a few to be boiled.
Their taste most resembled that of a parsnip, but I
thought them much better.   I found no vestige of the
plant attached to them, and anxious to ascertain the
species, I succeeded in obtaining information from
the squaws of the route by which they came to the
Fort, and immediately set out on the search.   After
much pains I found one of the places where they had
dug the plants, and to my surprise discovered, from
the tops broken off, that the plant was one I was well
acquainted with, having found it even in the vicinity
of St. Louis, where I had first discovered it, and determined it to be a new species of *psoralea*, which is now
known as *psoralea esculenta*.   On enquiry I was informed that this root is of the greatest importance, not
only to the Indians, but to the hunters, who, in case of
the failure of other food, from the want of success in
hunting, can always support life by resorting to it; and
even when not impelled by want, it cannot but be ex-

tremely grateful to those who otherwise must exist on animal food alone, without bread or salt; at least I then thought it so.   I found the country about the Fort, and especially the bluffs, extremely interesting.   It chiefly consists of argillaceous schistus, and a very tenacious and indurated yellow clay, exhibiting in many places the appearance of coal.   The land floods from the country behind the bluffs had cut through them, and left large [150] bodies of clay standing up, with the sides perpendicular, and resembling in appearance towers, or large square buildings, which it was impossible to ascend.   The incumbent soil appears to be of excellent quality, and was at this time covered with fine grass and a number of beautiful plants.   The roots and specimens of these I collected with the greatest assiduity, not having yet determined to remain any longer than until our party returned.   I soon found the number to increase so much, as I lengthened my excursions, that I resolved to remain at the Fort until Mr. Lisa came up with his boat, and obtain a passage with him down to the Aricaras, and this resolution I announced to Mr. Crooks.   The Missouri had overflowed its banks some time before our arrival, and on receding had left numberless pools in the alluvion.   In these the mosquitoes had been generated in numbers inconceivably great. In walking it was necessary to have one hand constantly employed to keep them out of the eyes; and although a person killed hundreds, thousands were ready to take their place.   At evening the horses collected in a body round the Fort, waiting until fires were made, to produce smoke, in which they might stand for protection.   This was regularly done, and a quantity of green

weeds thrown on each fire to increase the smoke.
These fires caused much quarrelling and fighting, each
horse contending for the centre of the smoke, [151] and
the place nearest the fire. In the afternoon we were
visited by She-he-kè, the Mandan chief, who came
dressed in a suit of clothes brought with him from the
United States. He informed us that he had a great
wish to go [to] live with the whites, and that several of
his people, induced by the representations he had made
of the white people's mode of living, had the same
intentions. We were able to converse with She-he-kè
through the medium of Jussum, the interpreter for
the Fort, who was a Frenchman, and had married a
squaw belonging to the second village of the Minetarees, or Gros Ventres Indians.[94] As I expressed a
wish to visit the villages, I spoke to Jussum on that subject, who readily consented to accompany me, but informed me that in a day or two there would be a dance
of the squaws, to celebrate the exploits of their husbands, when it was agreed we should go. The Fort
consisted of a square block-house, the lower part of
which was a room for furs: the upper part was inhabited
by Mr. Lewis and some of the hunters belonging to
the establishment. There were some small outhouses,

---

[94] Réné Jessaume (Jussomme) was a French Canadian who for many
years had lived among the Minitaree. In 1795 he acted as interpreter for
the North West Company; and again two years later accompanied David
Thompson's brigade. See Coues (ed.), *Henry-Thompson Journals*, index.
Lewis and Clark employed him during their winter among the Mandan
(1804-05), and he was the interpreter who accompanied the Mandan chief
to Washington. Upon their return up the river (1807), Jessaume was
severely wounded, but was restored by careful treatment at St. Louis.
Like most "squaw-men" he was a degraded character, and Henry speaks
of him in opprobrious terms.— ED.

and the whole was surrounded by a pallisado, or piquet, about fifteen feet high. I found attached to it a very pretty garden, in which were peas, beans, sallad, radishes, and other vegetables, under the care of a gardener, an Irishman, who shewed it to me with much self-importance. I praised his management, but expressed [152] my regret that he had no potatoes. ''Oh!'' said he, ''that does not signify; we can soon have them; there is plenty just over the way.'' I did not think the man was serious; but on mentioning the circumstance to Mr. Lewis, he told me that there really were potatoes at an English Fort on the river St. Peter's, distant *only* from two to three hundred miles.[95]

24th.— This morning I was informed by Jussum that the squaw dance would be performed in the afternoon, and he promised to have horses ready for us by mid-day. I packed up a few beads for presents, and spent the fore part of the day in my usual way, but took a more extended range into the interior from the river, as the air was calm, having discovered that the mosquitoes remain almost entirely in the valley of the river, where during calm weather it was nearly impossible to collect. On the top of a hill, about four miles from the Fort, I had a fine view of a beautiful valley, caused by a rivulet, being a branch of Knife River, the declivi-

---

[95] This English post upon St. Peter's (Minnesota) River appears to have been one founded by the independent traders of Mackinac. Lieutenant Pike met Cameron (1805), who had a post among the Sioux near the mouth of the Minnesota. Captain T. G. Anderson (*Wisconsin Historical Collections*, ix, pp. 158 ff.) describes his wintering station among the Sioux, upon St. Peter's River about fifty miles above its mouth. All of the Prairie du Chien traders, including Dickson, traded with the Sioux upon this stream. The exact location of the post to which Bradbury refers, has not been determined.— ED.

ties of which abound in a new species of *eleagnus*, intermixed with a singular procumbent species of cedar
(*juniperus*.) The branches are entirely prostrate on
the ground, and never rise above the height of a few
inches. The beautiful silvery hue of the first, con-
trasted with the dark green of the latter, had a most
pleasing [153] effect; and to render the scene more interesting, the small alluvion of the rivulet was so plenti-
fully covered with a species of lily, (*lilium catesbæi*) as
to make it resemble a scarlet stripe as far as the eye
could trace it. I returned to the Fort much gratified,
and prepared to accompany Jussum to the dance. On
our approach some fields of Indian corn lay betwixt us
and the village, which I wished to avoid, and proposed
that we should change our route, as the corn was now
nearly a yard high.[96] This proposal was absolutely refused by Jussum, and we rode on through the corn till
we came to where some squaws were at work, who
called out to us to make us change our route, but were
soon silenced by Jussum. I suspected that he committed [154] this aggression to show his authority or

---

[96] This is about the full height to which the maize grows in the Upper
Missouri, and when this circumstance is connected with the quickness
with which it grows and is matured, it is a wonderful instance of the power
given to some plants to accommodate themselves to climate. The latitude
of this place is about forty-seven degrees geographically, but geologically
many degrees colder, arising from its elevation, which must be admitted to
be very considerable, when we consider that it is at a distance of more than
three thousand miles from the ocean by the course of a rapid river. This
plant is certainly the same species of *zea* that is cultivated within the tropics,
where it usually requires four months to ripen, and rises to the height of
twelve feet. Here ten weeks is sufficient, with a much less degree of heat.
Whether or not this property is more peculiar to plants useful to men, and
given for wise and benevolent purposes, I will not attempt to determine.—
BRADBURY.

importance. On our arrival at the village we went into several of the lodges, which were constructed exactly in the same form as those of the Aricaras. We smoked at every lodge, and I found by the bustle among the women that they were preparing for the dance, as some of them were putting on their husbands' clothes, for which purpose they did not retire into a corner, nor seem in the least discomposed by our presence. In about half an hour the dance began, which was performed in a circle, the dancers moving round, with tomahawks in their hands. At intervals they turned their faces all at once towards the middle of the circle, and brandished their weapons. After some time one of them stepped into the centre of the ring, and made an harangue, frequently brandishing her weapon, whilst the rest moved round her. I found that the nature of all the speeches was the same, which was to boast of the actions of their husbands. One which made Jussum smile I requested he would interpret. He briefly informed me, that she had said her husband had travelled south-west to a country inhabited by white people, which journey took him twenty days to perform: that he went to steal horses, and when he came to the white people's houses, he found one where the men were gone out, and in which he killed two women, and stole from them a number of horses. She corrected [155] herself, by denying that they were women whom her husband had killed, and the reasons she assigned to prove they were not, was what caused Jussum to smile. The dance did not last more than an hour, and I was informed by Jussum that it would be followed by a feast of dog's flesh, of which it was

expected I should partake. I excused myself by saying I wished to collect some plants, and set out alone.
In my way to the Fort I passed through a small wood,
where I discovered a stage constructed betwixt four
trees, standing very near each other, and to which the
stage was attached, about ten feet from the ground.
On this stage was laid the body of an Indian, wrapt
in a buffalo robe. As the stage was very narrow, I
could see all that was upon it without much trouble.
It was the body of a man, and beside it there lay a bow
and quiver with arrows, a tomahawk, and a scalping
knife. There were a great number of stages erected
about a quarter of a mile from the village, on which
the dead bodies were deposited, which, for fear of giving offence, I avoided; as I found, that although it is
the custom of these people thus to expose the dead
bodies of their ancestors, yet they have in a very high
degree that veneration for their remains which is a
characteristic of the American Indians.[97] I arrived
at the Fort about sunset. Soon afterwards we heard
the report of a swivel down the river, which caused us
all to run [156] out, and soon saw the boat belonging to
Mr. Lisa turning a point about two miles below us.
We returned the salute, but he did not arrive that
night, as the side on which we were, to within half a
mile of the Fort, consisted of high perpendicular
bluffs, and his men were too much exhausted to reach
us by the river.

25th.— This morning I had the pleasure of again
meeting Mr. Brackenridge, and of finding that it was

[97] For a further account of burial customs among the Mandan, see Smithsonian *Report*, 1885, part ii, pp. 276-278, 420, 421.— ED.

the intention of Mr. Lisa to stay at least a fortnight at the Fort. I was very glad to have so good an opportunity of examining this interesting country. I received by the hands of Mr. Brackenridge some small articles for trade, which I had delivered to him at the Aricaras. This enabled me to reward the gardener for his civility in offering me a place in the garden where I could deposit my living plants, and of this I availed myself during my stay.

27th.— The business relative to the horses having been arranged betwixt Mr. Lisa and Mr. Crooks, he set out early this morning on his return to the Aricara nation; and as he was not without his fears that the Gros Ventres Indians, headed by Le Borgne, or One Eyed, would attempt to rob him of his horses, he determined to proceed with as much celerity as we had travelled to the Fort, [157] and kept his departure as secret as possible. I was much pleased to see this chief at the Fort in a few hours afterwards, being satisfied that Mr. Crooks was now out of his reach. As it may give some idea of the tyrannic sway with which the chiefs sometimes govern these children of nature, I shall relate an instance of cruelty and oppression practised by this villain. He had a wish to possess the wife of a young warrior of his tribe, who was esteemed beautiful. She resisted his offers, and avoided him. He took the opportunity of the absence of her husband, and carried her off forcibly. The husband was informed on his return of the transaction, and went to the lodge of Le Borgne to claim his wife. The monster killed him. The young man had no father: his mother only was living, and he was her only son. The shock

deprived her of reason, and she reviles the wretch
whenever she meets him, and often seeks him to procure the opportunity of doing so.   Even amongst those
we term savages, the horror which the deed has occasioned is so great, and the pity which the situation of
the poor maniac has excited so prevailing, that he dares
not kill her.   How much then ought Christians to
detest a similar deed.   He has a most savage and ferocious aspect, and is of large stature.   He is chief of one
of the villages of the Minetarees, or, as the French call
them, Gros Ventres, and assumes a dominion over
both, although [158] there are several other chiefs.   It
is stated by Mr. Lewis that the two villages or bands can
raise six hundred warriors, but the number at this
time is probably much less.   The object of this wretch
in visiting the Fort was to make professions of friend-
ship, and to obtain a present.   Mr. Lisa knew very
well the value of his professions, but, notwithstanding,
he gave him some, with which he appeared satisfied.[98]

28th.— Having selected some silver ornaments which
I purposed, presenting to She-he-kè, Mr. Brackenridge
agreed to accompany me to the Mandan village.   We
obtained horses from Mr. Lewis for the journey, and
about ten o'clock set off.   We crossed Knife River
at the lower of the Minetaree villages, and paid the
accustomed price to the squaw who ferried us over;

---

[98] The reputation here given Le Borgne, the giant chief of the Minitaree,
is fully borne out by the reports of other traders and travellers.   Henry
speaks of him as "an astute and atrocious savage," and gives incidents of
his ferocity similar to those cited by Bradbury.   He also represents him as
a successful diplomat, and as being composed and deliberate in the midst
of trying circumstances.   Lewis and Clark, as they returned down the
river (1806), sought to propitiate this influential chieftain by presenting him
with their swivel gun.   The tradition is, that he was killed by a rival chief,
Red Shield.— ED.

which was, for each of us, three balls and three charges
of powder. Before we left the village, we were invited
into the lodge belonging to the *White Wolf*, one of the
chiefs of this village, with whom we smoked.[99] I was
surprised to observe that his squaw and one of his
children had brown hair, although their skins did not
appear to be lighter coloured than the rest of the tribe.
As the woman appeared to be above forty years of
age, it is almost certain that no intercourse had taken
place betwixt these people and the whites at the time
she was born. I should have been less [159] surprised
at the circumstance had they been one of those tribes
who change their places of residence; but they have
not even a tradition of having resided in any other
place than where the present village stands. The
White Wolf appeared to be much pleased with our visit,
and by signs invited us to call at his lodge whenever we
came that way. He shook hands very cordially with
us at parting. In our way to the Mandans we passed
through the small village belonging to the Ahwah-
haways, consisting of not more than eighteen or twenty
lodges. This nation can scarcely muster fifty warriors,
and yet they carry on an offensive war against the Snake
and Flathead Indians.[100] On our arrival at the Mandans, She-he-kè, as before, came to the door of his

[99] This Minitaree chief would seem to be the one called by Lewis and
Clark, ''Wolf Man Chief,'' a son of the famous Choke Cherry. Henry
calls him ''Chief of the Wolves,'' and describes his exploits. See *Henry-
Thompson Journals* (Coues's ed.), pp. 368-370.— ED.

[100] The Ahnahaways were called by the French Gens de Soulier, and
by the Mandan, Wattasoons (Wetersoons). They were kindred to the
Minitaree, claiming to be an offshoot of the Crows. A separate tribal
organization was maintained by them until about 1836, when they merged
into the Hidatsa. Their village was on the present site of Stanton, Mercer
County, North Dakota.— ED.

lodge, and said, "come in house." We had scarcely
entered when he looked earnestly at us, and said,
"whiskey." In this we could not gratify him, as we
had not thought of bringing any. I presented the silver
ornaments to him, with which he seemed much pleased,
and after smoking we were feasted with a dish consisting
of jerked buffalo meat, corn, and beans boiled together.
I mentioned to him my wish to purchase some mockasons, and he sent out into the village to inform the
squaws, who flocked into the lodge in such numbers,
and with so plentiful a supply, that I could not buy a
tenth part of them. I furnished myself with a dozen
pair at a cheap rate, for which I gave a little vermillion,
[160] or rather red lead, and a few strings of blue beads.
During our stay, She-he-kè pointed to a little boy in
the lodge, whom we had not before noticed, and gave
us to understand that his father was one of the party
that accompanied Mr. Lewis, and also indicated the
individual. On our return we crossed Knife River at
the upper village of the Minetarees. The old squaw
who brought the canoe to the opposite side of the river,
to fetch us over, was accompanied by three young
squaws, apparently about fourteen or fifteen years of
age, who came over in the canoe, and were followed
by an Indian, who swam over to take care of our horses.
When our saddles were taken off, and put into the
canoe, Mr. Brackenridge and myself stepped in, and
were followed by the old squaw, when the three young
ones instantly stripped, threw their clothes into the
canoe, and jumped into the river. We had scarcely
embarked before they began to practice on us a number
of mischievous tricks. The slow progress which the

canoe made enabled them to swim round us frequently, sometimes splashing us, then seizing hold of the old squaw's paddle, who tried in vain to strike them with it; at other times they would pull the canoe in such a manner as to change the direction of its course; at length they all seized hold of the hind part, and hung to it. The old squaw called out to the Indian that was following our horses, who immediately swam down to our [161] assistance, and soon relieved us from our frolicksome tormentors, by plunging them successively over head, and holding them for a considerable time under water. After some time they all made their escape from him, by diving and swimming in different directions. On landing, by way of retaliation, we seized their clothes, which caused much laughing betwixt the squaw and the Indian. We had many invitations to stay and smoke; but as it was near sunset, and we had seven miles to ride, they excused us.

29th and 30th.— I continued adding to my stock, and the latter day observed a vein of fine coal, about eighteen inches thick, in the perpendicular bluff below the Fort. On shewing specimens of it to some of the hunters in the Fort, they assured me that higher up the river it was a very common substance, and that there were places in which it was on fire. As pumice is often found floating down the Missouri, I made frequent inquiries of the hunters if any volcano existed on the river or its branches, but could not procure from them any information that would warrant such a conclusion. It is probable, therefore, that this pumice stone proceeds from these burning coal beds.

1st July.— I extended my researches up the river,

along the foot of the bluffs; and when at [162] the distance of three or four miles from the Fort, and in the act of digging up some roots, I was surprised by an Indian, who was within a few yards of me before I perceived him. He had a short gun on his shoulder, and came close to me. He shewed me by signs that he knew very well I was collecting those roots and plants for medicine, and laying hold of my shirt, made the motion usual when traffic or exchange is proposed. It consists in crossing the two fore fingers one over the other alternately. On his pointing to a little distance from us, I perceived a squaw coming up, followed by two dogs, each of which drew a sledge, containing some mockasons and other small articles. The signs which he afterwards made were of a nature not to be misunderstood, and implied a wish to make a certain exchange for my shirt, wherein the squaw would have been the temporary object of barter. To this proposition I did not accede, but replied, in the Osage language, *honkoska* (no) which he seemed to understand, and immediately took hold of my belt, which was of scarlet worsted, worked with blue and white beads, and repeated his proposition, but with the same success. After looking at me fiercely for a few moments, he took his gun from his shoulder, and said in French, *sacre crapaud*, which was also repeated by the squaw. As I had foreseen that he would be offended at my refusal, I took care, on the first movement [163] which he made with his gun, to be beforehand with him, by placing my hand on the lock of mine, which I held presented to him. In this situation we gradually withdrew from each other, until he disappeared with his squaw and the dogs.

2nd.— Mr. Brackenridge and I made an excursion into the interior from the river, and found nothing interesting but what has already been noticed, excepting some bodies of argillaceous schist, parts of which had a columnar appearance. They were lying in a horizontal position, and resembled in some degree the bodies of trees.

4th.— This day being the anniversary of the independence of the United States, Mr. Lisa invited us to dine on board of his boat, which was accepted by Messrs. Brackenridge, Lewis, Nuttall, and myself; and as Le Borgne and the Black Shoe, the two Minetaree chiefs, called at the Fort before dinner, they were invited also. They ate with moderation, and behaved with much propriety, seeming studiously to imitate the manners of white people. After dinner Mr. Lisa gave to each of them a glass of whiskey, which they drank without any hesitation; but on having swallowed it, they laid their hands on their stomachs, and exhibited such distortion of features, as to render it impossible to forbear laughing. As Jussum was present, I asked [164] him the meaning of some words which they spoke to each other, who informed me that they called the whiskey fire water.

Mr. Lisa having announced to us his intention to depart on the 6th for the Aricaras, I employed myself during the 5th in packing up carefully my collection, and on the morning of the 6th we set out. Our progress down the river was very rapid, as it was still in a high state. We did not land until evening, after making in the course of the day more than one hundred miles. In the evening and during the night the mosquitoes were exceedingly troublesome, which rendered it almost impossible to sleep.

7th.— We passed Cannon-ball River about ten o'clock, and stopped a short time at its mouth, where I noticed and procured some additional specimens. In the evening I had the pleasure of meeting my former companions, and was rejoiced to find that Mr. Crooks arrived safely with the horses, and that Mr. Hunt had now obtained nearly eighty in all. Soon after my arrival, Mr. Hunt informed me of his intention to depart from the Aricaras shortly. I therefore purposed returning down the river; and as the Canadians would not be permitted to take their trunks, or, as they termed them, their *caisettes*, by land, I purchased [165] from them seventeen, in which I intended to arrange my living specimens, having now collected several thousands. It had been a custom with us to keep a guard round our camp during the night, since our arrival at the Aricaras. Four of the party were stationed for this purpose until midnight, and were then relieved by four others, who remained on guard until morning. On the morning of the 10th, at day-break, some Indians came to our camp from the village, among whom was my friend the young warrior. As I happened to be on guard, he came to me, and by signs invited me to go and breakfast with him. Whilst we were sitting together, he suddenly jumped up, and pointed to the bluffs, at the distance of three or four miles down the river. On looking, I observed a numerous crowd of Indians. He gave me to understand that it was a war party on their return, and immediately ran to the village. In a few minutes the tops of the lodges were

crowded with Indians, who appeared much agitated.
Soon after an Indian gallopped past our camp, who I
understood was a chief. In a few minutes afterwards
parties began to come out of the village, on their
way to meet the warriors, or rather to join them,
as it is the custom for a war party to wait at a distance
from the village, when a victory has been gained,
that their friends may join in the parade of a triump-
phal entry; and on such occasions all their [166] finery
and decorations are displayed: some time also is re-
quisite to enable the warriors at home and their friends
to paint themselves, so as to appear with proper *eclat*.
During the time that elapsed before the arrival of the
procession, I walked into the village, where a universal
stillness prevailed. No business seemed to be going on,
excepting the preparing of something for the warriors
to eat on their return. The squaws were thus employed
in all the lodges into which I entered,[101] and I noticed
that not one of the poor creatures seemed in the least
solicitous about her own person; as they are [167] too

---

[101] I noticed over their fires much larger vessels of earthenware than any
I had before seen, and was permitted to examine them. They were sufficiently hardened by the fire to cause them to emit a sonorous tone on being
struck, and in all I observed impressions on the outside, seemingly made by
wicker work. This led me to enquire of them by signs how they were made ?
when a squaw brought a basket, and took some clay, which she began to
spread very evenly within it, shewing me at the same time that they were
made in that way. From the shape of these vessels, they must be under
the necessity of burning the basket to disengage them, as they are wider
at the bottom than at the top. I must here remark, that at the Great Salt
Lick, or Saline, about twenty miles from the mouth of the Wabash, vast
quantities of Indian earthenware are found, on which I have observed impressions exactly similar to those here mentioned. From the situation of
these heaps of fragments, and their proximity to the salt works, I am decid-
edly of opinion that the Indians practised the art of evaporating the brine,
to make salt, before the discovery of America.— BRADBURY.

insignificant to be thought an appendage to a triumph. It was near the middle of the day before the procession came in sight, when I went to meet it, in order that my view might be prolonged. A number of the old men and squaws were also moving down from the town to meet it. At the head of the procession were four standard bearers, followed by a band of warriors on foot; after which came a party on horseback: to these succeeded two of the principal chiefs, betwixt whom was a young warrior, who I understood had been severely wounded. Then came two other standard bearers, who were succeeded by another band of foot and horse; this order was observed until the four bands of which the party consisted had passed. They were about three hundred in number: each man carried a shield; a few were armed with guns, some with bows,[102] and

---

[102] The bows are short, but strong. Those which are esteemed the best, are made of the horns of the animal called by the French *gros corne*. This animal inhabits the Rocky Mountains, and is gregarious. All who have seen it, represent its agility in leaping from rock to rock as one of the most surprising things they ever beheld. The Americans call it the mountain sheep; but the probability is that it belongs to the genus antelope. The horns are exceedingly large for the size of the animal. The bows are made of three pieces, very neatly joined together by a long splice, and wound round with sinew in a very exact manner. The next in value, and but little inferior, are made of a yellow wood, from a tree which grows on Red River, and perhaps on the Arkansas. This wood is called *bois jaune*, or *bois d'arc*. I do not think the tree has yet been described, unless it has been found lately in Mexico. I have seen two trees of this species in the garden of Pierre Chouteau, in St. Louis, and found that it belongs to the class *dioecia*; but both of the trees being females, I could not determine the genus. The fruit is as large as an apple, and is rough on the outside. It bleeds an acrid milky juice when wounded, and is called by the hunters the Osage orange. The price of a bow made from this wood at the Aricaras is a horse and a blanket. Many of the war clubs are made of the same kind of wood, and have the blade of a knife, or some sharp instrument, fastened at the end, and projecting from four to six inches, forming a right angle with the club.— BRADBURY.

others with war clubs. [168] They were painted in
a manner that seemed as if they had studied to make
themselves hideous. Many of them had the mark
which indicates that they had drunk the blood of an
enemy. This mark is made by rubbing the hand all
over with vermillion, and by laying it on the mouth, it
leaves a complete impression on the face, which is
designed to resemble and indicate a bloody hand.
With every band some scalps were carried, elevated on
long sticks; but it was easy to perceive, on a close examination, that the scalps had been divided, to increase
the apparent number. The enemy that were killed
we suppose did not exceed in number seven or eight,
and they had themselves lost two, so that this engagement had not been a very bloody one. As the body
approached the town, the squaws and old men met
them, and, excepting the lamentations [169] of those
whose relatives had been killed or wounded, the expressions of joy became general, but without disturbing
in the least the order of the procession. I walked into
the village, which assumed a busy air. On the entrance
of the party, the warriors were conducted to the different lodges, that they might refresh themselves; and the
old men went among them, shaking hands with some,
and seemingly bestowing praises on others, who had
conducted themselves well in the battle. As the time
fixed on for the departure of Mr. Hunt and his party
by land was now approaching, I quitted this scene of
festivity, in order to resume my employment, and
returned to the camp, where I found the party busily
employed in preparing for their departure, by parching
and grinding corn, mixing it with sugar, and putting

it in bags. I now learned that the three men who had
promised to accompany me down the river had changed
their minds, and on account of the now determined and
inveterate hostility of the Sioux, they could not be prevailed on to venture, although I made them liberal
offers. Two of them had determined to join the expedition: the other, Amos Richardson, was very anxious to
descend the river, four years having elapsed since he
had seen the house of a white man; but we two would
not have been sufficient to navigate the boat. Notwithstanding this I commenced filling the caisettes
with plants, and placed them in my [170] boat, and in
the evening again walked up to the village, where I
met Mr. Brackenridge, who had amused himself during
the afternoon by attending to the proceedings consequent on the return of the war party. I was also met
by my friend the young warrior, who invited me into
his lodge, and repeated his request that I would be his
guest during my stay. I gave him a few yards of printed
calico and some gunpowder. In return he pressed me
to accept a bow and a quiver-full of arrows. Whilst we
were smoking, his sister prepared some buffalo meat
with hominy, of which we ate, and after shaking hands
with him, I joined Mr. Brackenridge. In the village
all kind of labour among the women was suspended:
the old men were going from lodge to lodge, probably
enquiring the particulars of the engagement, and bestowing praises on those who had behaved well. The
tops and entrances of the lodges were adorned with the
shields and arms of the warriors, and all seemed joy
and festivity, with the exception of those squaws who
were mourning the loss of the killed. It may not be

amiss to observe that these people had more reason to rejoice for this victory, than many European nations have had for those of infinitely more importance in appearance. For although it had not been attended with so much bloodshed as some battles in Europe have, yet it had for the present driven away an enemy, who [171] for two or three weeks had been hovering round, and threatened us all with starvation. This enemy is the oldest and the most implacable they have, and has already succeeded so far in effecting their extermination, that they are reduced from composing ten large tribes to their present number. These miscreants have been constantly their oppressors, and rob and murder them sometimes with impunity. The present number which the two villages contain is estimated at two thousand, and the warriors at five hundred, but I think it overrated. They are derived from the Panies, and are stout and well built. The men go mostly naked in summer, and when disposed to make use of a covering, it consists of only a part of a buffalo skin thrown over the shoulders, with a hole for the right arm to pass through. This can be thrown off in an instant. They scarcely ever appear without arms beyond the limits of the town. As the nature of the country renders it necessary that they should pursue their game on horseback, frequent practice renders them not only good horsemen, but also teaches them to handle their bows and strike an object with precision with their arrows, when at full speed   They chiefly subsist on the buffalo, and when a herd is discovered, a considerable number of the hunters dispose themselves in a manner so as to approach as near as possible unperceived by

them. This must always be done [172] with due
regard to the direction of the wind, on account of the
exquisite degree in which this animal possesses the
sense of smelling. The instant they are perceived by the
herd, they dash in amongst them, each singling out one.
The horse is taught to understand and obey the wishes
of his rider, although conveyed to him by the slightest
movement. When he has overtaken a buffalo, he does
not offer to pass it, but continues at an even pace until
the arrow is discharged, when the rider singles out another immediately, if he thinks the first arrow has
effected his purpose. If the horse has sufficient strength
and wind to enable his rider to kill three buffaloes, he
is held in great estimation. None of these would be
sold by the Aricaras to Mr. Hunt. After the horses
are out of breath, they pursue the wounded animals at
leisure, as they separate from the herd on being wounded, and are soon left behind from weakness, occasioned
by loss of blood. To produce a more copious discharge,
the heads of the arrows designed to be used in hunting
are much broader than those intended for war. The
heads of both are flat, and of the form of an isosceles triangle; the length of the two equal sides is three times
that of the base.[103] [173] In neither does the shaft of
the arrow fill up the wound which the head has made;
but the shaft of the hunting arrow is fluted, to promote
a still greater discharge of blood. On these occasions
they often kill many more than they can possibly dispose of, and it has already been observed that hunting

---

[103] Before the Indians had any intercourse with the whites, they made
the heads of their arrows of flint or horn stone. They now purchase them
from the traders, who cut them from rolled iron or from hoops.— BRAD-
BURY.

parties are frequently followed by wolves, which profit by this wanton destruction.

The Aricaras do not provide for their horses any better than the other nations of the Missouri. They cut down the cotton wood, (*populus angulosa*) and the horses feed on the bark and smaller branches. I have seen instances exhibiting proofs that these poor animals have eaten branches two inches in diameter. The women, as is the custom with Indians, do all the drudgery, and are excellent cultivators. I have not seen, even in the United States, any crop of Indian corn in finer order, or better managed, than the corn about these villages. They also cultivate squashes, beans, and the small species of tobacco (*nicotiana rustica.*) The only implement of husbandry used by them is the hoe. Of these implements they were so destitute before our arrival, that I saw several of the squaws hoeing their corn with the blade bone of a buffalo, ingeniously fixed in a stick for that purpose.

I am not acquainted with any customs peculiar [174] to this nation, except that of having a sacred lodge in the centre of the largest village. This is called the *Medicine Lodge*, and in one particular corresponds with the sanctuary of the Jews, as no blood is on any account whatsoever to be spilled within it, not even that of an enemy; nor is any one, having taken refuge there, to be forced from it. This lodge is also the general place of deposit for such things as they devote to the *Father of life:* but it does not seem absolutely necessary that every thing devoted shall be deposited here; for one of the chiefs, availing himself of this regulation, devoted his horse, or, in their mode of ex-

pressing it, "gave it to his medicine," after which he
could not, according to their rules, give him away.
This exempted him, in respect to that particular object,
from the tax which custom lays on the chiefs of this
nation and most of the other nations. This will be
explained by stating that generosity, or rather an indifference for self, forms here a necessary qualification
in a chief. The desire to acquire and possess more
than others, is thought a passion too ignoble for a *brave
man:* it often happens, therefore, that a chief is the poor-
est man in the community.

In respect to their general policy as regards property,
they seem to have correct ideas amongst themselves of
the *meum* and *tuum*; and when the [175] generally
thievish character of those we call savages is considered,
the Indians of the Missouri are superlatively honest
towards strangers. I never heard of a single instance
of a white man being robbed, or having any thing stolen
from him in an Indian village. It is true, that when
they find white men trapping for beaver on the grounds
which they claim, they often take from them the furs
they have collected, and beat them severely with their
wiping sticks; but so far is this from being surprising,
that it is a wonder they do not kill them, or take away
their rifles.

The chief part of their riches consists in horses, many
of which are obtained from the nations southwest of
them, as the Chayennes, Poncars, Panies, &c. who
make predatory excursions into Mexico, and steal horses
from the Spaniards. A considerable number of those
bought from the Aricaras were branded, and were

doubtless brought from Mexico, as the Indians do not practice branding.

There is nothing relating to the Indians so difficult to understand as their religion. They believe in a Supreme Being, in a future state, and in supernatural agency. Of the Great Spirit they do not pretend to give any account, but believe him to be the author and giver of all good. They believe in bad spirits, but seem to consider them rather [176] as little wicked beings, who can only gratify their malignity by driving away the game, preventing the efficacy of medicine, or such petty mischief. The belief in a future state seems to be general, as it extends even to the Nodowessies or Sioux, who are the furthest removed from civilization, and who do not even cultivate the soil. It is known, that frequently when an Indian has shot down his enemy, and is preparing to scalp him, with the tomahawk uplifted to give the fatal stroke, he will address him in words to this effect: ''My name is Cashegra. I am a famous warrior, and am now going to kill you. When you arrive at the land of spirits, you will see the ghost of my father; tell him it was Cashegra that sent you there.'' He then gives the blow.

In respect to laws, I could never find that any code is established, or that any crime against society becomes a subject of inquiry amongst the chiefs, excepting cowardice or murder. The last is, for the most part, punished with death, and the nearest of kin is deputed by the council to act the part of executioner. In some tribes, I am told, this crime may be commuted. It scarcely requires to be observed, that chastity in females

is not a virtue, nor that a deviation from it is considered
a crime, when sanctioned by the consent of their husbands, fathers, or brothers: but in some tribes, [177]
as the Potowatomies, Saukies, Foxes, &c. the breach
of it, without the consent of the husband, is punished
severely, as he may bite off the nose of his squaw if she
is found guilty.

No people on earth discharge the duties of hospitality
with more cordial good-will than the Indians.   On entering a lodge I was always met by the master, who first
shook hands with me, and immediately looked for his
pipe: before he had time to light it, a bear-skin, or that
of a buffalo, was spread for me to sit on, although they
sat on the bare ground.   When the pipe was lighted, he
smoked a few whiffs, and then handed it to me; after
which it went round to all the men in the lodge.   Whilst
this was going on, the squaw prepared something to eat,
which, when ready, was placed before me on the ground.
The squaw, in some instances, examined my dress, and
in particular my mockasons: if any repair was wanting,
she brought a small leather bag, in which she kept her
awls and split sinew, and put it to rights.   After con-
versing as well as we could by signs, if it was near night,
I was made to understand that a bed was at my service; and in general this offer was accompanied by that
of a *bedfellow*.

The two men, Jones and Carson, whom we met
descending the Missouri on the 22nd of May, had
[178] remained with the Aricaras during the winter, and
on our return, Carson was desirous of rewarding the
Indian with whom he had boarded during that period.
For that purpose he obtained some articles from Mr.

Hunt, and offered them to the *savage*, who refused to accept them, and as a reason for it, observed, that *"Carson was poorer than himself."*

I breakfasted with Mr. Lisa the day following, and found that he intended to send two of the boats purchased from Mr. Hunt to St. Louis, with skins and furs, and that Mr. Brackenridge purposed to descend with them. I knew also that in a week our party would take their departure for the Pacific Ocean. Messrs. Hunt, Crooks, and M'Kenzie invited me to go to the Pacific, and in the first instance I was inclined to accept the invitation; but finding that they could not assure me of a passage from thence to the United States by sea, or even to China, and considering also that I must sacrifice my present collection by adopting that measure, and that in passing over the Rocky Mountains, I should probably be unable to preserve or carry my specimens, I declined. There was now something of uncertainty whether Mr. Lisa would return to St. Louis in autumn, or remain during the winter.

On duly weighing all these circumstances, I resolved to return in the boats which were intended [179] to be dispatched down the river, although it did not exactly suit my views, as I had noticed a great number of species of plants on the river, that, from the early state of the season, could not then be collected advantageously. These I had reserved for my descent; but as no man would accompany me but Richardson, I applied to Mr. Lisa, informing him of my wish to descend in his boats; and on consideration of being permitted to land at certain places which I pointed out, I offered to give him my boat as a compensation. To this he readi-

ly agreed, and I commenced preparing for my departure.

It had been a matter of surprise to me on my return
from Fort Mandan, to find plenty of fresh buffalo meat
in our camp, although the fear of the Sioux had not yet
subsided. On enquiry, I found that Mr. Hunt had
hit upon an expedient which proved successful. This
was to dispatch a boat up the river in the night to some
miles distant, which afforded an opportunity to the
hunters to procure food. This boat returned with a
plentiful supply, and secured the party from starving,
as a considerable portion of the Indian dogs were already consumed. I was not less surprised on learning
that at least two-thirds of our Canadians had experienced unpleasant consequences from their intercourse
with the squaws, notwithstanding which [180] the traffic
before mentioned continued. I had been informed
by Jones and Carson of the existence of this evil, but
found it was of the mildest description, and that here,
where the natives do not use spirituous liquors nor
salt, it is not feared. I found some of the Canadians
digging up roots, with which I understood they made a
decoction, and used it as a drink. They mostly pre-
ferred the roots of *rudbeckia purpurea*, and sometimes
they used those of *houstonia longifolia*.

This morning a circumstance came to our knowledge
which gave serious alarm to Mr. Hunt and the leaders
of the party. During the night a cask of gunpowder
belonging to me had been stolen from amongst the baggage, and from the security of our situation, and the precautions we had taken, it was impossible the Indians
could have stolen it. Our camp was situated immedi-

ately on the bank of the river; the tents, together with
the men sleeping in their blankets, surrounded the baggage, and four men were constantly on guard during the
night, walking round the camp in sight of each other.
I had been on guard in the fore part of the night, and
Mr. Crooks on the latter watch. No collusion could
therefore be suspected; these and other circumstances
concurred in producing a belief that some of the party
intended to desert, and on examination I found that
one of my trunks had been [181] opened, and a pistol,
some flints, my belt, and a few shirts, taken out. In
confirmation of our opinions, John Day, one of the
hunters,[104] informed Mr. Hunt of his having overheard
some of the Canadians murmuring at the fatigues they
had already undergone, and expressing an opinion that
they should all be murdered in the journey they were
going to undertake. As the safety of the party depended, in a great measure, on its strength, a diminution in
the number, if considerable, might therefore defeat the
enterprize; a search was made in all the neighbourhood of the camp, and even in the bank of the river, but

---

[104] John Day was a Virginia backwoodsman who had hunted some time
on the Missouri, and had been in Crooks's employ. He joined the overland
Astorian party at their winter quarters on the Nodaway. Upon the outward
journey Day and Crook were left behind, being robbed and stripped by the
Indians on the Columbia. They were rescued and carried to Astoria by
Robert Stuart's party. Day started to return with the overland party in
1813, but was taken violently insane, and attempted his own life. He
was sent back to Astoria, where Irving says that he died the following year.
There is evidence, however, that he joined the North West Company and
lived until 1819. See Ross, *Adventures of the First Settlers on the Columbia*, comprising vol. vii of the present series. Two rivers in Oregon are
named for this traveller — a small creek in the western part of the state,
flowing into the Columbia, and a large affluent of the latter in eastern
Oregon.— ED.

without effect. As my boat might facilitate a deser-
tion, I caused it to be removed to Mr. Lisa's camp, who
moored it in safety with his own boats; and I employed
myself, for the remainder of the day, in filling some
boxes.

On account of my constant attention to plants, and
being regularly employed in collecting, I was considered as the physician of the party by all the nations
we saw; and generally the *medicine men* amongst them
sought my acquaintance. This day, the doctor, whom
Mr. Brackenridge and I saw in the upper village, and
who showed me his medicine bag, came to examine my
plants. I found he understood a few French words,
such as *bon*, *mal*, &c. I presented him with some small
ornaments of silver, with which he appeared to be very
much [182] pleased, and requested me to go to his lodge
and smoke with him. When I entered, he spread a
fine new buffalo robe for me to sit on, and showed
me that it was a present, which he wished me to accept.
I smoked with him, and regretted much that we could
only converse by signs, and he seemed also to feel the
same regret. He showed me a quantity of a plant
lately gathered, and by signs informed me that it cured
the cholic. It was a new species of *amorpha*. I returned to the camp, accompanied by the doctor, who
very politely carried the buffalo robe for me.

On the 17th I took leave of my worthy friends, Messrs.
Hunt, Crooks, and M'Kenzie, whose kindness and
attention to me had been such as to render the parting
painful; and I am happy in having this opportunity of
testifying my gratitude and respect for them: throughout the whole voyage, every indulgence was given me,

that was consistent with their duty, and the general
safety. Mr. Lisa had loaded two boats with skins
and furs, in each of which were six men. Mr. Brackenridge, Amos Richardson, and myself were passengers.
On passing our camp, Mr. Hunt caused the men to
draw up in a line, and give three cheers, which we returned; and we soon lost sight of them, as we moved at
the rate of about nine miles per hour. I now found,
to my great surprise, that Mr. Lisa [183] had instructed
Mr. Brackenridge not, on any account, to stop in the
day, but if possible, to go night and day. As this
measure would deprive me of all hopes of adding to my
collection any of the plants lower down the river, and
was directly contrary to our agreement, I was greatly
mortified and chagrined; and although I found that Mr.
Brackenridge felt sensibly for my disappointment, yet
I could not expect that he would act contrary to the
directions given by Lisa: I had in consequence the mortification during the day, of passing a number of plants
that may probably remain unknown for ages.

Our descent was very rapid, and the day remarkably
fine; we had an opportunity, therefore, of considering
the river more in its *tout ensemble* than in our ascent,
and the changes of scenery came upon us with a succession so quick, as to keep the eye and the mind continually employed. We soon came in sight of the
bluffs which border the Chayenne River, stretching as
far as the eye could reach, and visible only through the
low intervals in those bordering the Missouri. Before
night we passed the Chayenne, and during a few moments had a view of its stream, for two or three miles
above its junction with the Missouri. It is one of the

largest rivers that falls into it, being at least four hundred yards wide at its mouth, and [184] navigable to a great distance. The banks appear to be more steep than those of the Missouri, and are clothed with trees to the water's edge. On both sides of the river we saw numberless herds of buffaloes, grazing in tranquillity, some of them not a quarter of a mile from us when we passed them. We continued under way until late in the evening, and encamped on an island; a measure we determined to pursue when practicable, as we knew that to fall into the hands of the Sioux would be certain death.

18th.— We set out early, and continued under way during the whole of the day without interruption, and encamped on Great Cedar Island, where a French trader, named L'Oiselle, formerly had a post or trading house.[105] This island is about two miles in length, and chiefly covered with very fine cedar, and some rose and currant bushes, considerably overrun with vines, on which some of the grapes were already changing colour.

19th.— In the early part of the day we arrived at the upper part of the Great Bend, and continued to see innumerable herds of buffaloes on both sides of the river. I now found that although our *patron*, or steersman, who conducted the first boat, and directed our motions, was determined to obey strictly the orders of Lisa as regard-

---

[105] This post, commonly known as Fort aux Cèdres, and situated upon an island about thirty miles below Pierre, in Hughes County, South Dakota, was probably the earliest upon the upper Missouri. Lewis and Clark noted it in 1804.

Registre Loisel came to St. Louis in 1793 under the Spanish regime, and entered the fur-trade. He died in 1804, and his fort was abandoned.— ED.

ed expedition, [185] yet from his timidity I had some hope of opportunities to collect.

Before we entirely passed the Great Bend a breeze arose, which ruffled the surface of the river: He put ashore, not daring to proceed, and we lay to during the remainder of the day, having descended about two hundred and eighty miles in two days and a half. I determined not to lose this opportunity to add a few species to my collection, and was accompanied in my excursion by Mr. Brackenridge, who employed himself in keeping a good look out for fear of a surprise by the Sioux, a precaution necessary to my safety, as the nature of my employment kept me for the most part in a stooping posture. The track of land which is inclosed in the Bend probably contains about forty square miles, nearly level, and the soil excellent. It was at this time covered with fine grass and scattered groves of trees, betwixt which many herds of buffaloes were quietly grazing: we did not wish to disturb them, for fear of thereby enabling the Sioux to discover us.

20th.— About nine o'clock we discovered some buffaloes grazing near the edge of the river, about half a mile below us, and in such a position that we might apparently approach very near them without being discovered. We landed a little above [186] them, and approached within about sixty yards, when four of the party fired. It appeared that two were wounded, one of which fled towards the river, into which it plunged, and was immediately pursued by one of the boats, whilst the party ashore followed the other, among whom I ran, but I was much less intent on obtaining the buffalo, than on procuring some plants which I knew

were to be had on the bluffs, and actually succeeded.
In about half an hour the party gave up the pursuit,
being unsuccessful, and returned discouraged to the
place where they had left me. But as I had not
gone over the bluffs, and had observed what had
passed in the river, I gave them the pleasing intelligence that the boat had overtaken the other buffalo,
and that the men were now employed in dragging
the carcase ashore. We soon joined them, and in
a few minutes the animal was skinned and cut up.
It was by much the fattest we had seen, and the
tallow it contained was very considerable.[106]

[187] We soon passed White River, which is inferior
both in magnitude and beauty to the Chayenne, if we
may judge from its mouth, where it is not more than
three hundred yards wide. Soon after we passed the
river, we saw a buffalo running over the bluff towards
the Missouri, which put us on our guard, as we considered it a certain indication of Indians being near.
Immediately below the river the vast vein of iron ore
commences which has been before mentioned. I
again noticed its exact conformity on both sides of the
river, in point of elevation and thickness of the vein.

As the evening approached we noticed a succession
of flashes of lightning, just appearing over the bluffs,
on the opposite side of the river. This did not for
some time excite much attention, as it was by no means

---

[106] I am informed by the hunters, that in autumn the quantity of tallow or
fat in the buffalo is very great. It of course diminishes when food becomes
scarce. As the same thing obtains in a number of animals, by climate and
habit ordained to procure abundance of food in summer, and to suffer great
privation in winter, this collection of fat seems to be a kind of reservoir,
containing the means of existence, which is drained by absorbent vessels, and
returned into the system when necessary.— BRADBURY.

an uncommon occurrence; but we soon began to ap-
prehend impending danger, as we perceived that the
storm advanced with great rapidity, accompanied with
appearances truly terrific. The cloud was of a pitchy
blackness, and so dense as to resemble a solid body,
out of which, at short intervals, the lightning poured
in a continued stream for one or two seconds. It was
too late to cross the river, and, unfortunately for us, the
side on which we were was entirely bounded by rocks.
We looked most anxiously for some little harbour, or
jutting point, behind which we might shelter [188] ourselves; but not one appeared, and darkness came on
with a rapidity I never before witnessed. It was not
long that any choice was left us. We plainly heard the
storm coming. We stopped and fastened our boats to
some shrubs, (*amorpha fruticosa*) which grew in abundance out of the clefts of these rocks, and prepared to
save ourselves and our little barks if possible. At each
end of the boats there was a small deck: under these we
stowed our provisions, &c.: next to the decks were
piled the packs of skins, secured by ropes, and in the
middle a space of about twelve feet long was left for
the oarsmen. Fortunately for us, we had some broad
boards in each boat, designed as a defence against
arrows, in case of an attack by the Sioux. These
boards we placed on the gunwale of the boats, and
crammed our blankets into such parts as the lightning
enabled us at intervals to see did not fit closely. Before
we had time to lash our boards the gale commenced,
and in a few minutes the swell was tremendous. For
nearly an hour it required the utmost exertion of our
strength to hold the boards to their places, and before

the storm abated we were nearly exhausted, as also were those who were occupied in baling. As the river is in this place nearly a mile in breadth, and being on the lee shore, the waves were of considerable magnitude, and frequently broke over the boats. Had our fastenings given way, we must [189] inevitably have perished. When the wind abated the rain increased, and continued for the greater part of the night, during which my friend Brackenridge and myself lay on the deck, rolled up in our wet blankets, congratulating ourselves on our escape. For myself I felt but little: two years, in a great measure spent in the wilds, had inured me to hardships and inclemencies; but I felt much for my friend Brackenridge. *Poor young man*, his youth, and the delicacy of his frame, ill suited him for such hardships, which, nevertheless, he supported cheerfully.

In the morning the sun rose unobscured, which was to us extremely welcome, as its heat soon rendered us comparatively comfortable. We passed the river L'Eau qui Court, and shortly afterwards the place where we met the Poncar Indians, and as the wind began to blow fresh, we stopped five or six miles lower down, nearly at the place where I met the three Indians on the 24th of May. This enabled me to procure roots of the new species of currant, although with much pain and difficulty, having four miles at least to wade through water and mud, as the river had recently overflowed its banks. On my return to the boats, as the wind had in some degree abated, we proceeded, and had not gone more than five or six miles before we were surprised by a dull hollow sound, the cause [190] of which we could not possibly imagine. It seemed to be one or two miles below us; but as our descent was very rapid, it increased every moment in loudness, and before we had proceeded far, our ears were able to catch some distinct tones, like the bellowing of buffaloes. When opposite to the place from whence it proceeded, we landed, ascended the bank, and entered a small skirting of trees and shrubs, that separated the river from an extensive plain. On gaining a view of it, such a scene opened to us as will fall to the lot of few travellers to witness. This plain was literally covered with buffaloes as far as we could see, and we soon discovered that it consisted in part of females. The males were fighting in every direction, with a fury which I have never seen paralleled, each having singled out his antagonist. We judged that the number must have amounted to some thousands, and that there were many hundreds of these battles going on at the same time, some not eighty yards from us. It will be recollected that at this season the females would naturally admit the society of the males. From attentively observing some of the combats nearest to us, I am persuaded that our domestic bull would almost invariably be worsted in a contest with this animal, as he is inferior to him both in strength and ferocity. A shot was fired amongst them, which they did not seem to notice. Mr. Brackenridge joined me in [191] preventing a volley being fired, as it would have been useless, and therefore wanton; for if we had killed one of these animals, I am certain the weight of his carcase in gold would not have bribed us to fetch him. I shall only observe farther, that the noise occasioned by the trampling and bellowing was far beyond description. In the evening, before we encamped, another immense herd made its appearance, running along the bluffs at full speed, and although at least a mile from us, we could distinctly hear the sound of their feet, which resembled distant thunder.

The morning of the next day was very fine. We saw some buffaloes swimming, at which the men fired, contrary to our wishes, as we did not intend to stop for them. The stream was very rapid. We passed the Sulphur bluffs, and stopped a short time at Floyd's grave: shortly afterwards we arrived at the trading house opposite the Maha village, but saw no one, nor did we wish it, as Mr. Lisa had not called on the Big Elk when he ascended, who might probably be offended at his neglect. We encamped on some drift wood from necessity, not being able to get ashore. The navigation of the river had now become much more difficult, and we had in the two succeeding days some very narrow escapes. The river was considerably higher than at any former period, and from the Mahas to the River [192] Platte, is more crooked than in any other part. At every sudden turn the momentum of the boats had a continual tendency to throw them ashore on the outer bank, which it required all the skill of the steersman, and strength of the oarsmen, to prevent. In two instances we were very near being carried into the woods, in places where the river overflowed its banks. We arrived at Fort Osage, now Fort Clark, on the 27th in the afternoon, and were very politely received by Major Brownson. I had the pleasure to find that Mr. Sibley had returned a few days before from his tour to the Arkansas, to examine the vast body of salt in the neighbourhood of that river. He very politely furnished us with extracts from his journal, which are as follows:—

''After giving a number of medals to the Panie chiefs, and having various counsels with them, I left their villages on the 4th of June, and proceeded to the little Osage Camp, on the Arkansas, about seventy-five miles south, and sixteen east from the Panies, where I safely arrived on the 11th. I remained several days with the Osages, who had abundance of provisions, they having killed two hundred buffaloes within a few days. Where they had their camp, the Arkansas was about two hundred yards wide, the water shallow, rapid, and of a red colour. On the 16th, the Indians raised their camp, and proceeded towards the hilly country, on [193] the other side of the Arkansas. I continued with them about fifty miles west and thirty miles east, when we fell in with some men of the Chanier's Band, who informed us that their camp was at no great distance, and the camp of the Big Osage still nearer. In consequence, I determined to pass through both on my way to the Grand Salines. On the 21st I rode south forty miles, east thirty, to the Big Osage camp;[107] nearly all the warriors were at war, or abroad

[107] These Indians were abroad hunting, and the camps noted by Sibley were temporary. Their permanent villages were as follows: that of the Grand Osage, high up on the river of that name, in Vernon County, Missouri; that of the Little Osage, about six miles beyond; Chanier's Band was the Arkansas branch of the Osage, under the chief Cashesagra, whose village was on the Verdigris Branch of the Arkansas, about sixty miles from its mouth, in the present Cherokee nation, Indian Territory. Chouteau had had a fine trade with the Osage, when Manuel Lisa succeeded in obtaining the monopoly for that tribe on the Missouri and Osage rivers, whereupon Chouteau enticed one of the bands to the waters of the Arkansas. See Pike's *Expeditions* (Coues's ed., New York, 1895), pp. 556-558.— ED.

hunting. I was remarkably well treated by young
White Hair and family; I however remained but one
night with them. On the 22d I rode twenty miles
south, fifteen east, to the Chanier's camp, where we arrived about one o'clock. We were well treated by the
head men; and indeed, this is one of the tribes most
attached to the Americans. The chief's name is Clermont.[108] From hence it is forty miles to the Grand
Salines, which we reached early on the morning of the
24th. I hasten to give you a description of this cele-
brated curiosity.

"The Grand Saline is situated about two hundred
and eighty miles south-west of Fort Osage, between
two forks of a small branch of the Arkansas, one of
which washes its southern extremity; and the other, the
principal one, runs nearly parallel, within a mile of its
opposite side. It is a hard level plain, of reddish coloured sand, and of [194] an irregular or mixed figure.
Its greatest length is from north-west to south-east,
and its circumference full thirty miles. From the appearance of drift-wood that is scattered over, it would
seem that the whole plain is at times inundated by the
overflowing of the streams that pass near it. This
plain is entirely covered in hot dry weather, from two
to six inches deep, with a crust of beautiful clean white
salt, of a quality rather superior to the imported blown

---

[108] Clermont (Builder of towns) was said by Pike to be the hereditary
chief of the Great Osage, whose position was usurped by White Hair the
elder, while Clermont was still a child. Clermont seceded with Cashesagra
(see preceding note), and became the most influential chief of the Arkansas band. White Hair the elder remained at the original Great Osage
village. His son, young White Hair, accompanied Pike a short distance
on his journey, and then made an excuse to turn back. The explorer
calls him a "discontented young fellow, filled with self-pride."— ED.

salt: it bears a striking resemblance to a field of brilliant snow after a rain, with a light crust on its top. On a bright sunny morning, the appearance of this natural curiosity is highly picturesque: it possesses the quality of looming, or magnifying objects, and this in a very striking degree, making the small billets of wood appear as formidable as trees. Numbers of buffaloes were on the plain. The Saline is environed by a stripe of marshy prairie, with a few scattered trees, mostly of cotton wood; behind these is a range of sand hills, some of which are perfectly naked, others thinly clothed with verdure and dwarf plum bushes, not more than thirty inches in height, from which we procured abundance of the most delicious plums I ever tasted. The distance to a navigable branch of the Arkansas is about eighty miles, the country tolerably level, and the water-courses easily passed.[109] About sixty miles south-west of this, I came to the Saline, [195] the whole of this distance lying over a country remarkably rugged and broken, affording the most romantic and picturesque views imaginable. It is a tract of about seventy-five miles square, in which nature has displayed a great variety of the most strange and whimsical vagaries. It is an assemblage of beautiful meadows, verdant ridges, and rude, mis-shapen piles of red clay, thrown together in the utmost apparent confusion, yet affording the most pleasant harmonies, and presenting us in every direction an endless variety of curious and inter-

---

[109] The salines here described were on Cimarron River, where is now a saline reservation in Woodward County, Oklahoma. Lieutenant Wilkinson, in his descent of the Arkansas River, describes them as located about two days' march from that stream, and says the Indians obtain the salt by scraping the prairie with a turkey's wing.— ED.

esting objects. After winding along for a few miles
on the high ridges, you suddenly descend an almost
perpendicular declivity of rocks and clay, into a series
of level, fertile meadows, watered by some beautiful
rivulets, and here and there adorned with shrubby cotton wood trees, elms, and cedars. These meadows
are divided by chains formed of red clay and huge
masses of gypsum, with here and there a pyramid of
gravel: one might imagine himself surrounded by the
ruins of some ancient city, and that the plain had sunk,
by some convulsion of nature, more than one hundred
feet below its former level; for some of the huge columns
of red clay rise to the height of two hundred feet perpendicular, capped with rocks of gypsum, which the
hand of time is ever crumbling off, and strewing in
beautiful transparent flakes along the [196] declivities
of the hills, glittering, like so many mirrors, in the
sun.''[110]

Mr. Sibly also showed me a letter from his father,
Dr. Sibly, of Natchitoches, informing him of a mass of
native iron having been brought down the Red River,
which weighed about two thousand five hundred
pounds. In the fort we saw the young bears which we
left there in passing up the river; they had grown surprisingly, and were quite tame, except whilst feeding,
when all bears are more fierce than at other times.

28th.— After breakfasting at the fort, we set off, and
encamped near where Fort Orleans formerly was situated.

---

[110] The second saline, called "Grand Saline" on Pike's map, is located
by him on the head-springs of one branch of the Cimarron, which would
probably place it in northwestern Texas, or southeastern Colorado.— ED.

29th.— About noon we came in sight of a white man's house, at Boon's Lick, when our boatmen immediately set up a shout. Soon after, some men appeared at the edge of a field of Indian corn, close to the river: they invited us ashore, and we willingly complied. In passing through the corn, I was much struck with its luxuriance: I judged it to be not less than fourteen feet high, and the ears were far above my head. It was Sunday, and when we arrived at the house, we found three women there, all dressed in clean white gowns, [197] and being in other respects very neat, they formed a pleasing contrast to the squaws whom we had of late been in the habit of seeing. They soon spread the table for us, and produced bread, milk, and preserved fruits, which I thought the most delicious that I ever tasted. We arrived at St. Louis in safety, where I had the pleasure of shaking hands with my worthy friend, Mr. Abraham Gallatin, at whose house I slept. Early the next day, I called at the post-office, and found letters from England, informing me of the welfare of my family. This pleasing intelligence was damped by a letter from my son, who informed me that those who had agreed to furnish me with the means of prosecuting my tour, and to whom I had sent my former collection, had determined to withhold any farther supply. Early in the forenoon, my worthy and respected friend, Mr. S. Bridge, from Manchester, came to St. Louis, and invited me to take up my residence for the present with him. He informed me that during my absence he had bought a considerable quantity of land, on which he had built a house. He sent his waggon for my plants, and allotted me a piece of ground, which, with much labour, I prepared in a few days, got it surrounded by a fence, and transplanted the whole of my collection. I found the situation of Mr. Bridge's house extremely pleasant, and his plantation of the first quality of land. Within a hundred and fifty [198] yards of his house was a small vein of coal, from twelve to eighteen inches in thickness, and rising to the surface. For this land he had paid one dollar, sixty-five cents per arpent, or French acre.[111]

In about ten days after my arrival I was attacked by a bilious fever, which confined me to my bed. Its violence left me little hope of recovery. In about a month it became intermittent, and continued until the beginning of December.

During my illness a circumstance occurred, an account of which will tend to show the almost unconquerable attachment to the hunting life in those accustomed to it. It will be remembered that a man named Richardson accompanied us down the Missouri, and that it has been related of him that he had been several years in the wilderness. He had there suffered more than common hardships, having been often ill treated by the Indians, and once severely wounded by an arrow. This man, during our descent, seemed to look forward with great anxiety to the time when we should arrive in the settlements, and often declared his intention never again to adopt the hunting life. When I had been sick about three weeks, he came to see me, [199] and after some conversation, reminded me of my having mentioned a design to ascend the

---

[111] The arpent is to the statute acre nearly in the proportion of eighty-three to one hundred.— BRADBURY.

Arkansas River, and requested that I would admit him as my companion, if I persisted in my intention. I spoke of my doubts whether I should ever recover, and expressed my surprise at so sudden a change in his intentions. He replied, ''I find so much deceit and selfishness amongst white men, that I am already tired of them. The arrow head which is not yet extracted, pains me when I chop wood, whiskey I can't drink, and bread and salt I don't care about: I will go again amongst the Indians.''

Towards the latter end of November, I received a remittance from those who had previously determined to withhold it, together with a letter from the person[112] who managed the Botanic Garden at Liverpool, informing me that he had received my former collection, out of which he had secured in pots more than one thousand plants, and that the seeds were already vegetating in vast numbers. As I had now so far recovered as to be able to ride to St. Louis, I visited my friend Mr. Gallatin, and remained with him some days, during which period I often saw a young gentleman from Philadelphia, Mr. H. W. Drinker, who had frequently called to see me in my sickness, and whose talents and amiable [200] manners had created in me a strong attachment to him. In a tour through the country west of the Alleghanies, he visited St. Louis, and pleased with the beauty of the place, had resided there for some months. Finding that I was determined to descend the Mississippi to New Orleans, he invited me to take my passage with him, as he purposed taking a boat down to that place, loaded with lead, of which

[112] This man's name is Shepherd.— BRADBURY.

he had a sufficient quantity. This was a very favourable opportunity, and I made every exertion my weak
state would admit of, to be in readiness. À short time
afterwards Mr. Drinker ascertained that some debts
due to him, and contracted to be paid in lead, could not
be collected until the ensuing spring: he therefore
found himself necessitated to remain at St. Louis until
that period. But aware of the impossibility of my
detaining what yet remained of my collection till that
season, he offered to buy a boat, load it with lead, and
commit it to my care, with liberty to sell the lead at
Orleans, òr store it for his account. This kind and
generous offer I gladly accepted, and in a few days a
boat was procured, and her cargo put on board, amounting to about thirty thousand pounds weight of lead.
Her crew consisted of five French Creoles, four of whom
were oarsmen, and the fifth, who steered the boat, is
called the *patron*.

[201] On the evening of the 4th of December we were
in perfect readiness, when I took leave of my friends at
St. Louis, several of whom, from their polite attention
to me, I have reason to hold in lasting remembrance;
and in addition to those I have already mentioned, I
ought not to omit Mr. Josh. Charless, editor of the Missouri Gazette, whose disposition and manners gain him
the esteem of all who know him: mine he will always
retain.[113]   I find that I omitted stating, that in Novem-

---

[113] The *Missouri Gazette* was the earliest newspaper published west of
the Mississippi River, its first issue appearing in 1808. It was the pro-
genitor of the present St. Louis *Republic*, which took the latter title in 1822.
Joseph Charless, its first editor and proprietor, was an Irishman who became
involved in sedition and fled to America in 1796. He served as printer
under Matthew Carey at Philadelphia until 1800, when he removed to
Kentucky, and eight years later to St. Louis. Charless retired from the
conduct of this paper in 1820, and died at St. Louis in 1834.— ED.

ber Mr. Lisa arrived at St. Louis, and delivered me a letter from Mr. Hunt, who informed me, that after my departure from the Aricaras, whilst the men were still assembled to watch our boats descend, he addressed them on the subject of my cask of powder, which was stolen, and with such effect, that one of the Canadians came privately to his tent the night following, and informed him where it was buried in the bank of the river. Mr. Hunt caused a search to be made the day after, and found it. As Mr. Lisa was in want of powder, he bought it, and paid me for it on his return.

On the 5th of December I set off from St. Louis on the voyage to New Orleans, a distance of about one thousand three hundred and fifty miles. I was accompanied by Mr. John Bridge, whom I admitted as a passenger at the request of his brother. He purposed sailing from Orleans to the eastern [202] states. We arrived at St. Genevieve in the evening, and slept at the mouth of Gabarie, a small creek near the village, where boats trading to that place usually stop. Having some business to transact at St. Genevieve, I was detained till the afternoon of the following day. During my stay here, I became acquainted with a gentleman of the name of Longprie, a native of St. Domingo. He had a boat, in part loaded with lead, intended for Orleans. It was much wished by both of us that we should descend in company, as in case of an accident happening to one, assistance might be rendered by the other; but as he could not be ready in less than two days, I set out, intending to travel leisurely, that he might overtake me. It may be necessary to remark in this place, that the navigation of the Mississippi is attended with considerable danger, and in particular to boats loaded

with lead.   These, by reason of the small space occupied by the cargo, in case of striking against a *planter* or
a *sawyer*, sink instantly.   That these terms may be
understood, it must be observed that the alluvion of the
Mississippi is almost in every part covered with timber
close to the edge of the river, and that in some part or
other encroachments are continually made, and in
particular during the time of the floods, when it often
happens that tracts of some acres in extent are carried
away in a few days.   As in most instances a large body
of earth is attached [203] to the roots of the trees, it
sinks those parts to the bottom of the river, whilst the
upper parts, more buoyant, rise to the surface in an
inclined posture, generally with the heads of the trees
pointing down the river.   Some of these trees are fixed
and immoveable, and are therefore termed *planters*.
Others, although they do not remove from where they
are placed, are constantly in motion: the whole tree is
sometimes entirely submerged by the pressure of the
stream, and carried to a greater depth by its momentum than the stream can maintain.   On rising, its
momentum in the other direction, causes many of its
huge limbs to be lifted above the surface of the river.
The period of this oscillatory motion is sometimes of
several minutes duration.   These are the *sawyers*,
which are much more dangerous than the *planters*, as no
care or caution can sufficiently guard against them.
The steersman this instant sees all the surface of the
river smooth and tranquil, and the next he is struck
with horror at seeing just before him the *sawyer* raising
his terrific arms, and so near that neither strength nor
skill can save him from destruction.   This is not figura-

tive: many boats have been lost in this way, and more particularly those descending. From these and other risks, it is common for those carrying lead, to have a canoe with them, in which they may save themselves in case of any accident happening to the boat.

[204] Until the 14th, no occurrence happened worth noticing, excepting that we saw on the bank of the river four Indians, who beckoned to us to stop: we accordingly landed near them, and found they were Choctaws, who wanted to sell some venison and turkies. As they were acquainted with the use of money, I bought from them three turkies and two hind quarters of venison for three quarters of a dollar, being the sum they asked.

In the evening of the 14th, we arrived at New Madrid, and having occasion for some necessaries, I bought them in the morning.[114] I was much disappointed in this place, as I found only a few straggling houses, situated round a plain of from two to three hundred acres in extent. There are only two stores, which are very indifferently furnished. We set off about nine o'clock, and passed the Upper Chickasaw Bluffs; these bluffs are of soft sand-stone rock, of a yellow colour, but some parts being highly charged with oxyd of iron, the whole has a clouded appearance, and is considered as a curiosity by the boatmen. At the lower end of the bluffs we saw a smoke, and on a nearer approach, observed five or six Indians, and on the opposite side of the river, but lower down, we heard a dog howling. When the Indians perceived us, they held up some venison, to

---

[114] On the settlement of New Madrid, see Cuming's *Tour*, vol. iv of our series, p. 282, note 185.— ED.

show us that they wished to dispose of it. Being desirous of [205] adding to our stock of fresh meat, I hastily got into the canoe, and took with me one of the men, named La France, who spoke the Chickasaw language, as I supposed the Indians to be of that nation.[115] We very imprudently went without arms an omission that gave me some uneasiness before we reached them; especially as the boat, by my direction, proceeded leisurely on.

We found that the Indians had plenty of deer's flesh, and some turkies. I began to bargain for them, when the people in the boat fired a shot, and the dog on the other side of the river instantly ceased howling. The Indians immediately flew to their arms, speaking all together, with much earnestness. La France appeared much terrified, and told me that they said our people in the boat had shot their dog. I desired him to tell them that we did not believe that our people had done so, but if they had, I would pay them any price for him. They seemed too much infuriated to hearken to him, and surrounded us with their weapons in their hands. They were very clamorous amongst themselves, and, as I was afterwards told by La France, could not agree whether they should immediately put us to death, or keep us prisoners until we could procure goods from the boat to pay for the dog, on which it appeared they set high value. Most fortunately for us, the dog, [206] at this instant began to bark opposite to us, having run a considerable distance up the river after the shot was fired. The tomahawks were immediately

---

[115] For the early history of the Chickasaw Indians, see Croghan's *Journals*, vol. i of our series, p. 75, note 36.— ED.

laid aside, and I bargained for half a deer, for which I gave them a quarter dollar and some gunpowder. I was not very exact in measuring the last, being rather anxious to get away, and could perceive that La France had no desire to stay any longer.

On reaching our canoe we seized our paddles, and being told by La France that we were not yet out of danger, we made every exertion to get out of their reach. When we conceived ourselves safe, we relaxed, and he told me that even when we were leaving them, they were deliberating whether they should detain us or not; some of them having remarked that the dog might be wounded. We had been so long delayed by this adventure, that it was more than an hour before we overtook the boat. I blamed the boatmen much for firing, and charged them with having fired at the dog: this, however, appeared not to have been the case, as they fired at a loon, (*mergus merganser.*) In the course of this day, we passed no fewer than thirteen arks, or Kentucky boats, going with produce to Orleans; all these we left a considerable distance behind, as they only float with the stream, and we made considerable [207] head-way with our oars. In the evening we came in view of the dangerous part of the river, called by the Americans the *Devil's Channel*, and by the French *Chenal du Diable.* It appears to be caused by a bank that crosses the river in this place, which renders it shallow. On this bank, a great number of trees have lodged; and, on account of the shallowness of the river, a considerable portion of the branches are raised above the surface; through these the water rushes with such impetuosity as to be heard at the distance of some miles.

As it would require every effort of skill and exertion to pass through this channel in safety, and as the sun had set, I resolved to wait until the morning, and caused the boat to be moored to a small island, about five hundred yards above the entrance into the channel. After supper we went to sleep as usual; and in the night, about ten o'clock, I was awakened by a most tremendous noise, accompanied by so violent an agitation of the boat that it appeared in danger of upsetting. Before I could quit the bed, or rather the skin, upon which I lay, the four men who slept in the other cabin rushed in, and cried out in the greatest terror, "*O mon Dieu! Monsieur Bradbury, qu'est ce qu'il y a?*" I passed them with some difficulty, and ran to the door of the cabin, where I could distinctly see the [208] river agitated as if by a storm; and although the noise was inconceivably loud and terrific, I could distinctly hear the crash of falling trees, and the screaming of the wild fowl on the river, but found that the boat was still safe at her moorings. I was followed by the men and the *patron*, who, in accents of terror, were still enquiring what it was: I tried to calm them by saying, "*Restez vous tranquil, c'est un tremblement de terre,*" which term they did not seem to understand.

By the time we could get to our fire, which was on a large flag, in the stern of the boat, the shock had ceased; but immediately the perpendicular banks, both above and below us, began to fall into the river in such vast masses, as nearly to sink our boat by the swell they occasioned; and our *patron*, who seemed more terrified even than the men, began to cry out, "*O mon Dieu! nous perirons!*" I wished to consult with him as to what we could do to preserve ourselves and the boat, but could get no answer except *"O mon Dieu! nous perirons!"* and *"Allons à terre! Allons à terre!"* As I found Mr. Bridge the only one who seemed to retain any presence of mind, we consulted together, and agreed to send two of the men with a candle up the bank, in order to examine if it had separated from the island, a circumstance that we suspected, from hearing the [209] snapping of the limbs of some drift trees, which were deposited between the margin of the river and the summit of the bank. The men, on arriving at the edge of the river, cried out, *"Venez à terre! Venez à terre!"* and told us there was a fire, and desired Mr. Bridge and the *patron* to follow them; and as it now occurred to me that the preservation of the boat in a great measure depended on the depth of the river, I tried with a sounding pole, and to my great joy, found it did not exceed eight or ten feet.

Immediately after the shock we observed the time, and found it was near two o'clock. At about nearly half-past two, I resolved to go ashore myself, but whilst I was securing some papers and money, by taking them out of my trunks, another shock came on, terrible indeed, but not equal to the first. Morin, our *patron*, called out from the island, *"Monsieur Bradbury! sauvez vous, sauvez vous!"* I went ashore, and found the chasm really frightful, being not less than four feet in width, and the bank had sunk at least two feet. I took the candle to examine its length, and concluded that it could not be less than eighty yards; and at each end, the banks had fallen into the river. I now saw clearly that our lives had been saved by our boat being

moored to a sloping bank. Before we completed our
fire, we had two [210] more shocks, and others occurred
during the whole night, at intervals of from six to ten
minutes, but they were slight in comparison with the
first and second. At four o'clock I took a candle, and
again examined the bank, and perceived to my great
satisfaction that no material alteration had taken
place; I also found the boat safe, and secured my pocket compass. I had already noticed that the sound
which was heard at the time of every shock, always
preceded it at least a second, and that it uniformly
came from the same point, and went off in an opposite
direction. I now found that the shock came from a
little northward of east, and proceeded to the westward.
At day-light we had counted twenty-seven shocks during our stay on the island, but still found the chasm so
that it might be passed. The river was covered with
foam and drift timber, and had risen considerably, but
our boat was safe. Whilst we were waiting till the
light became sufficient for us to embark, two canoes
floated down the river, in one of which we saw some
Indian corn and some clothes. We considered this
as a melancholy proof that some of the boats we passed
the preceding day had perished. Our conjectures were
afterwards confirmed, as we learned that three had been
overwhelmed, and that all on board had perished.
When the daylight appeared to be sufficient for us, I
gave orders to embark, and we all went on board.
Two men [211] were in the act of loosening the fastenings, when a shock occurred nearly equal to the first
in violence. The men ran up the bank, to save themselves on the island, but before they could get over the

chasm, a tree fell close by them and stopped their progress. As the bank appeared to me to be moving rapidly into the river, I called out to the men in the boat, *"Coupez les cordes!"* on hearing which, the two men ran down the bank, loosed the cords, and jumped into the boat. We were again on the river: the *Chenal du Diable* was in sight, but it appeared absolutely impassable, from the quantity of trees and drift wood that had lodged during the night against the planters fixed in the bottom of the river; and in addition to our difficulties, the *patron* and the men appeared to be so terrified and confused, as to be almost incapable of action. Previous to passing the channel, I stopped that the men might have time to become more composed. I had the good fortune to discover a bank, rising with a gentle slope, where we again moored, and prepared to breakfast on the island. Whilst that was preparing, I walked out in company with Morin, our *patron*, to view the channel, to ascertain the safest part, which we soon agreed upon. Whilst we were thus employed, we experienced a very severe shock, and found some difficulty in preserving ourselves from being thrown down; another occurred during the time we were [212] at breakfast, and a third as we were preparing to re-embark. In the last, Mr. Bridge, who was standing within the declivity of the bank, narrowly escaped being thrown into the river, as the sand continued to give way under his feet. Observing that the men were still very much under the influence of terror, I desired Morin to give to each of them a glass of spirits, and reminding them that their safety depended on their exertions, we pushed out into the river. The danger we

had now to encounter was of a nature which they understood: the nearer we approached it, the more confidence they appeared to gain; and indeed, all their
strength, and all the skill of Morin, was necessary;
for there being no direct channel through the trees,
we were several times under the necessity of changing
our course in the space of a few seconds, and that so
instantaneously, as not to leave a moment for deliberation.   Immediately after we had cleared all danger, the
men dropped their oars, crossed themselves, then gave
a shout, which was followed by mutual congratulations
on their safety.

We continued on the river till eleven o'clock, when
there was another violent shock, which seemed to affect
us as sensibly as if we had been on land.   The trees
on both sides of the river were most violently agitated,
and the banks in several places fell in, within our view,
carrying with them [213] innumerable trees, the crash
of which falling into the river, mixed with the terrible
sound attending the shock, and the screaming of the
geese and other wild fowl, produced an idea that all
nature was in a state of dissolution.   During the shock,
the river had been much agitated, and the men became
anxious to go ashore: my opinion was, that we were
much safer on the river; but finding that they laid down
their oars, and that they seemed determined to quit the
boat for the present, we looked out for a part of the river
where we might moor in security, and having found
one, we stopped during the remainder of the day.

At three o'clock, another canoe passed us adrift on
the river.   We did not experience any more shocks until
the morning of the 17th, when two occurred; one about

five and the other about seven o'clock. We continued
our voyage, and about twelve this day, had a severe
shock, of very long duration. About four o'clock we
came in sight of a log-house, a little above the Lower
Chickasaw bluffs. More than twenty people came out
as soon as they discovered us, and when within hearing,
earnestly entreated us to come ashore. I found them
almost distracted with fear, and that they were composed of several families, who had collected to pray
together. On entering the house, [214] I saw a bible
lying open on the table. They informed me that the
greatest part of the inhabitants in the neighbourhood
had fled to the hills, on the opposite side of the river,
for safety; and that during the shock, about sun-rise
on the 16th, a chasm had opened on the sand bar opposite the bluffs below, and on closing again, had thrown
the water to the height of a tall tree. They also affirmed
that the earth opened in several places back from the
river. One of the men, who appeared to be considered
as possessing more knowledge than the rest, entered into
an explanation of the cause, and attributed it to the
comet that had appeared a few months before, which
he described as having two horns, over one of which
the earth had rolled, and was now lodged betwixt them:
that the shocks were occasioned by the attempts made
by the earth to surmount the other horn. If this
should be accomplished, all would be well, if otherwise,
inevitable destruction to the world would follow. Finding him confident in his hypothesis, and myself unable
to refute it, I did not dispute the point, and we went on
about a mile further. Only one shock occurred this
night, at half past seven o'clock. On the morning of

the 18th, we had two shocks, one betwixt three and four
o'clock, and the other at six. At noon, there was a
violent one of very long duration, which threw a
great [215] number of trees into the river within our
view, and in the evening, two slight shocks more, one at
six, the other at nine o'clock.

19th.— We arrived at the mouth of the river St.
Francis, and had only one shock, which happened at
eleven at night.

20th.— Detained by fog, and experienced only
two shocks, one at five, the other at seven in the
evening.

21st.— Awakened by a shock at half past four o'clock:
this was the last, it was not very violent, but it lasted
for nearly a minute.

On the 24th in the evening, we saw a smoke, and
knowing that there were no habitations on this part of
the river, we made towards it, and found it to be the
camp of a few Choctaw Indians, from whom I purchased a swan, for five balls and five loads of powder.[116]

25th.— Monsieur Longpre overtook us, and we encamped together in the evening. He was about two
hundred miles from us on the night of the 15th, by the
course of the river, where the earthquakes had also
been very terrible. It appeared from his account, that
at New Madrid the shock had been [216] extremely
violent: the greatest part of the houses had been rendered uninhabitable, although, being constructed of
timber, and framed together, they were better calculated to withstand the shocks than buildings of brick

[116] For the Choctaw Indians, see Cuming's *Tour*, vol. iv of our series,
p. 287, note 187.— ED.

or stone. The greatest part of the plain on which the town was situated was become a lake, and the houses were deserted.

The remainder of our voyage to Natchez was very pleasant, with the exception of two very narrow escapes from *planters* in the river. Without any occurrence that would excite much interest, we arrived at the port of Natchez on the afternoon of the 5th of January, and went to the city, which is situated about three quarters of a mile from the river, on the level behind the bluffs.[117] The port consists of thirty or forty houses, and some stores: for the size of it, there is not, perhaps, in the world a more dissipated place. Almost all the Kentucky men stop here on the way to Orleans, and as they now consider all the dangers and difficulties of their voyage as past, they feel the same inclination to dissipation as sailors who have been long out of port, and generally remain here a day or two to indulge it. I spent a pleasant evening in the city, in company with Dr. Brown, whom I found to be a very agreeable and intelligent man.

[217] In the morning of the 6th instant I went on board the steam boat from Pittsburg; she had passed us at the mouth of the Arkansas, three hundred and forty-one miles above Natchez; she was a very handsome vessel, of four hundred and ten tons burden, and was impelled by a very powerful steam engine, made at Pittsburg, whence she had come in less than twenty days, although nineteen hundred miles distant. About eighty miles above New Orleans, the sugar plantations

---

[117] For the early history of Natchez, see F. A. Michaux's *Journal*, vol. iii of our series, p. 254, note 53.— ED.

commenced, some of which I visited, accompanied by Mr. Longpre, who assured me that he had not seen the cane in higher perfection in any part of the West Indies. Many fields yet remained, from which the cane had not been got in: they were now covered with snow, an occurrence, as I was informed, very uncommon. From this part to New Orleans, groves of orange trees of great extent are seen on both sides of the river, and at this season, loaded with ripe fruit.

On the 13th we arrived at New Orleans, where I consigned the lead to the agent of Mr. Drinker, again met with my friend Brackenridge, and on the 20th set sail for New York.

APPENDIX

APPENDIX

No. I

VOCABULARY OF SOME WORDS

IN THE

OSAGE LANGUAGE

Man,	*Ne-ka.*
Woman,	*Wa-ko.*
Boy,	*Shin-zo shin-ga.*
Girl,	*She-ma shinga.*
Young man,	*Shen-don-sho.*
Young woman,	*Kas-ho-meĕ.*
Old man,	*Ke-sau-ga hin-ga.*
Old woman,	*Wa-ko hin-ga.*
Head,	*Wa-augh-reh.*
Nose,	*Pa-gĕ.*
Mouth,	*E-haugh.*
Chin,	*La-baugh.*
Face,	*In-ga.*
Throat,	*To-ja.*
Arm,	*Haugh.*
[222] Hand,	*Nom-ba.*
Breast,	*Mo-in-ga.*
Belly,	*Che-sa.*
Thigh,	*Sha-gaugh omba.*
Knee,	*Se-don-ja.*
Leg,	*Sha-gaugh.*
Calf of Leg,	*E-sho.*
Shin,	*Wa-haugh.*

Ancle,	*He-ka.*
Foot,	*See.*
Toe,	*See-paugh.*
Finger,	*Sha-ga.*
Finger nails,	*Sha-ga hugh*
Horse,	*Kou-o-lă.*
Mare,	*Kou-o-lă min-gă*
Colt,	*Kou-o-lă shin-ga.*
Bull,	*Shes-ka ton-ga.*
Cow,	*Shes-ka min-gă.*
Buffalo bull,	*Sha ton-ga.*
Ditto cow,	*Sha.*
Elk, male,	*O-pa ton-ga*
Do. female,	*O-pa min-gă.*
Deer, male.	*Taw ton-ga.*
Do. female,	*Taw min-gă.*
Fawn,	*Sha-ra-sha shin-ga.*
Bear, male,	*Was-saw-ba ton-ga.*
Do. female,	*Was-saw-ba min-gă.*
Wolf,	*Sho-ma ca-sa.*
Dog,	*Shon-ga.*
[223] Fox,	*Mou-shu lo-go-nĕ.*
Cat,	*E-gron-ga-sha.*
Beaver,	*Sha-ba.*
Otter,	*Tow-non-ja.*
Squirrel,	*Se-in-ja.*
Rabbit,	*Mos-tin-ja.*
Panther,	*E-gron-ga.*
Skunk,	*Mon-ga.*
Rattlesnake,	*Sha-kee.*
Black snake,	*Wait-saw sau-ba.*
Frog,	*Pa-nis-ka.*

Spider,	*Shaw-bas-ka.*
Turkey cock,	*Su-ka ton-ga.*
Ditto hen,	*Su-ka.*
Goose,	*Me-has-shaw-ba.*
Swan,	*Me-has-ka.*
Dunghill cock,	*Su-ga shu-ga ton-ga.*
Hen,	*Su-ka shu-ga.*
Crow,	*Ka-wa.*
Raven,	*Ka-wa ton-ga.*
Hawk,	*Was-sa shin-ga ton-ga.*
Eagle,	*Hu-ras-po-sa.*
Vulture,	*Ha-ja.*
Owl,	*Waw po-jă.*
Fish,	*Hoe.*
An American,	*Moi-hě ton-ga.*
An Englishman,	*Me-gra-sha.*
A Frenchman,	*Es-ta-wě.*
A Spaniard,	*Esh-pa-nuo.*
[224] Sugar,	*Shau-no.*
Salt,	*Ne-shu.*
Tobacco,	*No-ne-agh.*
Pipe,	*No-nem-ba.*
Gun,	*Wau-ho-ton.*
Cannon,	*Wau-ho-ton ton-ga.*
Pistol,	*Wau-ho-ton-da paugh.*
Gunpowder,	*Ne-hu-ja wa-ca-ja.*
Lead,	*Mos-sa ma-jos-ca.*
Flint,	*Moi-hu-sě.*
Powder-horn,	*Sha-ka.*
Knife,	*Moi-hě.*
Tomahawk,	*Moi-hě sa-pa shinga.*
Axe,	*Moi-hě shaw-a-ga-sa.*

Hoe,	*Mon-sa-vă.*
Kettle,	*Sha-ha.*
Tin cup,	*Kes-ne-la-tă.*
Saddle,	*Hon-ko-gra.*
Hair,	*Pa-us-ka.*
Beads,	*Hes-ka.*
Wampum,	*Hes-ka wa-num-pě.*
Vermillion,	*Wa-su-ga.*
Medal,	*Ca-ha-ga.*
Cloth,	*Hau.*
Red cloth,	*Hau shu-ja.*
White cloth,	*Hau ska.*
Black cloth, &c. &c.	*Hau-sau-ba.*
One,	*Mi-ne-hě.*
Two,	*Nom-baugh.*
[225] Three,	*Lau-be-na.*
Four,	*To-ba.*
Five,	*Sat-ta.*
Six,	*Sha-pa.*
Seven,	*Pa-nom-ba.*
Eight,	*Ke-lan-baugh.*
Nine,	*Shan-ka.*
Ten,	*Cra-bra.*
Eleven,	*Au-grě mi-ne-hě.*
Twelve,	*Au-grě nom-baugh.*
Thirteen &c. to twenty,	*Au-grě lau-be-na.*
One hundred,	*Cra-bra ton-ga.*
River,	*Nes-ka.*
Prairie,	*Ton-ja.*
Woodland,	*Son ja.*
A garrison,	*Nau-sa.*
Village,	*To-wa-ně.*

A commanding officer,	*Kaw-he-ja wau-ton-ga.*
Physician,	*Wa-ken-da-ga.*
Father,	*In-da-ja.*
Mother,	*E-naugh.*
Brother,	*Wee-shin-da.*
Sister,	*Wee-ton-ja.*
Uncle,	*Ween-ja-kĕ.*
Aunt,	*Wee-she-mee.*
Brother-in-law,	*Wee-ton-ha.*
Water,	*Nes-nigh.*
Ice,	*Non-ha.*
Snow,	*Pau.*
[226] Rain,	*Nigh-shu.*
Frost,	*Pau-sha.*
Winter,	*Bor-ra.*
Summer,	*To-ja-ton.*
Spring,	*Pa-ton.*
Autumn,	*Ton-da.*
Hot,	*Most-cha.*
Cold,	*Ne-wat-cha.*
Red,	*Shu-ja.*
White,	*Ska.*
Black,	*Sau-ba.*
Blue,	*To-ha.*
Yellow,	*Se-a.*
Green,	*Ne-a-ko.*
House,	*Tee-he.*
Door,	*Tee-he sha-ba.*
Robe,	*Mes-co-ba.*
Blanket,	*Aug-re.*
Mockasons,	*Hom-ba.*
Leggings,	*He-minca.*

Soldier,	*Has-ka-ke-da.*
Large,	*Gron-da.*
Largest,	*Ton-ga.*
Small,	*Wau-ho-ka.*
Smaller,	*Shin-ga.*
Ugly,	*Pe-sha.*
Handsome,	*Lo-go-ne.*
Yes,	*Hoy-a.*
No,	*Hon-kos-ka.*
[227] Good,	*Lo-go-ne,* or *Tou-ha.*
Bad,	*Pe-sha.*
President of the United States,	*Kow-a-ga Show-a-ga Wa-ge-shu.*
Large man,	*Ne-ka she-ka gronda.*
Large body of men,	*Ne-ka she-ga hugh.*
Flock of deer,	*Tau-hugh.*
Large flock of birds,	*Was-sa shin-ga hugh.*
Drove of buffaloes,	*Sha-to-ga ochĕ.*
Scalp,	*Ne-shu-ha-du-sa.*
Run,	*Tau-nĕ.*
Come,	*Ku-e-lo.*
To go,	*Mo-gre-na.*
Kill,	*Es-sa-ra.*
Leap,	*We-she.*
Me,	*We-ah.*
You,	*De-ah.*
Day,	*Hon-pa.*
Night,	*He-nĕ.*
Light,	*Hon-pa lo-go-nĕ.*
Dark,	*He-nĕ pe-sha.*
To part asunder,	*We-ta.*
To join,	*Sho-sho.*

To eat,	*Wa-num-bra.*
To drink,	*Ne-bra-ta.*
To sleep,	*A-shem-bra.*
To get up,	*Pau-haw.*
To walk,	*O-ga-sha.*
To lie down,	*Au-re-con-sha.*

ORATION DELIVERED BY THE BIG ELK
THE CHIEF OF THE MAHA NATION
OVER THE GRAVE OF THE BLACK BUFFALO
CHIEF OF THE TETONS
A TRIBE OF THE SIOUX, AT THE PORTAGE DES SIOUX[118]

14*th July*, 1813

Do not grieve — misfortunes will happen to the wisest
and best men. Death will come, and always comes
out of season: it is the command of the Great Spirit,
and all nations and people must obey. What is passed,
and cannot be prevented, should not be grieved for.
Be not discouraged or displeased then, that in visiting
your father here, you have lost your chief. A misfortune of this kind may never again befal you, but this
would have attended you perhaps at your own village.
Five times have I visited this land, and never returned
with sorrow or pain. Misfortunes do not flourish
particularly in our path — they grow every where.
(*Addressing himself to Governor Edwards and Colonel
Miller.*) What a misfortune for me that I could not
have died this day, instead of the [229] chief that lies
before us. The trifling loss my nation would have
sustained in my death, would have been doubly paid

---

[118] Portage des Sioux is in St. Charles County, Missouri, at the point
where the Mississippi most nearly approaches the Missouri River. Frequent councils with the Indians were held at this place. In 1815 there was
signed here the treaty which pacified the Western Indians.— ED.

for by the honours of my burial — they would have
wiped off every thing like regret. Instead of being
covered with a cloud of sorrow — my warriors would
have felt the sunshine of joy in their hearts. To me it
would have been a most glorious occurrence. Hereafter, when I die at home, instead of a noble grave and a
grand procession, the rolling music and the thundering
cannon, with a flag waving at my head, I shall be
wrapped in a robe, (an old robe, perhaps) and hoisted
on a slender scaffold to the whistling winds, soon to be
blown down to the earth — my flesh to be devoured by
the wolves, and my bones rattled on the plain by the
wild beasts, (*Addressing himself to Colonel Miller.*)
Chief of the soldiers — your labours have not been in
vain:— your attention shall not be forgotten. My nation
shall know the respect that is paid over the dead. When
I return I will echo the sound of your guns.

THE FOLLOWING INTERESTING NARRATIVE

OF THE

EXPEDITION OF MR. HUNT

MENTIONED IN THIS WORK, IS EXTRACTED FROM THE MISSOURI GAZETTE

"WE last week promised our readers an account of the journey of the gentlemen attached to the New York Fur Company, from the Pacific Ocean to this place.— We now lay it before our readers, as collected from the gentlemen themselves.

On the 28th of June, 1812, Mr. Robert Stewart, one of the partners of the Pacific Fur Company, with two Frenchmen, Mr. Ramsey Crooks, and Mr. Robert M'Clellan, left the Pacific Ocean with despatches for New York.[119]

After ascending the Columbia river ninety miles,

---

[119] Robert Stuart, one of the partners of the Pacific Fur Company, went to Astoria in the ship "Tonquin." For the adventures of that voyage, see Franchère's *Narrative*, in vol. vi of our series. Robert was a nephew of David Stuart, and being born in Scotland (1784) was educated at Paris. At the age of twenty-two he landed in Montreal and entered the service of the North West Company. After the perilous overland journey herein related, Stuart became a partner of Astor in the American Fur Company, and after 1819 was manager for that concern at Mackinac. Later (1834) he removed to Detroit, where he became a prominent citizen, serving for one term as state treasurer (1840-41), and thereafter for four years as federal Indian agent. He died in Chicago in 1848. Many of his letters, written during his residence at Mackinac, are now in the archives of the Wisconsin Historical Society.— ED.

John Day, one of the hunters, became perfectly insane, and was sent back to the main establishment, under the charge of some Indians: the [231] remaining six pursued their voyage upwards of six hundred miles, when they happily met with Mr. Joseph Miller, on his way to the mouth of the Columbia. He had been considerably to the south and east, among the nations called Blackarms and Arapahays, by the latter of whom he was robbed;[120] in consequence of which he suffered almost every privation human nature is capable of, and was in a state of starvation and almost nudity when the party met him.

They had now fifteen horses, and pursued their journey for the Atlantic world, without any uncommon accident, until within about two hundred miles of the Rocky Mountains, where they unfortunately met

---

[120] The Blackfeet and Arapaho are both of Algonquian stock, belonging to that branch of the great Indian family which had had its earlier habitat east of the Mississippi River. Together with the Cheyenne they had crossed into Siouan territory, and now occupied the Rocky Mountain region. The Blackfeet were the more northern of the two tribes, and quite numerous; they roved upon the upper waters of the Missouri — chiefly Milk and Maria rivers — and traded with the British fur-trade companies which operated throughout the vast region drained by the Winnipeg, Assiniboine, and Saskatchewan systems, which parallel the upper reaches of the Missouri and its northern tributaries. Upon his return journey, Lewis had a hostile encounter with one of their bands. To this unfortunate affair, in which a Blackfoot horse-thief was killed by one of Lewis's men, has been attributed the intense hostility of the tribe to the early American traders, causing much bloodshed and disaster. Later writers have thought, however, that their opposition arose from hunters who joined war-raids upon the Blackfeet. The latter now number about two thousand, upon a reservation in Montana.

The Arapaho occupied the central mountainous region, roaming through Wyoming and Southern Idaho. They traded with the Spaniards, and supplied their kindred the Cheyenne with Spanish horses. There are now about eighteen hundred of this tribe upon reservations in Oklahoma and Wyoming.— ED.

with a party of the Crow Indians,[121] who behaved with
the utmost unbounded insolence, and were solely prevented from cutting off the party by observing them
well armed and constantly on their guard. They, however, pursued on their track six days, and finally stole
every horse belonging to the party.

Some idea of the situation of those men may be
conceived, when we take into consideration, that
they were now on foot, and had a journey of two
thousand miles before them, fifteen hundred of which
was entirely unknown, as they intended and prose-
cuted it considerably south of Messrs. Lewis [232] and
Clarke's route. The impossibility of carrying any
quantity of provisions on their backs, in addition to
their ammunition and bedding, will occur at first view.
The danger to be apprehended from starvation was
imminent. They, however, put the best face upon
their prospects, and pursued their route towards the
Rocky Mountains, at the head waters of the Colorado,
or Spanish River, and stood their course E. S. E. until
they struck the head waters of the great River Platte,
which they undeviatingly followed to its mouth. It
may here be observed, that this river, for about two
hundred miles, is navigable for a barge; from thence to
the Otto Village, within forty-five miles of its entrance
into the Missouri, it is a mere bed of sand, without
water sufficient to float a skin canoe.

From the Otto Village to St. Louis, the party per-

---

[121] The Crows were of the Hidatsan sub-stock of the Siouan race, closely
related to the Minitaree. They were a wandering tribe, whose habitat
was the Big Horn range and valley, and they were exacting in their demands
upon traders. Their chief enemies were Blackfeet and Sioux. They now
number about eighteen hundred, upon a reservation in Montana.— ED.

formed their voyage in a canoe, furnished them by the natives, and arrived here in perfect health, on the 30th of last month (May.)

Our travellers did not hear of the war with England until they came to the Ottoes. These people told them that the Shawnoe Prophet had sent them a wampum, inviting them to join in the war against the Americans.[122] They answered the messenger, that they could make more by trapping beaver than making war against the Americans.

[233] After crossing the hills (Rocky Mountains) they fell in with a small party of Snake Indians,[123] from whom they purchased a horse, which relieved them from any further carriage of food, and this faithful four-footed companion, performed that service to the Otto village. They wintered on the river Platte, six hundred miles from its mouth.

By information received from these gentlemen, it appears that a journey across the continent of North America might be performed with a waggon, there being no obstruction in the whole route that any person would dare to call a mountain, in addition to its being

---

[122] The Shawnee Prophet was brother and partner of Tecumseh, in his confederacy against the Americans. The range of his operations is shown by this message to the distant Oto. After the close of the War of 1812-15, the Prophet received from the British authorities a pension for his services; later, he removed with his tribe to Indian Territory, and there died about 1834.— ED.

[123] The Snake Indians were the largest branch of the Shoshonian stock, and are frequently spoken of as Shoshoni. Their habitat was the upper waters of the Columbia, whose largest tributary takes its name from this tribe. They were first encountered and described by Lewis and Clark. As a rule they have been friendly Indians. They now number about twenty-five hundred, chiefly at the Fort Hall and Lemhi agencies in Idaho and the Shoshoni agency in Wyoming.— ED.

much the most direct and short one to go from this
place to the mouth of the Columbia river.   Any future
party, who may undertake this journey, and are tolerably acquainted with the different places where it would
be necessary to lay up a small stock of provisions, would
not be impeded, as in all probability, they would not
meet with an Indian to interrupt their progress, although
on the other route, more north, there are almost insur-
mountable barriers.''

*The following is Mr. Crooks's narrative of Mr.
Hunt's expedition from the Aricaras to the Pacific:*

Messrs. Hunt, Crooks, Miller, M'Clellan, M'Kenzie, and about sixty men, who left St. Louis [234] in the
beginning of March, 1811, for the Pacific Ocean,
reached the Aricara village on the 13th day of June,
where meeting with some American hunters, who had
been the preceding year on the waters of the Columbia
with Mr. Henry, and who, giving such an account of
the route by which they passed, as being far preferable
in point of procuring with facility an abundant supply
of food at all times, as well as avoiding even the probability of seeing their enemies, the Black Feet, than by
the track of Captains Lewis and Clarke, the gentlemen
of the expedition at once abandoned their former ideas
of passing by the Falls of the Missouri, and made the
necessary arrangements for commencing their journey
over land from this place.

Eighty horses were purchased and equipped by the
17th of July, and on the day following they departed
from the Aricaras, sixty persons in number, all on foot,
except the partners of the company.— In this situation

they proceeded for five days, having crossed in that time, two considerable streams, which joined the Missouri below the Aricaras, when, finding an inland fribe of Indians, calling themselves Shawhays, but known among the whites by the appellation of Chiennes, they procured from these an accession of forty horses, which enabled the gentlemen to furnish a horse for every two [235] men. Steering about W. S. W. they passed the small branches of Big River, the Little Missouri, above its forks, and several of the tributary streams of Powder River, one of which they followed up. They found a band of the Absaroka, or Crow nation, encamped on its banks, at the foot of the Big Horn Mountain.

For ammunition and some small articles, they exchanged all their lame for sound horses, with these savages; but although this band has been allowed by every one who knew them, to be, by far, the best behaved of their tribe, it was only by that unalterable determination of the gentlemen to avoid jeopardizing the safety of the party, without, at the same moment, submitting to intentional insults, that they left this camp (not possessing a greater force than the whites) without coming to blows.

The distance from the Aricaras to this mountain, is about four hundred and fifty miles, over an extremely rugged tract, by no means furnishing a sufficient supply of water: but during the twenty-eight days they were getting to the base of the mountain, they were only in a few instances without abundance of buffalo meat.

Three days took them over the plains of Mad River, (the name given to the Big Horn above this [236] mountain) which following for a number of days, they left it where it was reduced to eighty yards in width, and the same evening reached the banks of the Colorado, or Spanish River. Finding flocks of buffaloes at the end of the third day's travel on this stream, the party passed a week in drying buffalo meat, for the residue of the voyage, as in all probability those were the last animals of the kind they would meet with. From this camp, in one day, they crossed the Dividing Mountain, and pitched their tents on Hoback's Fork of Mad River, where it was near one hundred and fifty feet broad; and in eight days more, having passed several stupendous ridges, they encamped in the vicinity of the establishment made by Mr. Henry, in the fall of 1810, on a fork about seventy yards wide, bearing the name of that gentleman;[124] having travelled from the main Missouri, about nine hundred miles, in fifty-four days. Here, abandoning their horses, the party constructed canoes, and descended the Snake, or Ky-eye-nem River, (made by the junction of Mad River, south of Henry's Fork) four hundred miles; in the course of which they were obliged, by the intervention of impassable rapids, to make a number of portages; till at length they found the river confined between gloomy precipices, at least two hundred feet perpendicular, whose banks for the most part were washed by this turbulent stream, which for thirty miles was a continual succession of falls, cascades, [237] and rapids. Mr. Crooks' canoe had split and upset in the middle of

---

[124] For biographical sketch of Andrew Henry, one of the partners of the Missouri Fur Company, see Chittenden, *American Fur Trade*, pp. 251, 252. His fort was the first trading post west of the Rocky Mountains, being situated about where the village of Egin, Idaho, now stands.— ED.

a rapid, by which one man was drowned, named Antonie Clappin, and Mr. Crooks saved himself only by extreme exertion in swimming. From the repeated losses by the upsetting of canoes, their provisions were now reduced to a bare sufficiency for five days, totally ignorant of the country where they were, and unsuccessful in meeting any of the nations from whom they could hope for information.

Unable to proceed by water, Messrs. M'Kenzie, M'Clellan, and Reed set out in different directions down the river, for the purpose of finding Indians, and buying horses: Mr. Crooks, with a few men, returned to Henry's Fork for those they had left, while Mr. Hunt remained with the main body of men, entrapping beaver for their support. Mr. Crooks, finding the distance much greater by land than he had contemplated, returned at the end of three days; where waiting five more, expecting relief from below, the near approach of winter made them determine on depositing all superfluous articles, and proceeding on foot. Accordingly, on the 10th of November, Messrs. Hunt and Crooks set out, each with eighteen men; one party on the south side of the river. Mr. Hunt was fortunate in finding Indians, with abundance of salmon and some horses; but Mr. Crooks saw but few, and [238] in general too miserably poor to afford his party assistance. Thirteen days brought the latter to a high range of mountains, through which the river forced a passage, and the banks being their only guide, they still, by climbing over points of rocky ridges projecting into the stream, kept as near to it as possible, till in the evening of the 3d of December, impassable precipices, of immense height, put an

end to all hopes of following the margin of this water
course, which here was no more than forty yards wide,
ran with incredible velocity, and was withal so foam-
ingly tumultuous, that even had the opposite bank been
fit for their purpose, attempts at rafting would have
been perfect madness, as they could only have the inducement of ending, in a watery grave, a series of hardships and privations, to which the most hardy and determined of the human race must have found himself
inadequate.   They attempted to climb the mountains,
still bent on pushing on, but after ascending for half a
day, they discovered to their sorrow, that they were not
half way to the summit, and the snow already too deep
for men in their emaciated state to proceed further.

Regaining the river bank, they returned up, and on
the third day met with Mr. Hunt and party, with one
horse, proceeding downwards. A canoe was soon
made of a horse hide, and in it they transported [239]
some meat, which they could spare, to Mr. Crooks'
starving followers, who, for the first eighteen days,
after leaving the place of deposit, had subsisted on half
a meal in twenty-four hours, and in the last nine days
had eaten only one beaver, a dog, a few wild cherries,
and some old mockason soles, having travelled, during
these twenty-seven days, at least five hundred and fifty
miles.   For the next four days, both parties continued
their course up the river, without any other support
than what little rose-buds and cherries they could find;
but here they luckily fell in with some Snake Indians,
from whom they got five horses, giving them three guns
and some other articles for the same.

Starvation had bereft J. B. Provost of his senses

entirely, and on seeing the horse flesh on the opposite side of the river, he was so agitated in crossing in a skin canoe, that he upset it, and was unfortunately drowned. From hence Mr. Hunt went on to a camp of Shoshonies, about ninety miles above, where procuring a few horses and a guide, he set out for the main Columbia, across the mountains of the south west, leaving the river where it entered the range, and on it Mr. Crooks and five men, unable to travel. Mr. Hunt lost a Canadian, named Carrier, by starvation, before he met the Shyeye-to-ga Indians, in the Columbia plains;[125] from whom, getting a supply of provisions, he soon reached the [240] main river, which he descended in canoes, and arrived without any further loss at Astoria in the month of February.

Messrs. M'Kenzie, M'Clellan, and Reed, had united their parties on the Snake River Mountains, through which they travelled twenty one days, to the Mulpot River, existing on an allowance by no means adequate to the toils they underwent daily; and to the smallness of their number (which was in all eleven) they attribute their success in getting with life to where they found some wild horses. They soon after reached the Forks, called by Captains Lewis and Clarke, Koolkooske; went down Lewis's River and the Columbia wholly by water, without any misfortune except the upsetting, in a rapid, of Mr. M'Clellan's canoe: and although it happened on the first day of the year, yet, by great exertion, they clang to the canoe till the others came to their assist-

---

[125] These Indians were probably some branch of the populous Salishan family. Irving speaks of them as ''Sciatogas,'' and associates them with the ''Tushepaws'' — a tribe well-known to Lewis and Clark. Apparently they were encountered near Umatilla River, in eastern Oregon.— ED.

ance, making their escape with the loss of some rifles. They reached Astoria early in January.

Three of the five men who remained with Mr. Crooks, afraid of perishing by want, left him in February, on a small river on the road, by which Mr. Hunt had passed, in quest of Indians, and have not since been heard of. Mr. Crooks had followed Mr. Hunt's track in the snow for seven [241] days; but coming to a low prairie, he lost every appearance of a trace, and was compelled to pass the remaining part of the winter in mountains, subsisting sometimes on beaver and horse meat, and the skins of those animals, and at other times on their success in finding roots. Finally, on the last of March, the other only Canadian being unable to proceed, was left with a lodge of Shoshonies, and Mr. Crooks, with John Day, finding the snow sufficiently diminished, undertook, from Indian information, to cross the last ridge, which they happily effected, and reached the banks of the Columbia in the middle of April; where, in the beginning of May, they fell in with Messrs. Stewart and Co. having been, a few days before, stripped of every thing they possessed, by a band of villains near the Falls. On the 10th of May they arrived safe at Astoria, the principal establishment of the Pacific Fur Company,[126] within fourteen miles of Cape Disappointment.

---

[126] This establishment has since been broken up.— BRADBURY.

[242] No. IV

DESCRIPTION

OF THE

MISSOURI TERRITORY

THE Missouri Territory is bounded by the state of Louisiana on the south, the Mississippi on the east, the British Territory on the north, and the Rocky Mountains and Mexico on the west. It was first discovered by Sebastian Cabot, in the year 1497, and in the year 1512 it was visited by John Pontio de Leon, a Spaniard, who attempted to form a settlement. In 1684, Monsieur de la Salle, a Frenchman, discovered the mouth of the Mississippi, and built Fort Louis; but being assassinated, it was again abandoned. In the year 1698, Captain Ibberville sailed up the Mississippi, formed a settlement, and named the country Louisiana. About twenty-two years afterwards Monsieur de la Sueur also sailed up the Mississippi, and proceeded to the distance of two thousand two hundred and eighty miles from its mouth.[127]

[243] In 1762 France ceded it to Spain by a secret treaty, and a small force was sent to take possession; but the inhabitants not having been officially made acquainted with the cession, refused to submit to the dominion of that power. Some time afterwards the Spanish government commissioned a man named

---

[127] This should be two years later, not twenty-two; Le Sueur's voyage was in 1700. See *Wisconsin Historical Collections*, xvi, pp. 177-193.— ED.

O'Reilly, who, at the head of three thousand men, took possession of it, and from motives of revenge, put several of the principal inhabitants to death. In 1800, 1801, Spain ceded it back to France, and by a treaty of April 30th, 1803, the French government sold it to the United States for the sum of fifteen millions of dollars, payable in fifteen years, at one million annually. The extent of country purchased for this sum is not yet known with any considerable degree of accuracy, but it is calculated to contain at least 1,026,-312 square miles, or 656,839,680 acres, and it must be remembered that for this sum not only the political dominion, but the reversionary property in the land, was purchased. If we suppose the money to apply to the purchase of the land only, the cost will fall short of $1\frac{1}{4}d$. per acre, or £3, 6s. 8d. sterling per square mile, without one drop of blood being shed.[128]

[244] The Mississippi receives the water furnished by almost the whole of this area, and as the extent of country from whence it derives its water is pretty accurately known, I shall state it, that an adequate idea may be formed of that mighty river; previously observing, that the name is of Indian origin, and signifies "*The mother of waters.*"

From the extremity of the most eastern branch to

---

[128] By the most accurate calculation, the surface of the globe contains 198,976,786 square miles, one-fifth of which only is land, or 39,795,357 square miles, the value of which, at £3, 6s. 8d. per square mile, is £132,651,-190 sterling; from whence it appears that at this price the cost of seven worlds, as large as this we inhabit, would be only £928,558,330!!! Should any one doubt the wisdom of Mr. Jefferson, after being acquainted with this fact, let him enter into a calculation of the expenses incurred in the *old mode* of acquiring territory by the sword. He will soon convince himself that this is a very much improved plan.— BRADBURY.

that of the most western, it is one thousand six hundred
and eighty miles in a direct line; and from the commencement of the most northerly to its mouth, it is one
thousand six hundred and fifty, also in a direct line.

Amongst the immense advantages which the United
States will derive from the purchase of Louisiana, the
possession of this river is one of the greatest. The
whole territory of the United States is 1,205,635,840
acres. The following table will show that the area
dependent on the Mississippi for a communication with
the ocean, is 1,344,779 square miles, or 860,658,560
acres. The whole [245] empire of China is only estimated at 800,000,000 of acres!

The area of the states or territories, or of the portions of such as contribute to the waters of this river
are as follows:—

	Sqr. Miles.
Missouri Territory	985,250
North-West Territory, $\frac{1}{2}$	53,415
Illinois Territory (the whole)	52,000
Indiana State, $\frac{18}{20}$	37,050
Ohio State, $\frac{4}{5}$	35,088
Pennsylvania, $\frac{1}{3}$	16,493
New York, $\frac{1}{100}$	521
Maryland, $\frac{1}{100}$	140
Virginia, $\frac{2}{3}$	28,200
Kentucky (the whole)	40,110
Tennessee (ditto)	43,200
Mississippi Territory, $\frac{1}{3}$	29,560
State of Orleans, $\frac{1}{2}$	20,500
Georgia, $\frac{1}{30}$	2,000
North Carolina, $\frac{1}{50}$	1,100
South Carolina, $\frac{1}{150}$	152
Square miles	1,344,779

This area is nearly twenty-eight times the extent of England and Wales, and eleven times that of the whole of Great Britain and Ireland.

Mr. Mellish[129] made a calculation of the quantity of water discharged by this river at its mean [246] height; but notwithstanding his usual accuracy, I think he has erred in this case, by taking wrong data. In the first place, he has made his estimate of the magnitude of the river by considering it at its mouth, without taking into account the great number of *bayoux* that have previously issued from it. Even at Orleans its magnitude is much diminished. Amongst other *bayoux* that take water from this river above that city, are *bayou Chiffalie*, *bayou Tunica*, *bayoux Manchac*, *La Fourche*, and *Placqmines*. In other places, any one of these five *bayoux* would be considered as a great river; but here a comparison with their vast parent destroys their consequence. It is singular that the Mississippi maintains its full magnitude only for the length of three miles. At that distance from the mouth of Red River issues bayou Chiffalie.

The second error consists in not allowing sufficient depth to the river. He assumes forty feet as the average depth from Orleans to the mouth, whereas it is well known that at that city the depth is sixty fathoms, or three hundred and sixty feet, and in no part from thence to the bar at its mouth is it less than thirteen fathoms, or seventy-eight feet. But although he has

---

[129] John Melish was a Scotchman who travelled extensively in the United States after 1807, and published a number of geographical works and descriptions of this country and the adjacent territories in North America. He died in Philadelphia in 1822.— ED.

assumed the dimensions of the river at too little, he has erred greatly in the calculation founded thereon, by making the discharge of water five times more than his own [247] data will produce. He considers the river at two miles in breadth, forty feet in depth, and to run four miles per hour. This gives, he says, 94,000,000 of gallons per second, whereas it is only 18,537,325 gallons. Perhaps about 60,000,000 of gallons per second, at a mean state betwixt Red River and bayou Chiffalie, may not be far from the true quantity.

The territory west of the Mississippi belonging to the United States, and extending from that river to the Rocky Mountains, has evidently two characters, so distinct, as regards the external appearance, that they cannot justly be included in one general description. The part which lies immediately on the Mississippi, and extends from one hundred to two hundred and fifty miles westward from that river, has a thin covering of timber, consisting of clumps and of scattered trees. From the western limits of this region to the Rocky Mountains, the whole is one vast prairie or meadow, and, excepting on the alluvion of the rivers, and, in a few instances, on the sides of the small hills, is entirely divested of trees or shrubs. The extent of this region is not accurately known, on account of the real situation of the Rocky Mountains not yet being truly ascertained; but it appears from the account of hunters and travellers, that in some of our best maps and globes they are laid down considerably [248] too far to the eastward. The course of the Mississippi is nearly from north to south, and its average longitude nearly ninety degrees west. The coast of the Pacific, in the medium latitude of the Mississippi from its source to its mouth, is about one hundred and thirty degrees west, a difference of forty degrees, making in that latitude the distance from the Mississippi to the Pacific to be two thousand, one hundred and twenty-four miles. It is the opinion of all whom I have consulted, and who have crossed the Rocky Mountains to the Pacific, that from the eastern limits of that chain to the Mississippi, the distance is at least twice as great as from the western limit to the Pacific.[130] If this is admitted to be correct, the distance from the summit of the Rocky Mountains to the Mississippi is one thousand four hundred and sixteen miles, from which if one hundred and fifty be subtracted for the half breadth of the chain, and two hundred for the woody region on the Mississippi, the breadth of the prairie will appear to be one thousand and sixty-six miles, and its length, from north to south, is at least eighteen degrees of latitude, or one thousand, two hundred and fifty-one miles.

Excepting towards the foot of the Rocky Mountains, the whole of this extent is what is usually [249] termed a plain, being destitute of those elevations that in other parts appear to have resulted from convulsions. But although the *general* surface corresponds almost exactly with the convexity of the earth, the agency of water has produced innumerable shallow valleys; and of the elevated places which separate them, those termed dividing ridges[131] are the highest. From the top of any of these ridges the limits of the visible hori-

---

[130] Mr. Mellish asserts that one branch of the Missouri rises within four hundred and fifty miles of the Pacific Ocean.— BRADBURY.

[131] See note in page 82.— BRADBURY.

zon are as exactly defined, and the view as extensive
as at sea, the undulations on the surface of the earth
here bearing no greater proportion in the scale than
the waves of an agitated ocean. The deviation from
the true curvature of the earth is much greater on the
approach to the Rocky Mountains. This gives an increased velocity to the currents of water, and produces
a more powerful attrition on their beds. The consequence is, the valleys in that part are deeper, and the
surface more rugged and broken.

Several geological facts tend to prove that this portion of the globe has been peculiarly exempted from
the operation of local and disorganizing convulsions,
and that it has remained for a vast length of time in its
present state. The most prominent of these facts is
the undisturbed uniformity of the strata, and their
general parallelism to the surface [250] of the earth, as
exemplified in the vast stratum of iron ore on the Missouri, and in the limestone rocks, wherever they occur.
The depth and extent of the valleys of the river, together with the peculiar formation of the hills, tend to
confirm the opinion, that whatever changes have taken
place on the surface have been effected by the operations of a slow, but continually acting cause.

Some of the mineral deposits are of wonderful
extent. Of these the deposit of salt on the Arkansas
River is the most remarkable. So little of this is yet
known, that an adequate idea of its magnitude can
only be formed by taking into view the number of
rivers constantly impregnated by it, and the extent of
country from which they derive their sources. The
most southerly of the salt rivers that rise in the region,

containing this salt deposit, is a branch of Red River, called by the Indians *Ba-ha-cha-ha*, and by the French *Fouxoacheta*. It is a considerable stream, and salt rock is found on its banks. No fewer than three salt rivers or streams flow into the Arkansas, the least of which is fifty yards in breadth; another is seventy-five, and the largest is one hundred and fifty yards wide. This last is called by the Osages *New-sew-kĕ tonga*, which signifies in their language, "*The largest salt river.*" These streams all rise in the same region, as also does a branch of the Canadian Fork of the [251] Arkansas, another large river mentioned by Mr. Pike, the name of which he writes *Ne-sout-che-bra-ra*,[132] which name indicates that either the water is salt, or that salt is found in the neighbourhood.[133]

It appears that this salt deposit passes under the Arkansas to the north-west, and impregnates two branches of the Kanzas River of the Missouri, both of considerable magnitude. There are several salt deposits on our globe, of vast extent; but perhaps when

---

[132] Fouxoacheta River is that now known as Washita, a large affluent of Red River, in Indian Territory. Bradbury derived his information from the explorations of Dr. John Sibley, published (1807) in connection with the *Statistical View* of Lewis and Clark.

The two names of the Arkansas affluents are derived from Pike's map, accompanying his journals of 1805-07. The Newsewketonga is the Cimarron River (see *ante*, note 109). The Nesoutchebrara appears to be the main fork of Canadian River, in its upper course.— ED.

[133] As the whole of this region is the property of the Osage Indians, it may justly be inferred that all the names of the rivers have originated with them. It is evident that Pike wrote the name from hearing the pronounciation, as the Indians do not write; and had he attended to the derivation in this instance, he would have followed the same orthography as in the former, both being derived from *ne-shu*, or *new-sew*, (salt) and *nes-ka*, or *nes-ke*, (river.) He would then have written it *New-sew-ke-bra-ra*.— BRADBURY.

this deposit becomes better known, it will be found inferior to none in point of magnitude; for if its continuity in one body is a fact, the area it covers must amount to several thousand square miles.[134]

[252] It is worthy of notice that gypsum and clay are found abounding with the salt of this deposit, and that in this instance, as well as in many others, the substances which are concomitant with each other on this continent, correspond with the order observed in other parts of the world. Salt springs are very abundant in other parts west of the Mississippi. The body of iron ore on the Missouri is another instance of the magnitude of mineral deposits in this country. Some account of it may be seen in page 101.

From the accounts of hunters, the various indications of coal, and its frequent appearance, we may justly conclude that no portion of the earth is more abundant in that useful mineral than this region. It appears in various parts, at the foot of the bluffs of the Missouri. On the Osage River, a bed of very great but unknown thickness shows itself. On Red River it comes to the surface in several places, and the hunters speak of it as being one of the most common substances on the Little Missouri and the Roche Jaune Rivers.

The existence of silver ore about the head of the Arkansas and Red River is believed by the [253]

---

[134] Mr. Sibly says the extent of this salt region is seventy-five miles square, which gives an area of five thousand, six hundred and twenty-five square miles. Of the degree to which the water of these salt rivers is saturated, some idea may be formed when it is stated, that in the dry seasons the water of the Arkansas and Red Rivers are rendered very brackish by them. It appears also that it is the overflowing of one of these salt rivers that fills the Great Lake, which is evaporated every summer, and leaves the incrustation mentioned in page 192, 193.— BRADBURY.

inhabitants of Upper Louisiana, and various accounts
are current amongst them of its having been discovered
there by hunters. As those rivers rise in the range of
mountains in which the mines of Santa Fe are situated,
and not far distant from them, the account is probable;
but the frequent occurrence of pyrites in America, the
deceptive appearance of that substance, and the inability of men so little acquainted with mineralogy to
discriminate, should induce great caution in admitting
the fact.[135]

The part which lies betwixt this vast meadow and
the Mississippi river, it has already been stated, is of a
different character so far as it regards the external
appearance of the country; not merely [254] owing to
the presence of trees in that part, but the surface of
the country wears quite another aspect. The numerous rivers which fall into the Mississippi in this region,
together with their various ramifications, run in deep
and comparatively narrow valleys, which give to this
country a very uneven appearance. This is a necessary
consequence of the number of small rivers that fall
immediately into the great trunk of the Mississippi.

---

[135] In the interior of America, specimens of pyrites have been often shown
to me as the ore of silver or gold, and I have frequently found it an unpleasant task to undeceive those who were in possession of them, as they were
persuaded that they had made a valuable discovery.

Immediately after I left the mouth of the Kenhawa river, I was followed
to Galliopolis by a Quaker of the name of Kenzie, who showed me some
specimens of whitish pyrites, which he said was silver ore, and offered me a
considerable sum of money if I would instruct him in the method of sepa-
rating the metal. I attempted to undeceive him, but he became angry,
and intimated that he knew the value of the mine too well to be *taken in
that way*, and that it was no uncommon thing for Englishmen to discourage
the working of mines in America, that they might get hold of them for themselves.— BRADBURY.

The general level of its bed being at least one hundred and fifty or two hundred feet below that of the surrounding country, gives a fall of that extent to the minor streams, besides that which is occasioned by the natural declivity of the country, and, of course, causes an increased velocity, and a more powerful action on their beds; and this effect extends to the smallest of the collateral branches. But although this portion differs so much from the other in its external appearance, still there are good reasons for thinking that they differ but little in their subterranean conformation, because many instances occur to prove, that although the surface is more broken and uneven, it is entirely owing to the more powerful action of the streams. The frequent instances of thin horizontal strata of limestone rock appearing on both sides of a valley, corresponding in all the circumstances of elevation, thickness, and their component parts, prove that the hills have not been formed by convulsions.

[255] With a few exceptions only, of isolated sandstone rock, the whole of this portion of the Missouri territory that I have seen is calcareous; the rocks being of a whitish limestone, containing organic remains in abundance, which consist of the casts of *entrochii*, *anomiæ*, &c. In this particular, an exception must be made to the rock forming the matrix of the lead in the mine region, in which I could not find any trace of organic remains whatever.

When the subterranean geography of this country shall become better known, it will probably be found to be one of the most interesting in the world. Besides the evidence furnished by the caves known to

exist in the incumbent rock, there are other facts tending to prove, that, beneath the surface, there are a
great many others, and of vast extent. A considerable
number of the minor streams are entirely lost under
ground, except in time of floods, and no place where
they re-appear can be traced out. The Merrimac and
Gasconade rivers have each a spring rising in their bed,
either of which would be sufficient of itself to form a
considerable river; and about three hundred miles
S. S. W. of St. Louis, there is a branch of White River,
composed entirely of one spring, so copious, that I am
credibly informed a boat of thirty or forty tons burthen
might sail to the source.[136]

[256] In many parts of this country, there are great
numbers of what the inhabitants call "*sink holes.*"
These are all of the same form, but differ in magnitude,
some not being more than thirty yards in diameter at
the top; others exceed two hundred.   They are circular,
but diminish towards the bottom, and resemble an inverted hollow cone; some of the large ones are so deep,
that tall trees, growing at the bottom, cannot be seen
until we approach the brink of the cavity. I have
examined many of these sink holes, and in several have
heard the noise of water, as of a considerable stream,
running below the bottom of the cavity. In others,
the subterranean stream is visible, and affords evidence
that it has caused the cavity, by carrying away the
incumbent earth, which has fallen in from time to time.

---

[136] Meramec and Gasconade rivers are affluents of the Missouri, in the
state of that name. The former signifies "catfish," in the local Indian
tongue, and was frequently spelled Marameg. White River is a western
branch of the Mississippi, in Arkansas.— ED.

The abundance of nitre, generated in the caves of this country, is a circumstance which ought not to be passed over unnoticed. These caves are always in the limestone rocks; and in those which produce the nitre, the bottom is covered with earth, which is strongly impregnated with it, and visible in needle-form crystals. In order to obtain the nitre, the earth is collected and lixiviated: the water, after being saturated, is boiled down, and suffered to stand till the crystals are formed. In this manner, it is no uncommon thing for three [257] men to make one hundred pounds of salt-petre in one day. As these caves may probably have been the resort of wild animals in former times, the accumulation of nitre, in the first instance, is not surprising; but that the earth, on being again spread on the bottom of the cave, should be re-impregnated in the space of four or five years, is not so easily accounted for: that this is a fact, many who have been employed in making salt-petre have assured me. In the spring of 1810, James M'Donald of Bonhomme, and his two sons, went to some caves on the Gasconade River to make salt-petre, and in a few weeks returned with three thousand pounds weight to St. Louis.

It is very probable that coal is here in great abundance. About four miles west of St. Louis, a vein, from twelve to eighteen inches in thickness, breaks out at the edge of a creek, and is used by the blacksmiths. In the year 1810, the grass of the prairie on the American Bottom, in the Illinois Territory, took fire, and kindled the dry stump of a tree, about five miles east of St. Louis: this stump set fire to a fine bed of coal on which it stood, and the coal continued to burn for several months, until the earth fell in and extinguished it. This bed breaks out at the bottom of the bluffs of the Mississippi, and is about five feet in thickness: I visited the place, and by examining the indications, [258] found the same vein at the surface several miles distant. Near the village of St. Ferdinand, on the edge of the Missouri, the bank is one solid bed of fine coal, of unknown thickness, but certainly more than twenty feet: this bed is called by the French *La Charbonniére*.

The lead mines of St. Genevieve[137] occupy an extent of country, the limits of which have not yet been ascertained: they commence about thirty miles west of the Mississippi, and extend west and north-west. That which more particularly indicates the existence of lead, is a redness of the soil, which appears to result from the decomposition of an hæmatitic iron ore, found there in great abundance, intermixed with pyrites, and in some [259] of its states exhibiting evident proofs of being a transition from that substance. The indications are still stronger, if this earth contain sulphate of barytes, crystalized carbonate of lime, and aggregated crystals of quartz. All these are in some parts

---

[137] It was the discovery of these lead mines that gave rise to the famous Mississippi scheme, projected by Law in 1719, which ruined hundreds of families in France. It was then supposed that it was a silver mine; and although the bubble burst immediately, it is surprising that Du Pratz, who wrote thirty-nine years afterwards, should still persist in the error. He not only lays down a silver mine on the Marameg in his map of Louisiana, but mentions it in his description. The Marameg is now called the Mirramac, on a branch of which, called the Negro Fork, the mines of St. Genevieve are situated. Du Pratz says, "The mine of Marameg, which is silver, is pretty near the confluence of the river which gives it name; which is a great advantage to those who would work it, because they might easily, by that means, have their goods from Europe. It is situate about five hundred leagues from the sea."— BRADBURY.

very abundant, and generally of a red colour, probably occasioned by the oxide of iron contained in the soil.[138]

These mines have been worked since about the year 1725, and until of late the ore has not been sought for in the rock, but has been found in the earth in detached lumps, intermixed with the substances above mentioned. The workmen employed, have no other implements than a pick-axe and a wooden shovel, and when at work, appear as if employed in making *tan pits*, rather than in mining. When they come to the rock, or to such a depth that it is no longer convenient to throw the dirt out of the hole, they quit, and perhaps commence a new *digging*, as they term it, within a few feet of that which they have previously abandoned. Each *digger* works separately for himself, and sells the ore to the proprietor of the soil, at two dollars per hundred pounds. It is evident from the nature of the employment, that the gain to the *diggers* must be very precarious, but in general they appear to live comfortably. They are almost all Creole French who are [260] employed, and if I may judge from a single instance, retain as much fondness for showy dress as the most foppish of their ancestors.[139]

The proprietors who buy the ore, cause it to be

---

[138] On the early history of these mines, see Thwaites, "Notes on Early Lead Mining," *Wisconsin Historical Collections*, xiii, pp. 271-292; or the revision thereof, "Early Lead Mining on the Upper Mississippi," in *How George Rogers Clark won the Northwest*, etc. (Chicago, 1903).— ED.

[139] On a Saturday evening I arrived at the mine *Belle Fontaine*, and employed myself until night in examining the substances thrown out by the *diggers*, and found the most interesting specimens amongst the refuse of one man, who, on that account, I particularly noticed. On the following morning I met him in the village, dressed in a white gown, with red slippers, and a blue silk waistcoat, embroidered with silver lace.— BRADBURY.

smelted in furnaces constructed of two parallel walls, one about eight, the other four, feet high, and three and a half asunder: these are joined by two sloping side walls, and into this inclosed area the fuel and ore are thrown.   In this way they obtain from sixty to seventy per cent of lead: the ore is said to contain eighty.

The mines belong to a number of proprietors, and are mostly held by grants from the Spanish governors who formerly resided at St. Louis, and are worked with more or less spirit, as the ore happens to be abundant or otherwise, for the workmen quit one *digging* without ceremony, when they hear of better success at another. The profits of the proprietors are commensurate with the quantity of ore raised on their property: therefore, [261] when the *diggings* become less productive than usual, they make trials on different parts of their land, to discover where the ore is more abundant, that the *diggers* may be induced to remain with them.   These trials consist in nothing more than digging a hole in some part of the woods, to the depth of three or four feet, and judging by the quantity of ore (*galena*) what degree of success may be expected.

A little time before I visited Richwood mines, the property of Monsieur Lebaume, of St. Louis, he had made forty trials, by simply digging holes, not more than four feet deep, in places remote from each other, on his land.   In thirty-eight of these he found ore, and from one hole more than half a hundred weight was raised.   This gentleman owns a square league.[140]

---

[140] Louis Labaume de Tateron came to St. Louis under the Spanish regime, and acted as secretary for Governor Trudeau. In accordance with democratic principles he dropped the aristocratic preposition ''de,'' being

As soon as any particular district is found so abundant as to warrant a furnace to be erected near it, they give it a name. Whilst I was at St. Louis, one of these places was discovered, and named *Mine au Shibboleth*, from which, I was credibly informed, four millions of pounds weight of ore was raised in the manner I have described, in one summer. The *diggings* which I visited were *Mine au Burton, Mine Belle Fontaine, Richwood Mines, Old Diggings, New Diggings*, and *Elliot's* [262] *Diggings*. Some of these *diggings* are ten or twelve miles distant from each other. *Mine la Motte*, on the waters of the river St. Francis, is thirty or forty miles south of all the rest. Some of these mines have fallen into the hands of Americans, who have ventured to penetrate the rock, which is always found at a depth of from six to twelve feet below the surface, and have been amply rewarded for their enterprize.

I remained a few days with Mr. Elliot, who at that time had only just commenced on the rock, but had the most promising prospects of success. He had raised a considerable quantity of ore, and many tons of *blende*, and with the last had repaired the road to his works, not knowing what substance it was. Mr. Moses Austin, proprietor of *Mine au Burton*, had been very successful, having found large masses of ore in the caves of the rock into which he had penetrated.[141]

known as Louis Tateron Labaume. After the transfer of Upper Louisiana to the United States (March 9, 1804), he was made judge of the court of common pleas, and colonel of militia. A man of fortune and ability, he was one of the prominent citizens of early St. Louis.— Ed.

[141] Moses Austin was the Texan pioneer for whom the capital of that state was named. Born in Connecticut, Austin came west in 1798 and for a

At the *New Diggings* a great deal had been raised
out of the rock, and a considerable quantity was lying
on the bank in very large lumps.— When I visited that
place, they were impeded by water, and had no better
means of getting rid of it, than those which buckets,
raised by a windlass, afforded. I was prevented from
descending by the quantity of water then in the mine.

[263] Although the district of country which contains the present *diggings* is considered as comprising
the mines, I am of opinion that the lead extends to a
very great distance beyond those limits. I have seen
all the indications on the upper part of the Mirramac
River, fifty or sixty miles west of the present workings,
and still further to the northward, at the mouth of the
Gasconade, on the Missouri. It is supposed by some
that it extends to the mines belonging to the Saukee
and Fox nations of Indians, which are situated on the
Mississippi, six hundred miles above St. Louis.—
These mines are known to extend over a space of
eighty miles in length, and nine miles in breadth.[142]

-----

number of years engaged in lead-mining. About 1820 he obtained a con-
cession from the Spanish authorities to plant a colony in Texas. Upon his
return to Missouri to secure emigrants, he was deserted by his party and
robbed on the road, from the effects of which he died in 1821. His son
Stephen founded the colony that his father had planned.— ED.

[142] These mines are of great value to the Saukee and Fox nations. As the
game on the lands which they claim is nearly destroyed, they have therefore
been compelled to commence the business of mining, or rather digging. The
ore is raised by the men, but the operation of smelting is done by the squaws.
The method by which they extract the metal was described to me by Mr.
Prior, who was of Messrs. Lewis and Clarke's party, and who traded with
these Indians for lead. They first dig a deep cavity in the ground, near a
perpendicular bank of the Mississippi, and from the face of the bank make
a horizontal hole to meet the bottom of it. A quantity of dry wood is then
thrown into the cavity, and set fire to, after which the ore is thrown in, and

[264] Some of the isolated and sand-stone rocks in this territory, alluded to, are remarkable for their purity, being so white as to exactly resemble the purest lump sugar. These would furnish an excellent material for the manufacture of glass.

[265] About five miles west of Herculaneum, which is situated on the Mississippi, thirty miles below St. Louis, there is a limestone rock, about a quarter of a mile in length, and in some parts forty or fifty feet high. This rock is so completely perforated in almost every part as to resemble a honey-comb, and the perforations are from one-eighth to three-quarters of an

the supply of both continued. The metal runs out at the horizontal opening, and is received in holes made by the Indians with their heels in the sand of the river. In this state it is bought by the traders from St. Louis, who afterwards cast it into pigs in their own moulds. Formerly, these Indians gave permission to a person of the name of Dubuque to dig lead: he resided at their village, being much respected by them, and acquired some property, the management of which, after his death, fell into the hands of Augustus Choutou, of St. Louis, who in 1810 advertised for sale Dubuque's property in the mines, or his right of digging lead. It was bought by Colonel Smith, the proprietor of *Mine Belle Fontaine*, and Mr. Moorhead, of St. Louis, for about three thousand dollars. They ascended the Mississippi with an armed party, to take possession, but were roughly handled by the Indians, and happy in having escaped with their lives. The Indians immediately afterwards called a council, and being fearful of giving offence to the American government, sent deputies to St. Louis, to plead their cause before Governor Howard and General Clarke, who performed their mission with great ability; first disclaiming any intention to continue the grant beyond the life of Dubuque, and, secondly, any wish to offend the government of the United States, by driving away Smith and Moorhead. They next stated, that when the *Great Spirit* gave the land to the Red Men, their ancestors, he foresaw that the White Men would come into the country, and that the game would be destroyed; therefore, out of his great goodness, he put lead into the ground, that they, their wives and children, might continue to exist: they lastly appealed to the justice of their *Great Father*, the President of the United States. Governor Howard and General Clarke approved of their conduct, and assured them of the protection of the government.— BRADBURY.

inch in diameter. It has exactly the appearance of marine rocks, perforated by *mytilus lithophagus*, or *rugosus*.

Fossil bones have been dug up in various places in Upper Louisiana. At a salt lick, about three miles from the Mirramac River, and twelve from St. Louis, several bones have been discovered, evidently belonging to the same species of mammoth as those found on the Ohio, and in Orange County, state of New York. I have frequently been informed of a place on Osage River, where there is an abundance of bones of great magnitude. General Clarke[143] showed me a tooth brought from the interior: it was a grinder, and belonged to the animal mentioned by Cuvier, called by him masto donté, *avec dents carrés*.

The general character of this country is that of prairie, with scattered trees and interspersed clumps. On the summits of the ridges, the timber is generally red cedar (*juniperus virginiana*), [266] on the prairie, post oak (*quercus obtusiloba*), black jack (*quercus nigra*), black walnut (*juglans nigra*), and shell bark

---

[143] General William Clark, the well-known explorer, was born in Virginia, August 1, 1770. While yet a lad, his father's family removed to Kentucky, where they had a plantation not far from Louisville, named "Mulberry Hill." William Clark campaigned with Scott in 1791, and joining the regular army served as lieutenant in the 4th sub-legion, under Wayne, 1793-95. After the treaty of Greenville, he resigned from the army and was engaged in private business until invited by Lewis to accompany him on the expedition to the Pacific (1804-06). Early in 1807 Clark was commissioned brigadier-general of the Louisiana militia, and Indian agent for the same territory. From that time, he made his home in St. Louis. From 1813 to 1820, he was governor of Missouri Territory. After the admission of the latter as a state, General Clark was appointed (1822) superintendent of Indian affairs for all the Western territory, which office he held until his death at St. Louis, September 1, 1838.— ED.

hickory (*juglans squamosa*). The alluvion of the
rivers contains a greater variety, of which the principal
are — cotton wood (*populus angulosa*), sycamore (*pla-
tanus occidentalis*), over-cup oak (*quercus macrocarpa*),
nettle tree, or hackberry (*celtis crassifolia*), hoop ash
(*celtis occidentalis*), honey locust (*gleditsia triacanthos*),
black locust (*robinia pseudacacia*), coffee tree (*guilandina dioica*), peccan (*juglans olivæformis*), and many
of the trees common in the states east of the Alleghanies.[144]

The soil is generally excellent, being for the most
part black loam, and is tilled without much trouble.

The climate is very fine: the spring commences
about the middle of March in the neighbourhood of
St. Louis, at which time the willow (*salix*), the elm
(*ulmus Americana*), and maples (*acer rubrum* and
saccharinum) are in flower. The spring rains usually
occur in May, after which month the weather continues fine, almost without interruption, until September, when rain again [267] occurs about the equinox,
after which it remains again fine serene weather until
near Christmas, when the winter commences. About
the beginning or middle of October the Indian summer[145] begins, which is immediately known by the
change that takes place in the atmosphere, as it now
becomes hazy, or what they term smoky. This gives
to the sun a red appearance, and takes away the glare
of light, so that all the day, except a few hours about

---

[144] A list of some of the herbaceous plants of the Missouri territory will
be found annexed.— BRADBURY.

[145] Indians begin to provide for the winter when this state of the weather
commences, as they know it will soon approach.— BRADBURY.

noon, it may be looked at with the naked eye without pain: the air is perfectly quiescent and all is stillness, as if nature, after her exertions during the summer, was now at rest. The winters are sharp, but it may be remarked that less snow falls, and they are much more moderate on the west than on the east side of the Alleghanies in similar latitudes.

The wild productions of the Missouri Territory, such as fruits, nuts, and berries, are numerous: of these the summer grape (*vitis æstivalis*) appears to be the most valuable, as the French have made a considerable quantity of wine from it by collecting the wild fruit.[146] This species grows in abundance [268] on the prairies, and produces a profusion of fine bunches. The winter grape (*vitis vulpinum*) is remarkable for the large size of its vine, which climbs to the tops of the highest trees, and takes such full possession of their tops, that after the fall of the leaf, the tree to which it has attached itself seems to be loaded with fruit. The vine at the bottom is commonly six or eight inches in diameter. I measured one near the Mirramac River, that was thirty-seven inches in circumference near the ground, after which it divided into three branches, each branch taking possession of a tree. The fruit is very good after the frosts have commenced. Another fruit found here is the persimon (*dyospyros virginiana*), which in appearance resembles a plum, excepting that the permanent calyx of the flower remains. It is so astrin-

---

[146] Mr. James Berry, with whom I resided, about four miles from St. Louis, told me that he made eight quarts of wine from the grapes of one of these vines, which ran up a small tree, about 150 yards from his house.— BRADBURY.

gent until ameliorated by the frosts, that on being eaten, it draws up the mouth, and when swallowed, contracts the throat in such a manner as to cause a sensation similar to that of choking.

The papaw (*anona triloba*) is found in plenty on the alluvion of the rivers. The fruit is of the magnitude and shape of a middling sized cucumber, and grows in clusters of three, four, or five [269] together: when ripe the pulp is of the consistence of a custard, and is very agreeable to some palates; but the hogs will not touch them. Strawberries are in vast abundance on the prairies, and are very fine. The pecan, or Illinois nut, is a kind of walnut, but very different from all the other species, both in the form and texture of its shell, which is so thin as to be cracked between the teeth with the greatest ease. It is of an oblong form, and from that circumstance the tree which produces it has obtained the name of *juglans olivæformis*. There are several other species of hickory and walnut, which yield nuts in great abundance. These, together with acorns from the various species of oak, furnish abundance of food for hogs.

The quadrupeds found in parts inhabited by the whites, of which the flesh is eaten, are bear, deer, hares, racoon, opposum, and a variety of squirrels. With bear, deer, and turkeys, the town of St. Louis is frequently supplied by a tribe of the Shawanee nation of Indians, who live about seventy miles west of that place. They usually charge a quarter of a dollar for a turkey or a quarter of venison.

It is necessary to observe that Upper Louisiana was settled from Canada, not by way of Orleans, but by

proceeding along the Lakes, and descending the Illinois or Miami rivers, and may be considered [270] as
a distinct colony, the history of which, so far as may
be gathered from themselves, does not present those
horrid examples of treachery and injustice to the Indians, which will for ever disgrace the memory of
those who first formed the lower settlement.   The consequence has been, that although individual acts of
injustice or aggression, committed against the Indians,
have met with due and appropriate punishment, yet
no general act has been committed of a nature so atrocious as to provoke general extermination; a thing
extremely easy to have been effected by the Indians in
the early part of the settlement, as there were several
powerful tribes in their vicinity.   The inhabitants of
Kaskaskias say that it was coeval with Philadelphia,
and the common term for Vincennes, (Old Post) shows
that it must have been one of the first settlements, if
not the first.   Both these are on the east side of the
Mississippi, as also are Cahokia and the small settlement of Prairie du Roche.   Besides these four, on the
west side, there were five villages originally settled,
each of which, besides its proper name, has a nick-
name given to it.   St. Genevieve is *Misère*; Carondolet, *Vuide Poche*; St. Louis, *Pain Court*; St. Ferdinand, *Florissante*; and St. Charles, *Petit Cote*.   These
nine villages were scattered some more than a hundred
miles distant from each other, and no two of them were
so situated as to be capable of rendering mutual aid, in
case of [271] attack from the Indians, and for more
than sixty years five of them existed, isolated in a wil-

derness, six hundred miles at least from any other white settlers.[147]

The villages were regularly laid out in squares of three hundred feet on each side, the houses standing towards the streets, and the interior of the area composed of gardens and orchards. To each of these villages was appropriated a large space of ground, fenced in the form of a parallelogram. In this space allotments are laid out, correspondent in number and relative magnitude with the town lots. These allotments extend the whole length of the field; but their magnitude is determined by the breadth, which is marked on one of the fences, being once, or once and a half, or twice, &c. the length of the side of a square arpent of land. In the common field belonging to Carondolet, these narrow stripes are more than a mile and a half in length. Besides the appropriation of land for cultivation, an extensive tract was laid out for each town as a forest, or demesne, from which each individual cuts what wood he thinks proper. All these appropriations have been ratified by the commissioners appointed to examine into claims by the government of the United States, since the cession of Louisiana. The French, who are the descendants of the first settlers, are very indolent, and so [272] much attached to the manners of their ancestors, and even to their practices in husbandry, that although they see their

[147] For the founding and early history of Vincennes, see Croghan's *Journals*, vol. i of this series, p. 141, note 113. This was known as "O post," not "Old Post," from the French "au poste" (at the fort). For Kaskaskia, Cahokia, Prairie du Rocher, and St. Louis see André Michaux's *Journals*, vol. iii of our series, notes 132, 133, 135, 138.— ED.

American neighbours, by the application of improved
implements and methods, able to cultivate double
the quantity of ground in the same time, nothing
can induce them to abandon their old practices:
and if any one attempts to reason with them on the
subject, their constant reply is, "As it was good enough
for our forefathers, it is good enough for us;" whence
it appears that even veneration for ancestry may become an evil.   They cultivate maize, wheat, oats, barley, beans (*phaseolus*), pumpkins, water and musk
melons, and tobacco and cotton for their own use.
Apples and peaches are very fine: the former are
abundant, and do not require to be engrafted.   They
pay great attention to gardening, and have a good
assortment of roots and vegetables.   Notwithstanding
their want of industry, there is an appearance of comfort and independence in their villages, as, from the
richness of the soil, and fineness of the climate, the
labours attendant on agriculture, and attention necessary to their cattle, are comparatively trivial.   They
have abundance of horses, cows, and hogs, all of which
run at large on the prairies, as they have no inclosures
but for the purpose of agriculture.   They mow a little
grass on the prairie, which they make into hay, and
give it to their horses and cattle when the ground is
covered [273] with snow: at other times they leave
them to provide for themselves.   The hogs live on
strawberries, hazle and hickory nuts, acorns and roots,
and must be occasionally sought for in the woods, to
prevent them from becoming entirely wild.   On these
occasions, the proprietor fills his saddle bags with the
ears of Indian corn, with which he mounts his horse,

generally with his rifle on his shoulder. If he finds them within three or four miles of his house, he thinks himself fortunate; but it sometimes happens that he is two days in ''hunting them up,'' as they term it. When he finds them, he throws down an ear of corn, which they devour, and he rides gently towards home, with the whole herd screaming after him. When they are almost inclined to give up the chase, he throws down another ear, which practice he continues until he brings them into his yard, where he shuts them up, and feeds them. Here they remain until the morning, when he again feeds them, marks the young pigs, sets them at liberty, and probably does not see them again for a fortnight or three weeks. That each planter may identify his own hogs, he marks them in the ear, and in each township an office is established, in which these marks are registered. They are either holes or slits, or both, differently arranged, so that no two marks are alike; and it is against the laws of the territory to expose the [274] carcass of a hog for sale without having the ears upon it.

St. Louis, the capital of this territory, is very pleasantly situated on the Mississippi, about eighteen miles below the mouth of the Missouri, in latitude 38° 5′ and longitude 89° 55′ W. It has a decided advantage over any of the other towns, on account of its being situated on a rock, but little elevated above the high floods of the river, and immediately on its border. Such situations are very rare, as the Mississippi is almost universally bounded either by high perpendicular rocks or loose alluvial soil; the latter of which is in continual danger of being washed away by the annual floods, to such an extent that a whole plantation, situated on the border of the river, has been known to have been swept away during one flood.   Fort Chartres, erected at a vast expence by the French government, on the border of the river, prior to the cession of Louisiana in 1763, is now almost entirely swept away.[148]   The fur trade of the Mississippi and the Missouri, together with that of the tributary streams, almost wholly centers in this town; and after the return of Messrs. Lewis and Clarke from the Pacific Ocean, a fur company was formed, for the purpose of trading with the nations on the head waters of the Missouri, which, from a variety of [275] untoward events, but principally from the hostile and bloody disposition of the Indians, has miscarried.[149]

There is no part of the western country that holds out greater advantages to the new settler than the Missouri Territory.   It is inferior to no part in point of soil or climate, and has a decided advantage over the country on the Ohio, as the transit to Orleans may be made at any season of the year, whereas the Ohio is not navigable during the months of August, September, and October.   It is also from six hundred to a thousand miles nearer to that city than the upper part of the Ohio.   Opportunities of purchasing settlements, or

[148] For the history of Fort Chartres, see André Michaux's *Travels*, vol. iii of our series, p. 71, note 136.— ED.

[149] The Missouri Fur Company was formed at St. Louis early in 1809; William Clark, Reuben Lewis, Manuel Lisa, the Chouteau brothers, and Andrew Henry were the leading partners.   For the disasters brought upon the trading parties by hostile Indians, see details in Chittenden, *American Fur Trade*, pp. 137-158.   The company maintained an existence under various managements until 1830.— ED.

plantations already formed, are very frequent, and at very moderate terms, as the rage of retiring back prevails here in as great a degree as in the other new countries. Wild land, as it is here called, may either be had from the government of the United States, or from the old French inhabitants, several of whom possess very large tracts, obtained by grants from the Spanish governors. The titles of these lands are now undoubted, as they have been ratified by the commissioners appointed by the government of the United States to examine into claims. The price of land is various, but may frequently be obtained on better terms from the land owners than from the government, or for less than two dollars per acre. [276] In the reclaiming of wild land, or the forming of a plantation from a state of nature, the trouble and labour is much less than in clearing a forest, as here the trees are not more abundant on the upland than would be necessary for fuel and for fences. They naturally stand at a sufficient distance from each other to admit a fine undergrowth of grass and herbage. This country, as well as the western region, will reap incalculable benefit from the application of steam boats on the Mississippi. Of these a great many are now building in the different ports of the Ohio. This mode of conveyance will also be much facilitated by the abundance of excellent coal so universally spread over these regions.

It is necessary to observe, that what has been stated relative to the climate, duration of winter, agriculture, &c. &c. relates more particularly to the region included betwixt the mouths of the Ohio and Missouri, or from thirty-seven to thirty-nine and a half degrees of latitude; but this territory extends from twenty-nine to fifty degrees, and therefore proper allowances must be made for the differences of latitude. In an agricultural point of view, it may be divided into three regions, suitable for the culture of as many great staple articles, viz. sugar, cotton, and corn. The sugar region reaches from the coast to latitude thirty-one [277] or thirty-one and a half degrees. The culture of sugar only commenced about fifteen years ago, and until of late has been confined to the alluvion of the Mississippi; but there is an extensive tract, suitable for that culture, lying west of that river, and reaching to the Sabine river, comprehending the countries of the Oppelousas and Atacapas, which is now settling fast, and in point of soil can scarcely be equalled. In the year 1811, some of the plantations on the Mississippi produced as much as five hundred hogsheads of sugar; and the cultivation is rapidly increasing, as many of the planters have already made immense fortunes.

The region proper for the cultivation of cotton, and too cold for that of the sugar-cane, extends from thirty-one and a half to about thirty-six degrees of latitude: the species cultivated is *gossypium annuum*. It will grow many degrees north of thirty-six; but it will not yield a sufficient crop, nor is the cotton so good, for the following reasons:—of the pods containing the cotton, the terminal pods of the principal branches are the first ripe: the next in succession are those of the secondary branches, which are followed by those of the tertiary ones, &c. &c.; but in each successive generation, the number is increased in something like the ratio of a geometrical progression. In the northerly part of the cotton region, the winter [278] comes on before the cotton in the pods on the lateral branches is ripe, and a great portion of the crop is destroyed, which a few degrees further south would have ripened. But the avarice of some planters prompts them to continue the gathering of their crops too long, and the quality of their cotton is deteriorated thereby, as the sun is too feeble to give the last part of their crop sufficient strength. The culture of the cotton plant is not attended with much trouble. The seeds are planted from three to three and a half feet asunder; and after the plants have acquired a little strength, they are weeded and earthed up: no further care is required until the gathering of the pods commences. The cotton is then separated from the seeds by a machine, called the *saw gin*.[150]

───

[150] From observation I am led to believe that the staple of cotton is sometimes injured in the gin; and as this machine is now universally used to separate the cotton from the seed, I shall describe it. The saws are circular, about six or eight inches in diameter; they are made of thin steel plates, and are toothed like those used for cutting wood, excepting that they make a more acute angle with the radii. Twenty-four, thirty, thirty-six, or more of these saws are placed on an iron shaft, at about one inch asunder. This shaft is fixed in a frame, three feet, or three feet six inches high, and parallel to it is placed a trough, not unlike a manger. One side of the trough is composed of thin plates of iron, exceeding in number that of the saws by one. This admits one of these plates betwixt each two saws, and they are so near each other as barely to admit the saw to pass between them. A fourth part of the saw works within the trough. Beneath the saws a cylindrical brush turns the same way, but with greater velocity. On the end of the shaft on which the saws are, there is a fast and loose pulley for driving the machine, with a belt for stopping it at pleasure. When the gin is intended to be set to work, a quantity of cotton, as taken from the pods, is thrown into the trough, and the belt is put on the fast pulley. The saws, in passing through the troughs, continue to load their teeth with cotton, which is instantly thrown off by the brush, and in a few minutes nothing remains in the trough but bare seeds. The management of this gin is mostly committed to negroes,

[279] As there are public gins established almost in every part, to which a planter may take his cotton, and have it cleaned and packed on moderate terms, it is in the power of a poor man to turn cotton-planter; and if he has a numerous family, so much the better, as females, and even children, can be employed in gathering the pods, and in taking the cotton from them. If he settles on wild land, he can enter upon the culture of cotton with more facility than on any other crop, as the ground requires less preparation.

This part of Louisiana as yet contains but very few white settlers, although, for the most part, the [280] soil is excellent, and the climate charming. Two very large rivers, Red River and the Arkansas, enter the Mississippi in this region, and run their whole course through it: they are both navigable to the confines of the internal provinces of New Mexico, and furnish to those parts the best means of communication with the ocean. Of these means, when Mexico shall break its chain, it will avail itself, and this will become one of the richest and most valuable parts of the United States.

In an agricultural point of view, the vast tract of prairie extending through all these regions, is an important object of consideration. Amongst intelligent Americans, the question of — whether it can or cannot be peopled by civilized man? has often been agitated. Accustomed, as they are, to a profusion of timber, for buildings, fuel, and fences, they are not aware of the

---

who, anxious to finish their task, drive the machine with too great velocity, by which, I conceive, not only the staple of the cotton is injured, but the green lumps, which are in fact the abortive seeds, are broken, and carried through along with the cotton. From this cause, in a great measure, arises the difference of quality of cotton from the same plantation.— BRADBURY.

small quantity of that article that may be dispensed with, in a country abounding in another substance for fuel; nor can they conceive, that fences, and even buildings, may be constructed with the application of a very small portion of timber. Under these impressions, the belief in America is, that the prairie cannot be inhabited by the whites; even Mr. Brackenridge says it cannot be cultivated. My own opinion is, that it can be cultivated; and that, in process of time, it will not only be peopled and [281] cultivated, but that it will be one of the most beautiful countries in the world.

If I may be permitted to judge from travelling nearly five hundred miles through it, I must pronounce the soil to be excellent, and in almost every part where I saw it in a state of nature, it was covered with the finest verdure imaginable. The stratum immediately below the vegetable soil is almost universally a very tenacious clay, and extremely well calculated to form a material for brick, or, in the first instance, for such habitations as are made in Ireland, many of which are very comfortable. In time timber would be raised; for to suppose it would not grow there because it does not, would be absurd. Whenever this region shall commence to be peopled, the first settlements will be made at the edge of the woody region, or on the borders of the rivers, where a little timber may be found, and probably the first wave in the tide of population will be formed of shepherds and herdsmen. The tacit compact mutually binding betwixt man and the animals he domesticates, implies a duty connected with an interest to both parties. Man furnishes to them food and protection, and enables them to pass a few years

of comfortable existence: they repay him with their
lives or their services. In all cases, the domestication
of animals is of the most value to man in those parts
where he can perform his duty to them at the least
expense [282] to himself. In no part of the world can
it be done with less trouble than in the southern part of
this region. A convincing proof of this is, that here
domesticated animals have dissolved the contract, and
that thousands and tens of thousands of their descendants still maintain their independence. If, besides
yielding food and protection to herbivorous animals,
other means of reducing them to a state of dependence
on man could not be found, domestication without inclosures (which imply coercion) would be in these parts
impracticable, because food is at all times in abundance, and the want of protection would be obviated by
an association in numbers. But salt furnishes those
means, by the aid of which the shepherd or the herds-
man obtains a complete dominion over the will of his
flock or his herds, and in the midst of this vast region
can call them round him at his pleasure.[151]

[283] I shall close this article by a few observations
on the state of this country before it was transferred to

---

[151] In a fertile country, and when not circumscribed by fences, there is a
continued tendency in animals to return to the state of nature. Besides
the accounts of others tending to prove this, I had evidence of it in my
horse, on the prairie near St. Louis, in the summer of 1810. He was usually
remarkably docile, and although there was not a single fence to obstruct his
passage to the Pacific Ocean, he was easily caught when often wanted: but
during the time I was attacked by the ague, sometimes he was not sought
for during a fortnight. At those times he would let no one come near him,
and showed an utter contempt for corn, when offered to him; but a display
of salt was at all times a temptation too great to be resisted, and he quietly
resigned his liberty.— BRADBURY.

the United States, and of the immense value and importance it is to that government. If a person who visited this country, and witnessed its fertility, did not at the same time witness the want of industry and enterprize in the descendents of the old inhabitants, he would be surprised that its advancement towards improvement has been so slow. But besides this, the political circumstances under which it has been placed, have been such as to preclude any possibility of prosperity; as the very nature and design of the principles by which it was governed, whilst under the dominion of Spain, was to prevent it. The invariable policy of that government, as regards her colonies, is to prevent, as much as possible, all intercourse betwixt them and other nations; and anxious only to raise *immediate* revenue, it is in the continued habit of sacrificing futurity to the present. The governors were petty tyrants, who considered their situations as the means only of aggrandizing themselves; to which, as well as the interest of the province, that of the Spanish government, must always give way. Anxious only to enrich themselves, and vested with almost unlimited power, the interest or prosperity of the colony was an object of very remote consideration. The most depressing regulations were made to shackle the internal trade of [284] the country; no man could sell the smallest article, not even a row of pins, without a licence, and those licences were sold at the most extravagant rates. A stranger coming into the province, and offering goods at a fair price, was certain to be sent to prison, and to have his goods confiscated. All favours from these governors, all grants of land, or even common privi-

leges, could only be obtained by bribery. Some of the
governors, not satisfied with the fruit of their rapacious
exactions on the province, were guilty of the most
shameful acts of villany towards their own government. A little above St. Louis stands a small trian-
gular fort, which, I was assured by one of the old settlers, was built by the inhabitants without one shilling
of expense to the governor; who rewarded some by
grants of land, and others by certain privileges; and,
for building this fort, a bill was sent to the Spanish
government to a large amount, which was paid.[152]

[285] Under so detestable a system of government the
energies of man must for ever remain dormant, and the
most fertile regions eternally unproductive to the world.

The political and commercial advantages that will
arise to the United States from the acquisition of Louisi-

---

[152] Schultz relates the following anecdote in his travels, which proves
that the above instance is not a solitary one:—

"At the lower end of the town of St. Genevieve, the remains of a Spanish
fort are still to be seen, which, being erected on an eminence, corresponded
with that of Kaskaskias by signals.

"It seems after the fort was completed, the commandant had to wait
upon the governor of the province to present his charges. They were
accordingly presented, and amounted to four hundred and twenty-one
dollars. The governor, after examining the account, returned it to the
commandant, informing him there was some mistake. The commandant
retired and examined it again; but finding it entirely correct, presented it
once more. The governor, on looking it over, informed him it was still
incorrect, and advised him to consult with some friend, as he had omitted
a figure or two. The commandant then called upon a friend to look over
his accounts with him, who no sooner saw the amount than he burst into a
loud laugh, and taking up a pen, added an o to the sum already stated. The
commandant presented his accounts a third time, when his excellency replied
that it was not quite right yet. The commandant was amazed: but what
was his astonishment, when he related the affair to his friend, to see him add
another o to the last sum, making it 42,100 instead of 421! On presenting
the account the fourth time, it was graciously received, and for the discharge
of the whole a very small part was paid to the commandant."— BRADBURY.

ana are incalculable, besides the vast revenue that will arise from the sale of lands. The exclusive right to the Mississippi river is an object of the highest importance. The acquisition of the sugar region alone would have sufficiently indemnified the American government. But without considering the positive advantages that will arise to the United States from the possession of Louisiana, the evils that might, and would have arisen [286] from its being in the possession of another power, which could have maintained the dominion of the Mississippi, are also incalculable. The most prominent of these evils would have been the separation of the States west of the Alleghanies from the Union, as, without the free navigation of the Mississippi, the products of their fertile soil must have perished on their hands for the want of a market. So far is a navigable river from being a boundary calculated to prevent collision betwixt two different states, that it affords the greatest possible opportunities for invasion or predatory excursions; and in case of war with the power possessing Louisiana, a line of more than two thousand miles in length of the United States would have been subject to be invaded in half an hour after the enemy left his own territory. But besides the devastations incident on regular warfare, this extended border would have been subject to the depredations of the various tribes of warlike Indians residing west of the Mississippi, who would have been a terrible engine in the hands of the power possessing the dominion of that country. In a state of hostility, they would have rendered the eastern bank of the Mississippi wholly uninhabitable.

No. V

REMARKS

ON

THE STATES OF OHIO, KENTUCKY, AND INDIANA

WITH

THE ILLINOIS AND WESTERN TERRITORY

AND ON THE

EMIGRATIONS TO THOSE COUNTRIES

IN a tour across the Alleghanies, and through the regions west of these mountains and east of the Mississippi river, I did not keep a regular journal, but contented myself with making general remarks, without any expectation that they would ever be submitted to public view. From these remarks I shall briefly extract such matter as may be useful to those who wish to visit the western country, or be read with interest by those who do not.

The committee appointed by the government of the United States, in the year 1816, to examine into the state of American manufactures, in speaking of the western country, say, "The rapidity of its growth is such, that even whilst we are employed in drawing the portrait, the features continue to [288] enlarge, and the picture becomes distorted." As nothing can be more true than the above observation, it is therefore evident that a traveller, in speaking of this country as acted upon by the operations of man, can only speak with confidence of *what was*. It is only on its natural formation that he can speak of *what is* as far as is known.

The region to which these observations will more particularly apply, is bounded by the Alleghanies to the south-east, by the Mississippi on the west, and the Great Lakes to the north. The Kaatskill Mountains, on the Hudson River, about one hundred and thirty miles from New York, are considered as the northern termination of the chain of mountains called the Alleghanies, from which point they proceed in a south-west direction to the Floridas, a distance of nine hundred miles, and parallel with the general direction of the Atlantic coast. The country west of this chain is in so many points of view different from that comprehended betwixt it and the Atlantic, as to demand a separate and distinct description. As almost the whole of the population of this country is confined to the vicinity of the Ohio or its tributary streams, the portion which furnishes water to that river will first be considered. West and north-west there is a vast tract on which that river is not dependent. That tract, as regards its natural formation, has [289] a distinct character, which will also be particularly noticed.

The Ohio, from Pittsburg to its mouth, is supposed to be eleven hundred and eighty-eight miles in length, and receives in its course a considerable number of streams, of which the following are the principal:—

Tennessee,	Sciota,
Cumberland,	Big Sandy River,
Green River,	Great Kenhawa,
Salt River,	Little Kenhawa,
Kentucky River,	Muskingum,
Little Miami,	Wabash.
Great Miami,	

Its name Ohio is of Indian origin, and signifies beautiful. The French have not adopted the term, but call
it in their maps of this country *La Belle Rivière*. Although it is a small stream when compared with the
Mississippi, some idea of its magnitude may be formed
by those who are only accustomed to see rivers in
miniature, by examining the following statement of
the area from which it derives its waters:—

[290]	*Sqr. Miles.*
Illinois Territory, $\frac{1}{10}$	5,200
Indiana Territory (the whole)	37,050
State of Ohio, $\frac{4}{5}$	35,088
Pennsylvania, $\frac{1}{3}$	16,493
New York, $\frac{1}{100}$	521
Maryland, $\frac{1}{100}$	140
Virginia, $\frac{2}{5}$	28,200
North Carolina, $\frac{1}{50}$	1,100
South Carolina, $\frac{1}{150}$	152
Georgia, $\frac{1}{30}$	2,000
Kentucky (the whole)	40,110
Tennessee $\frac{3}{4}$	32,400
Square miles	198,454

The area of England and Wales is 49,450 square
miles: it therefore appears that this river receives the
water of a surface four times that extent. This surface is comprehended betwixt the parallels of 35 and 43
degrees of latitude; a climate perhaps the best on the
globe as regards the comforts of man.

The seasons and the general state of the weather
correspond with what has been mentioned of Upper
Louisiana in similar latitudes:— in spring heavy rains;
in summer an almost cloudless sky, with heavy dews

at night; in autumn some rain, followed by the
Indian summer; and the winter from ten weeks to three
months long, which is dry, sharp, [291] and pleasant.
From the Alleghanies to the Lakes there are no mountains, or scarcely an elevation deserving the name of
a hill, the bluffs which border the rivers excepted. It
is nevertheless relieved from the dull monotony of a
level plain by numberless valleys, through which the
streams flow, and by small elevations, termed ridges.
The soil is much superior to that of the countries east of
the Alleghanies, and varies in quality. These varia-
tions are denoted by the term first, second, and third
rates. In the early stage of the transition of a fertile
country from a state of nature to that of improvement
and the arts, but little can be known as respects its geological formation, or, in other words, what it may contain as regards minerals. In general the first settlers
are only cultivators of the soil, and never examine to
any considerable depth below the surface, except by
digging wells. All that is known of this country on
those subjects has been discovered in that way, or has
manifested itself on the surface, and is confined, as
regards useful articles, to coal, salt, iron, lead, and
nitre. From the numerous and general indications
and the known existence of coal, it may be presumed
to be very abundant. In examining the beds of most
of the rivers, rounded nodules of coal may be found
mixed with the stones and gravel, and beds of argillaceous schist, containing vegetable impressions, are
frequent: in some instances these [292] beds contain
masses of pyrites. Coal is actually found at Pittsburg,
at Zanesville, on Green River, in the Illinois, and in the

western territories. It is uniformly bituminous, and highly charged with that substance.[153] In all these instances it has manifested itself on the surface of the earth, and indicates almost inexhaustible beds.

Salt, the most useful article at present, is found in various places, but as yet only in a state of solution, and has mostly been indicated by the excavations made by wild animals before the country was discovered by the whites. These animals, and in particular the herbivorous kind, have a strong predilection for salt; they resorted in immense numbers to every place where a salt spring existed, and not only drank the water, but licked up all the earth in its vicinity, that was impregnated with saline particles. Some of these excavations are of a surprising extent, when the means by which they have been effected is considered. The salt spring called the Ohio Saline, about twenty miles from the mouth of the Wabash, is several [293] acres in extent, and from six to ten feet in depth. On viewing these, and contemplating the length of time necessary for such a mass to be carried away in the stomachs of animals, the mind is struck with astonishment.[154] The existence of salt on the Kenhawa was not pointed out by these indications. On sinking a well, the per-

---

[153] This fact is remarkable in a geological point of view, when connected with another, which is, that almost all, if not the whole, of the coal discovered east of the Alleghanies is of the kind called by Kirwan mineral carbon, containing no bitumen. Vast beds of this description of coal exist on the Susquehannah and Delaware rivers. It contains ninety per cent. of carbon. — BRADBURY.

[154] Salt is made at various places in the western country, and the manufacture is rapidly increasing. The principal establishments are on the Kenhawa, at Bullet's and at Mann's Licks, Kentucky, and at the Ohio Saline, at the mouth of the Wabash.— BRADBURY.

sons employed came to a red sandstone rock before they had obtained a sufficiency of water, and perforated the rock, when the salt water immediately issued up with great force. This rock is now found to extend for several miles on both sides of the river. Wherever it is perforated salt water is found beneath, and several works for the manufacture of salt are already established.[155]

---

[155] In passing down that river I had an opportunity of seeing the manner in which they construct their wells for the salt water, which, on account of its singularity, I shall describe. They first ascertain by boring at what depth they shall come to the rock, and afterwards look out for a hollow tree, which must be at least from three to four feet in diameter. This they cut down carefully for fear of splitting, and saw off such a length as will reach from the surface of the ground to the rock. If the hollow of the tree is not large enough to allow room sufficient for a man to work within, they enlarge it. A well is next dug, and when so deep that there is danger of the earth falling in, the trunk is put down, and sunk to the surface of the rock. After the influx of fresh water is prevented by calkings round the edges at the bottom of the trunk, the perforation is made, and the salt water immediately rises to the surface. Besides the use here mentioned, hollow trees were applied to other purposes, being cut across in different lengths, and used by the first settlers as tubs to hold grain, &c. Any portion so cut off is called a gum, a name probably arising from the almost exclusive application of the gum trees to these purposes; for although many species of trees are liable to become hollow, yet none are so perfectly hollowed as the gum tree (*liquidamber styraciflua*). These trees, as I am informed, are often found so completely hollow as to leave the sound part not more than an inch in thickness, and the inside surface perfectly smooth.

Having mentioned the Kenhawa, I must observe, that on arriving at the falls of that river, ninety miles from the Ohio, I found a boat going from thence to Kenhawa Court-house, with some goods that had been brought over the Alleghanies. A passage was cheerfully granted to me, during which I enquired for the burning well, and expressed a wish to see it. The boatman informed me it was four miles from the river, and it would not be convenient for them to wait until I visited it, but promised to show me what would equally gratify my curiosity. Accordingly, near the edge of the river, and about fifteen miles farther down, they landed, and conducted me to where there was a hole dug in the sandy bank of the river, about a foot in diameter. From this hole a flame issued at least two feet high. Several stones were placed round the margin, on which some other boatmen had set

[294] Iron ore is found in many places, but chiefly in the neighbourhood where foundries have been established. [295] About fourteen miles west of the Ohio Saline, in the Illinois Territory, there is a lead mine, which was discovered by a gentleman from Tennessee, of the name of Guest. It is not yet worked, but seems to promise well. Some small excavations have been made, and a quantity of galena found. It appears to have no connection or affinity with the mines of St. Genevieve, not only on account of the distance being about a hundred and fifty miles, but from the marked difference in the rock which is the matrix of the ore, and in the substances which are concomitant with it. The rock in this mine is of that species of limestone called kettonstone, or compact limestone of Kirwan, and consists of very small accreted round granulations. The ore is mixed with very beautiful fluor spar, of several colours, as blue, brown, yellow, and pellucid. The caves yielding salt petre are still more abundant than those of Upper Louisiana, or rather they are better known, and some of them are of surprising extent. They abound chiefly on Green, Tennessee, and Cumberland rivers.

[296] The country is generally calcareous; but many

---

their kettles to cook their meat. I had noticed for several miles above a vein of iron ore appearing at the surface, about the height of the highest floods, and in almost every part of the bank great quantities of ochre. The same appearances continued to the distance of several miles below. From noticing this circumstance, I was led to form a conjecture on the formation of the gas that supplied the flame, and was persuaded that there is a vast body of iron ore, which, from the appearance of so much ochre, is in a continued state of oxydization, and produces a constant decomposition of water, with the oxygen of which it unites, and consequently a quantity of hydrogen is evolved.— May not this be the cause? — BRADBURY.

rocks of freestone occur. One producing excellent flags may be observed near the place where the battle was fought at Point Pleasant, on the Kenhawa.[156]

Near the mouth of Cabin Creek, about six miles above Limestone, on the Ohio, there is a hill almost covered with detached petrified casts of marine shells, in which a great many species may be observed.

In the state of nature, this country was almost wholly covered with trees, many of which are of great magnitude. More than one hundred species are found, and the timber is of various qualities, affording to the farmer, ship-builder, carpenter, cooper, and cabinet-maker great opportunities of selecting what is most suitable for their different purposes. Of the oak only, there are fourteen or fifteen species, of which the over cup (*quercus macrocarpa*,) affords the best timber. The post oak (*quercus obtusiloba*,) is also much esteemed for the durability of its timber when put into the ground. The black locust (*robinia pseud-acacia*,) and the honey locust (*gleditsia triacanthos*,) are excellent for the ship-builders, and are much esteemed by them, particularly for the making of tree-nails. For furniture, they chiefly use the wild [297] cherry (*prunas Virginia*,) and black walnut (*juglans nigra*;) the former is little inferior to mahogany in beauty.

Nothing so much surprises the European on his first

---

[156] This was the battle fought by the confederated Northern Indians with General Andrew Lewis's division of the Virginia army, on October 10, 1774. It was the chief engagement of Lord Dunmore's War, and one of the most hotly-contested conflicts during the history of our Indian wars. The result of the battle was indecisive; but during the following night the Indians withdrew, leaving the Virginians victorious. Shortly after, they made peace with Dunmore, governor of Virginia, upon his own terms.— Ed.

entrance on the western country, as the grandeur and
beauty of many of these trees, and more particularly
if he happens to arrive in the Spring; not fewer than ten
species produce a profusion of beautiful blossoms, and
the underwood consists mostly of some of our finest
flowering shrubs.   The trees comprise five species of
Magnolia, with *liriodendron tulipifera*, or tulip tree,
robinia pseudacacia, or black locust, *guilandina dioica*,
or coffee nut, and two species of horse chesnut, *æsculus
pavia* and *flava*.   Amongst the shrubs are found the
rhododendrons, *kalmias*, and *azaleas*, with *cercis Canadensis*, and *cornus florida*.

The wild animals have mostly disappeared from the
vicinity of the inhabited parts; none now remain
that are dangerous, and but few that are destructive.
The wolves sometimes take a sheep, or a small pig, but
they are already becoming scarce, and will soon disap-
pear.   The squirrels are the greatest enemies the farmers have now to contend with, but they are prevented
from an inordinate increase by the frequency of *squirrel
hunts* [298] by the riflemen, which are encouraged by
the landholders.[157]

---

[157] The squirrels have greatly increased since the country has become
peopled by the whites, owing to the greater quantity of food afforded, and
by the opportunities they have of robbing the corn and wheat fields; but
the farmers occasionally give what they call *"a barbique"* in the woods, to
the young riflemen, on the condition that they make a match at squirrel
hunting, of six, eight, or ten, against a similar number, who also make a
wager amongst themselves.   The hog is killed, dressed, and roasted after
the Indian method; this consists in digging a hole, the bottom of which
they cover with hot stones; on these the hog is laid, and covered over also
with heated stones.   There is plenty of liquor, and the *frolic* ends in shooting at a mark.   I have heard of more than two thousand squirrels being killed
at one of these hunts, all with ball.   Perhaps this circumstance contributes to
render these people such skilful marksmen; and as every man is necessitated

[299] The price of land is so much varied by quality and situation, that no certain data can be given. Near the large towns, land is as dear as near the cities in the eastern states, and in the most populous towns, the lots sell at a very high price. In February, 1816, land in the town of Louisville sold at the rate of 30,000 dollars per acre. The lands belonging to the United States government are sold at one uniform price, viz. two dollars per acre, with five years to pay it in, or one dollar, sixty-four cents cash. There are but few European families, who have been accustomed to sedentary employments, that could submit to the fatigues incident on clearing a forest, and converting it into arable land. To such, a resource is always open, as opportunities are never wanting to purchase from the *Backwoodsman* what he calls *his improvement*. He is alarmed at the approach of population, and is anxious to remove farther back into the woods. The improvement consists in a log house, a peach, and perhaps an apple, orchard, together with from ten, to thirty or forty acres of land, inclosed, and partially cleared. For this, seldom more than from fifty to a hundred dollars is asked, ex-

---

to appropriate a portion of his land to timber for fuel and fences, the squirrels having refuge there, will long continue to exercise their skill. Another enemy they keep within bounds, perhaps without designing it; before the peaches are naturally mature, great quantities fall from the trees, apparently ripe; to consume these, they turn the hogs into their orchards. On examining these peaches, there may be found in each a small worm, of course produced by a winged insect, probably a *cynips*. Those who are acquainted with the amazing powers of reproduction vested in insects, need not to be informed of the consequences if these were all suffered to arrive at maturity. Some of the farmers consider the woodpecker as an enemy, on account of the great number of perforations it makes in their apple trees, but as its food is insects, I think it may be considered to them an invaluable friend.— BRAD-BURY.

clusive of the value of the land, which in most cases belongs to the United States, and may be purchased at the land office on the usual terms. Besides the land belonging to the United States, there are large tracts in the hands of speculators, [300] from whom it may sometimes be purchased upon as good terms as from the government, and as liberal in point of credit; but in this case, care should be taken to examine if the title is good. Many of the speculators are anxious to sell, as the land-tax, although comparatively light, becomes heavy on very extensive purchases: it amounts to one dollar, twenty cents, per annum, on one hundred acres of first-rate land; one dollar on one hundred acres of second-rate; and sixty cents on third-rate. These sums are nearly in the proportion of $\frac{14}{20}$ of a penny per acre for first-rate; one halfpenny per acre for second rate; and $\frac{7}{10}$ of a halfpenny per acre for third-rate. Some districts of upland may be purchased of the speculators at half a dollar, or 2s. 3d. per acre: these would answer well for sheep. No land tax is expected until five years after the purchase, when land becomes liable. They have two modes of clearing land; one by cutting the trees round, so as to kill them, and afterwards clearing away the underwood, the quantity of which is very small: this mode is called *girdling*, and is only resorted to by those who, to use their own phrase, are "*weak-handed.*" The other mode is by cutting down the trees, dragging them into heaps, and burning them. This operation is almost always the subject of what they term a *frolic*, or in some places a *bee*. It is necessary to remark, that [301] in the early part of the settlement of a country like this, a great number of things occur necessary to be done, which require the united strength of numbers to effect. In those parts, money cannot purchase for the new settler the required aid; but that kind and generous feeling which men have for each other, who are not rendered callous by the possession of wealth, or the dread of poverty, comes to his relief: his neighbours, even unsolicited, appoint a day when as a *frolic*, they shall, for instance, build him a house. On the morning of the appointed day they assemble, and divide themselves into parties, to each of which is assigned its respective duty; one party cuts down the trees, another lops and cuts them to proper lengths, a third is furnished with horses and oxen, and drags them to the spot designed for the scite of the house: another party is employed in making *shingles* to cover the roof, and at night all the materials are ready upon the spot; and on the night of the next day, he and his family sleep in their new habitation. No remuneration is expected, nor would it be received. It is considered the performance of a duty, and only lays him under the obligation to discharge the debt by doing the same to subsequent settlers. But this combination of labour in numbers, for the benefit of one individual, is not confined to the new comer only, it occurs frequently in the course of a year amongst the *old settlers*, [302] with whom it is a continued bond of amity and social intercourse, and in no part of the world is *good neighbourship* found in greater perfection than in the western territory, or in America generally.

As the climate has already been spoken of, I shall only observe, that here, as in Upper Louisiana, the shortness and mildness of the winter is of immense advantage to the farmer. In parts where the winter is five or six months long, a great portion of time must necessarily be employed in providing food for the cattle during that season. Here very little time or land is necessary to be devoted to that purpose. The greatest part of the farmers scatter the seeds of pumpkins in the fields when planting the corn: no farther care is required, except throwing the pumpkins into the waggon when ripe. These, with the tops of the Indian corn, cut off when the ears are formed, give sufficient food for all the stock during winter. The pumpkins are raised with so little trouble, that they sell for a dollar per waggon load, and generally weigh from thirty to fifty pounds each, although some have been raised to exceed two hundred pounds. Cattle and hogs eat them with avidity.

The vine flourishes in this region, and the [303] wheat can scarcely be surpassed, either for quality or abundance. With the exception of beans (*vicia faba,*) and cauliflower, the culinary vegetables of Europe are raised in as much perfection as in England. In addition to these, they cultivate in their fields, amongst other crops, water melons, musk-melons, squashes, and sweet potatoes, (*convolvulus batatus*.) Cucumbers and beans (*phaseolus,*) grow in much greater perfection than in England. The fruits are excellent, and in great abundance, particularly peaches and apples.

Very little of the agricultural labour falls on the women, who employ themselves in their domestic manufactures, in which they are both expert and industrious. Almost all grow some flax, and south

of latitude 39° they have what they call a *cotton patch*.[158]
Few are without sheep. By these means the women
are furnished with three staple articles, out of which
they spin sufficient to produce almost all the clothing
and other articles necessary for a family. Some have
looms, and weave it themselves; others employ weavers,
who follow that business as an occupation.[159]

[304] In the towns, many of the trades or manufactories are already established, that are calculated to
furnish articles of the first degree of necessity; and
some of those which produce articles necessary in a
more advanced state of refinement. Amongst the first,
are masons, stone-cutters, brick-makers, smiths, carpenters, wheelwrights, cabinet-makers, saddlers, boot
and shoe makers, ship and boat builders, nailors, cop-
persmiths and brass-founders, wire-drawers and wire-
makers, screw and hinge makers, gunsmiths, cutlers,
machine makers, clock and watch makers, curriers,
glovers, distillers, butchers, bakers, brewers, stocking
makers, rope makers, coffee-mill makers, and a great
number of others. There are also glass manufactories,
cotton and woollen manufactories, iron foundries,
potteries, floor-cloth manufactories, steam engine makers, glass cutters, silversmiths, looking-glass makers,
printers, bookbinders, &c. &c. There is no part of
the world where labour finds a better market than in
the western country; this results from a state of things
that will not admit of a speedy change. A very mod-

---

[158] Cotton does not become an object of culture as a crop north of 36°.
— BRADBURY.

[159] The manufacture of their woollens is much facilitated by the establishment of carding machines: almost generally throughout the United
States, some proprietors have two or three machines.— BRADBURY.

erate sum of money enables a man to procure one or
two hundred acres of land; the savings of [305] two or
three years will enable a working man to effect this,
if he is prudent; and although he can only cultivate a
small part of it, and perhaps for the first two or three
years, not more than will maintain his family, yet the
accumulation of property by the regular and rapid
advance in the value of his land, forms more than an
equivalent to the savings of the labourer or mechanic.
From this cause there is a continued tendency in the
labourers to turn to farming, as soon as they have acquired a little property: they are well aware that, by
undertaking to bring *wild land* into a state of cultivation, they must undergo some hardships, and suffer
some privations, but the state of ease, security and independence which will assuredly follow, makes ample
amends.

That produce of every kind, of the nature of provisions, will for a very long time remain low, may be
presumed by attending to the following circumstances:
first the distance from a foreign market, causing a great
expense in exportation: secondly, the great predominance of scattered population employed in farming,
over that which is condensed in towns, or otherwise
employed: and thirdly, the vast extent of land remaining west of the Alleghanies yet unoccupied; this will
appear from the following statement of the area and
population, in which all that part attached to the
[306] Atlantic States is excluded. The population is
taken as it stood in the census of 1810, since when,
although there has been a great increase, yet it makes

no very sensible difference when the extent of the country is considered.

	Area in Square Miles.	*Population.*
Ohio State	43,860	230,760
Indiana State	39,000	24,520
Illinois Territory . . .	52,000	12,282
Michigan Territory . . .	34,820	4,762
North West Territory . . .	106,830	1,000
Kentucky State	40,110	406,511
Tenessee State	43,200	261,727
Mississippi Territory . . .	88,680	40,352
Missouri Territory . . .	985,250	20,845
	1,433,750	1,002,759

By this statement, it appears that in 1810, there was only one inhabitant in near one and a half square miles, or, (as there are six hundred and forty acres to the square mile) one inhabitant in every nine hundred acres; not one-tenth of these are residents in towns, nor one-fifth have any employment but agriculture.

The average population of England and Wales is one hundred and ninety-two to the square mile. In Lancashire there are four hundred inhabitants to the square mile, which allows but little more than an acre and a half to each individual.

[307] Wages in the Western Country, to a labourer or husbandman, are about fifteen dollars, or £3. 7s. 6d. per month, and his board, washing, &c. Carpenters, masons, and other handicraft men, average about one dollar and twenty-five cents per day, equal to 5s. 7½d. or one dollar and board. Shoemakers have about 4s. sterling for making a pair of shoes, and for a pair of

boots about 11s.   In the present state of things, flour,
and other produce that is transferable to a foreign
market, is higher than usual, but when not affected by
a scarcity in Europe, will fall to the usual price, which
is pretty near the following statement.

	American Money.		Eng. Money.	
	Dols.	Cents.	Shils.	Pence.
Flour, *per barrel*	4	0 or 18	0	
Indian corn meal, *per* 100 *lbs*. .	0	40 — 1	9½	
Potatoes, *per bushel* . . .	0	31 — 1	4½	
Beef, mutton, and veal, *per lb*. .	0	5 — 0	2½	
Pork, *per lb*.	0	4 — 0	2	
Bacon, *per lb*.	0	8 — 0	4½	
Venison, *per lb*. . . .	0	4 — 0	2	
Fowls, *each*	0	12½— 0	7	
Ducks, *each*	0	25 — 1	1½	
Geese, *each*	0	62½— 2	10	
Turkies, *each*	0	75 — 3	4½	
Cheese, *per lb*.	0	10 — 0	5¼	
Butter, *per lb*.	0	14 — 0	7¼	
Cider, *per barrel* . . .	3	0 — 13	6	
Whiskey, *per gallon* . . .	0	40 — 1	9½	
Peach brandy, *per gallon* . .	0	80 — 3	7	
Maple sugar, *per lb*. . . .	0	10 — 0	5¼	

[308] By a comparison of this table with the rate of
wages, it will appear, that an industrious working man
may support a family with great ease in this country.

Mellish, in his description of these parts, gives a
statement of the prices of provision and labour, which
he closes with the following observations.

"From this list of prices, taken in connexion with
the value of labour, it will be seen, that an ordinary
workman can procure for a day's work, fifty pounds of
flour,— or twenty pounds of beef,— or three bushels

of potatoes,— or twenty-seven pounds of pork,— or eight fowls,— or four ducks,— or two ordinary geese,— or one very large turkey.''

The constitution of the state of Ohio declares that

1. All men are born equally free and independent.

2. All men have a natural right to worship God according to the dictates of their own conscience.

3. Trial by jury shall be inviolate.

4. Printing-presses shall be free.

[309] 5. Unwarrantable searches shall not be permitted.

6. Unnecessary rigor shall not be exercised.

7. Excessive bail shall not be required in bailable offences.

8. All penalties shall be proportioned to the nature of the offence.

9. The liberty of the people to assemble together, to consult for the public good, and to bear arms in their own defence, is guaranteed.

10. Hereditary emoluments, honours, and privileges are for ever prohibited.

11. Slavery is for ever prohibited, and it is declared that ''No indenture of any negro or mulatto, hereafter made and executed out of the state, or if made in the state, where the term of service exceeds one year, shall be of the least validity, except those given in the case of apprenticeship.''

12. ''Religion, morality, and knowledge being essentially necessary to the good government and happiness of mankind, schools, and the means of instruction, shall be for ever encouraged by [310] legislative provision, not inconsistent with the rights of conscience.''

The government is legislative and executive, and regulates the judicial and military authorities.

The legislature consists of a senate and house of representatives. The senators are elected *biennially*, the representatives *annually*, by the people, and one half vacate their seats every year. Every free white male, who is a citizen of the United States, and has resided in that state one year, has a vote for a representative; if he has resided two years, he can vote for a senator.

Every citizen qualified to vote for a representative, and above twenty-five years of age, is also eligible to be himself elected: if above thirty years of age, he is eligible to become a senator.

The governor is also chosen by the people, and serves for two years: he cannot by law be elected more than three times in succession.

The election is carried on throughout the state on the same day, and during the same hours, viz. from ten to four o'clock. There is a poll in every township, and it is conducted by ballot; each elector hands in a slip of paper, containing the [311] name of the candidate to whom he gives his vote, at which time his own name is registered. By this means, the whole business of election is begun and terminated in one day, without any noise or disturbance.

The justices are appointed by the people of their respective townships, and retain their office only three years, unless re-elected.

In the military of the state, the captains and the subaltern officers are chosen by those in their respective company districts, who are subject to military duty.

Majors are elected by captains and subalterns.

Colonels are elected by majors, captains, and sub-alterns.

Brigadier-generals are elected by the commissioned officers of their respective brigades.

Major-generals and quarter-master-generals are ap-pointed by joint ballot of both houses of the legislature.

The governor is commander-in-chief, and appoints the adjutants.

[312] In regard to the manners of the people west of the Alleghanies, it would be absurd to expect that a general character could be now formed, or that it will be for many years yet to come. The population is at present compounded of a great number of nations, not yet amalgamated, consisting of emigrants from every state in the Union, mixed with English, Irish, Scotch, Dutch, Swiss, Germans, French, and almost from every country in Europe. In some traits they partake in common with the inhabitants of the Atlantic States, which results from the nature of their government. That species of hauteur which one class of society in some countries show in their intercourse with the other, is here utterly unknown. By their constitution, the existence of a privileged order, vested by birth with hereditary privileges, honours, or emoluments, is for ever interdicted. If, therefore, we should here expect to find that contemptuous feeling in man for man, we should naturally examine amongst those clothed with judicial or military authority; but we should search in vain. The justice on the bench, or the officer in the field, is respected and obeyed whilst discharging the functions of his office, as the representative or agent of the law,

enacted for the *good of all*; but should he be tempted
to treat even the least wealthy of his neighbours or
fellow-citizens with contumely, he would soon find
that he could not do it with impunity. [313] Travellers from Europe, in passing through the western
country, or indeed any part of the United States, ought
to be previously acquainted with this part of the
American character, and more particularly if they
have been in the habit of treating with contempt, or
irritating with abuse, those whom accidental circumstances may have placed in a situation to administer to
their wants.   Let no one here indulge himself in abus-
ing the waiter or hostler at an inn: that waiter or hostler
is probably a citizen, and does not, nor can he, conceive
that a situation in which he discharges a duty to society,
not in itself dishonourable, should subject him to insult: but this feeling, so far as I have experienced, is
entirely defensive.   I have travelled near ten thousand
miles in the United States, and never received the
least incivility or affront.

The Americans in general are accused by travellers
of being inquisitive.   If this be a crime, the western
people are guilty; but for my part I must say that it is a
practice that I never was disposed to complain of, because I always found them as ready to answer a question as to ask one, and therefore I always came off a
gainer by this sort of barter; and if any traveller does not,
it is his own fault.   As this leads me to notice their general conduct to strangers, I feel myself bound in gratitude and regard to truth, to speak of their hospitality.
In [314] my travels through the inhabited parts of the

United States, not less than two thousand miles was through parts where there were no taverns, and where a traveller is under the necessity of appealing to the hospitality of the inhabitants. In no one instance has my appeal been fruitless, although in many cases the furnishing of a bed has been evidently attended with inconvenience, and in a great many instances no remuneration would be received. Other European travellers have experienced this liberal spirit of hospitality, and some have repaid it by calumny. These calumnies have reached them: they are well acquainted with what Weld and a person who calls himself Ashe have said of them.[160] In respect to their moral character, my experience [315] reaches chiefly to the western, middle, and some of the southern states. In the western states, I noticed that very few of the houses in which I slept had either locks or bolts on the doors, and that the jails were in general without a single tenant.

It has already been observed that no people discharge the social duties, as respects the character of neighbours, better, and I believe no country, having a

---

[160] As the book published by this Ashe contains numberless statements, bearing in themselves such evidences of being void of truth as to deprive him of all claim to veracity, and as it has already sunk into the oblivion it merits, the malignant falsehoods propagated by him, respecting America and the American people, should have remained unnoticed by me, had I not witnessed the just indignation it has excited in that country, and also found that Ashe had been received and treated with the greatest kindness by the very people whom he has so grossly libelled. His statements are too numerous, and many of them too absurd, to deserve a serious refutation; but I think it a duty due both to myself and my country to state, that his description of the American people, and the accusations he makes against them, are void of foundation. If Mr. Ashe saw any instance to warrant his observations, he must have kept the worst of company.— BRADBURY.

population equal to the United States, can exhibit the records of their courts containing fewer statements of crimes committed against the laws.

The more northerly parts of the states of Ohio and Indiana, together with the whole of the Illinois and western territories, including an area of about 128,-130,000 acres, comprehend that part which, in the beginning of this article, has been noticed as possessing a different character in its natural state. The original state of the region already spoken of was that of a continued forest, not convertible into a state fit for cultivation without great pains and labour. This region is an assemblage of woodland and prairie or savannas intermixed; the portions of each varying in extent, but the aggregate area of the prairies exceeding that of the woodland in the proportion of three or four to one. The soil of this part is inferior to none in North [316] America, or perhaps in the world. In a state of nature, these prairies are covered with a luxuriant growth of grass and herbaceous plants, affording a most abundant supply of food for the stock of the new settler; and it is worthy of notice, that any part of these prairies, when constantly fed on by cattle, becomes covered with white clover and the much esteemed blue grass, (*poa compressa*) as frequent pasturing seems to give those plants a predominance over all others.

In the geological formation, this country also differs in some degree from the one entirely covered with wood in its natural state. The surface is much more level, and the strata more regular and undisturbed. In general the order of the strata is sand lying on sandstone, afterwards lime-stone, beneath which is argillaceous schist lying on coal. For the settler who is not habitually accustomed to the felling of trees, and who has the courage to fix himself on wild land, this is by much the best part of the United States, excepting Upper Louisiana. If he places his house at the edge of one of these prairies, it furnishes him food for any number of cattle he may choose to keep. The wood-land affords him the materials necessary for his house, his fire, and fences, and with a single yoke of oxen, he can in general immediately reduce any part of his prairie land to a state of tillage. Had this portion [317] of the country been placed at no greater distance from the Alleghanies than the woody region, it would undoubtedly have been the first settled; but being situated from five hundred to a thousand miles beyond those mountains, and separated from them by one of the most fertile countries in the world, the consequence is, that emigrants are so well satisfied with what advantages a first view of the country presents, that they are anxious to sit down as soon as possible. Another reason why this portion of the wild lands has not been more rapidly settled, is the total indifference of the American farmer to the present or future value of coal. This arises in part from his prejudice against the use of it for fuel, but more from his want of knowledge of its vast importance to other countries, and a consequent want of foresight. The farmer who is possessed of five hundred acres of land, expects that in time it will probably be divided into ten properties or farms by his posterity, each of which must be supplied with timber for fuel and fences: he wishes, therefore, that the land unreclaimed may remain covered with timber, as a reserve for posterity, although perhaps he has an excellent bed of coal at no great distance beneath the surface.

Nothing so strongly indicates the superiority of the western country, as the vast emigrations to it from the eastern and southern states. In passing [318] through the upper parts of Virginia, I observed a great number of farms that had been abandoned, on many of which good houses had been erected, and fine apple and peach orchards had been planted. On enquiring the reason, I was always informed that the owners had gone to the western country. From the New England States the emigrations are still more numerous. They mostly cross the Hudson river betwixt Albany and Newburg, and must pass through Cayuga in their way to Pittsburg. I was informed by an inhabitant of Cayuga, in April, 1816, that more than fifteen thousand waggons had passed over the bridge at that place within the last eighteen months, containing emigrants to the western country.

In making the following remarks, and in giving such instructions and information as will be useful to those who purpose to emigrate to America, I disclaim any wish to promote emigration. Much distress has arisen to emigrants, either from having entertained false conceptions, or from a want of knowledge how to conduct themselves after their arrival in the United States. I have witnessed that distress, and traced it to the cause: my wish is to obviate it.

The remarks that follow will only apply to such as the law permits to expatriate themselves, and [319] of course the present state or future prospects of manufactures in the United States will form no part of the subject to be considered. But the inutility of the law, prohibiting the emigration of manufacturers or machinists to the United States, is so obvious to persons acquainted with the interior of the country, that they are [at] a loss to conceive why it continues to exist. It is still more surprising that it should yet be enforced in a country where excess of population is a subject of complaint, where means have been devised to check the rapidity of its progress, and where the classes denied the privilege of expatriation are complained of as being an incumbrance, and are daily adding more and more to the distress of the nation, in the picture of which they stand the most prominent figure. Whoever is intimately acquainted with the interior of the United States, knows that cotton and woollen manufactories are spread throughout the Union, and that they have found their way even to the west of the Alleghanies. At Nashville, in Tenessee; Lexington, in Kentucky: at Cincinnati, Beaver, and at Pittsburg, and many other places, there are large cotton and woollen establishments.

In the eastern and middle states there are many hundreds of factories, abundantly supplied with managers and machine makers from Britain, of [320] whom there is such a redundancy, that a very considerable number have resorted to agriculture. Whether manufactories will succeed in America, or to what degree, time alone can determine; but that their progress can be in the least impeded by restrictive laws, prohibiting the emigration of manufacturers or machinists from this country, is now absolutely impossible.

The first step that an emigrant ought to take, should
be to provide himself with a proper certificate, setting
forth his trade or profession, and testifying that he has
never been employed in manufactures, or machine
making, or in works of brass, iron, or steel, appertain-
ing to manufactures. This certificate must be signed
by the minister and churchwardens of the parish to
which he belongs; and if also by a magistrate, it will
render it of more effect.

Most articles of furniture being cheaper in the
United States than in Britain, nothing of that kind
ought to be taken, as they would, in all probability,
suffer damage. Feather beds and bedding, on the contrary, ought to be preserved; and for packing clothes,
&c. trunks are preferable to heavy and clumsy boxes.
On arriving at the port from whence the emigrant
expects to sail, his first care should be to ascertain if
his certificate is sufficient, [321] which he may be
acquainted with at the custom-house; and he must be
careful not to pay for his passage until he be well
assured that he shall be permitted to proceed.

The port in the United States to which it will be the
interest of the emigrant to sail, will depend on his
views or his prospects. A wide field is open to him,
and he ought to make himself acquainted with its
geography before he decide on this point.

For a very great portion of emigrants, the countries
west of the Alleghanies, say Ohio, Indiana, Kentucky,
Tennessee, or the Illinois; offer by much the best prospects; and to get to those countries, Philadelphia and
Baltimore are the best ports. If the intention be to
proceed to the lower part of the Ohio, Baltimore is

preferable to Philadelphia, and the best way will be to
go from thence to Wheeling, on the Ohio, ninety-five
miles below Pittsburg, and the road is much less difficult. The port to which the emigrant will sail being
determined, the next consideration is sea store; and he
will do well to recollect that most probably both himself and his family will be sea sick for some days, and
that, during its continuance, if he is a steerage passenger,
both he and his wife will have an utter aversion to the
trouble of cooking: he must, [322] therefore, provide
some cold meat to last during that time: either fowls or
veal would be the best. For the general sea store it is
difficult to prescribe rules. The quantity will of course
depend on the number of persons to be provided for, and
the quality, on their taste, and in some measure on the
season of the year. If there are small children, some oat-
meal and molasses will be found very·useful and whole-
some, as it will furnish a food much more conducive to
their health than salt provisions. For the general sea
store, tea, coffee, sugar, biscuits, butter, cheese, a few
hams, salt, soap, candles, &c. will be necessary. Sufficient should be laid in to last at least eight weeks, in particular for Baltimore, as sometimes vessels are a week
or ten days in going up the Chesapeake after passing
the Capes. A proper regard to cleanliness during the
voyage is recommended; to admit as much air between
decks as the weather will permit, and to take a few
bottles of vinegar to sprinkle on the floor occasionally;
and if it can be practised, fumigation, by putting a red
hot piece of iron in a kettle of pitch, will be found
salutary. On arriving at the desired port, if the emigrant has any letters of introduction, he should deliver

them immediately: his friends may probably assist him in finding a proper place where his family may rest a few days after the fatigues of the voyage. His next care will be to land his trunks, bedding, &c. [323] and get them deposited in a place of safety. If he has not a letter of introduction to some person in the city where he first lands, he ought to be on his guard. In every one of the maritime cities in America, a great number of small stores are established for the sale of spirituous liquors, &c. Many of these are kept by natives of Great Britain, some of whom are so devoid of principle as to induce emigrants to remain in cities, under various pretences, but chiefly by holding out a prospect of employment, when their real purpose is to tempt them to spend their money with them.

So many emigrants arrive at all the principal ports in the United States, that there is very little chance of employment, and almost the whole of the distress that has been reported to exist in America, has arisen from the number of emigrants who have foolishly lingered in the cities until they have spent all their money.

It shall be supposed that the design of the emigrant is to proceed to the countries east of the Alleghanies, therefore he ought not to stay more than two or three days in the city, which he can leave when he pleases, as great numbers of waggons start from Philadelphia to Pittsburg, or from Baltimore to Pittsburg or Wheeling, every day. The charge is by the hundred weight, both for passengers [324] and their luggage, and the rate varies from five to seven dollars per hundred; but the men may go cheaper if they chuse to walk over the mountains, which is recommended. The waggon-

ers travel with great economy: many of them carry a
small camp-kettle with them to cook their provisions,
and some have even a bed in their waggons, in which
they sleep at night. A traveller who chooses to adopt
a similar mode, may travel very cheap; or, as there are
plenty of inns on the roads, he can be accommodated
every night with beds, at a very reasonable rate. When
the emigrant arrives at Pittsburg or Wheeling, he will
find that numbers of Europeans and Americans are
arriving there every day, and the same causes that
operated against them in the maritime cities, as respects employment, will, in some degree, have an effect
here; but as he will have occasion for information, it
would be advisable for him to stop a few days to make
enquiries. If he find it necessary to descend the Ohio,
the best mode of proceeding will be to enquire for one
or more families, who have intentions of going to the
same neighbourhood as himself, who may join him in
the purchase of an *ark*, one of the kind of vessels in
which families descend. These arks are built for sale,
for the accommodation of families descending the river,
and for the conveyance of produce. They are flat-
bottomed, [325] and square at the ends, and are all
made of the same dimensions, being fifty feet in length,
and fourteen in breadth; which last is limited, because
it often happens that they must pass over the falls at
Louisville, when the river is at a low state, at which
time they pass betwixt two rocks in the *Indian schute*,
only fifteen feet asunder.[161] These arks are covered,

[161] There are regular pilots resident at Louisville, who conduct the boats
over the falls, and deliver them safe at Shipping Port:— they charge two
dollars for pilotage.— BRADBURY.

and are managed by a steering oar, which can be lifted out of the water. The usual price is seventy-five dollars for each, which will accommodate three or four families, as they carry from twenty-five to thirty tons: and it frequently happens that the ark can be sold for nearly what it cost, six or eight hundred miles lower down the river.

After the arrival of the emigrant on the Ohio, the next step he takes is a very important one:— much depends on his movement, and it is at that point when he has the greatest need of counsel and advice. From Europe until he arrives on the Ohio, general rules may apply, but now his future destination depends on his choice, and no general rule can be given to direct that choice, because emigrants are of so many different descriptions. [326] In order that these remarks may have a general application, emigrants shall be considered as consisting of several classes, the remarks shall be applied to each class separately, and terminate with some general observations.

The first class of emigrants may be composed of labourers, who have no other trade or profession, and from whose services, more is expected to result from bodily strength, than from ingenuity or education. If a man of this class will work, he has nothing to fear in the interior of America:— he possesses all the requisites for a farmer excepting skill, and that he may soon obtain. A great number of farmers have more land inclosed in fence than they can well manage: ask one of these the reason, he replies, "I want help." An assistant enables him to cultivate a portion of his land that would otherwise become overrun with weeds.

The emigrant cannot expect full wages at the commencement, but if he be attentive, he may in one year become so expert as to be entitled to what is usually paid to husbandmen, from twelve to fifteen dollars per month, and board.

But when employment is obtained, the most difficult thing remains yet to be done. The man he lives with, and for whom he works, most probably makes his own cider, a portion of which is distilled [327] into brandy: both these articles are kept, in considerable quantities, in the farmer's house. The emigrant is liberally supplied with them, and can obtain them at a cheap rate elsewhere; but he must avoid indulging too much, particularly in the spirits. He is not accustomed to a profusion of this article, and may, by too frequent use, acquire a habit that will ruin all his future prospects in life. If his conduct is proper, he may associate with the sons of the neighbouring farmers, many of whom know that their ancestors became proprietors of land, from a beginning not more promising than his: even his employer was probably the helper to some one formerly. Before this man can become a complete American farmer, he must learn a number of things, not connected with agriculture in some other countries. He must learn to handle the axe dexterously, as he will often be employed to cut down trees. He must also learn, not only to distinguish the different species of trees, but also to know by their appearance whether they will suit the purpose for which they are wanted.

The second class of emigrants to be considered, are those who have trades or professions, and yet are too poor to enter into business for themselves. The primary object of a person of this description is, of course, employment: the commodity he has to dispose [328] of is *labour*, for which he wants a market. So much of this is daily brought into the sea-ports by the arrival of emigrants, that they are always overstocked; he must look for a better chance:— this chance the country will afford him. If his trade or profession be such as is followed in a city, he may remain two days before he goes to the country; if unsuccessful in his enquiries for work, he ought not to remain longer. During his stay, he ought to enquire amongst those of his own profession, where he may hope to obtain employment, as it is very likely they may furnish references which will be of great use to him. In travelling, this man ought not be sparing in his enquiries; he is not in the least danger of receiving a rude or an uncivil answer, even if he should address himself to a *squire*, (so justices are called.) It is expected in America, that every man shall attend to his own concerns; and if a man who is out of work ask for employment, it is considered as a very natural thing.

He ought to make his situation and profession known at the taverns where he stops, and rather to court than to shun conversation with any that he may find assembled there. He will seldom or never meet with a repulse, as it gives them an opportunity of making enquiries respecting the "*old* [329] *country*," (the term usually applied to the British Islands.)

Should he fail in procuring employment at his own business, he has all the advantages of the first man, in agriculture. The countries west of the Alleghany Mountains afford the greatest advantages of any part of the United States, to emigrants of this or the preceding description; and when they arrive at the head of the Ohio, the facility of descending that river opens to them a vast field, in which labour must, for ages to come, find a good market, as the vast tract of fine land yet unsettled will induce so great an avidity for farming, that labourers, or men who have trades or professions, will adopt that line of life whenever they can raise the means of purchasing land. For this reason a very long time must elapse before there can be such a redundancy of labour as to reduce its value. Some of the trades that are carried on in the large towns are enumerated at page 285.

The man possessed of some property, say from £200 to £1000, has more need of cautionary advice than either of the former. But no knowledge can be conveyed to him, that will be so valuable as what results from his own experience and observation. He is advised to deposit his money in a bank, or vest it in government stock immediately [330] on landing. His next object is to determine in what line of life he shall employ himself and his capital. In this he should avoid being too hasty. If it is known that he has money, he will probably be tempted to enter into speculations, both by his own countrymen and others. Designing men are much more likely to hold out temptations than men with honest and honourable intentions; and until he has acquired a competent knowledge of men and things, it is dangerous for him to embark in business. It should have been premised, that he ought, if possible, to take with him letters of introduction to some persons in the United States, experienced in matters of business, whom he might occasionally consult. If he decide on mercantile business, or keeping a store, he ought, by all means, to procure a situation in a merchant's counting-house or in a store for one year at least: even if with only trifling wages, he will still be a gainer. If he adopt agriculture, he ought to obtain, if possible, an assistant who knows the management of crops, and the mode of working the ground: such a person will be necessary for at least two years. If he should not succeed in procuring such a man, he must keep on good terms with his neighbours, who will cheerfully tell him what is necessary to be done. In purchasing his land, he ought not to depend entirely on his own judgment, unless he has made an extensive tour through the country, [331] and attentively considered the subject of land. He will find some remarks applicable to that head amongst those addressed to a farmer.

In a great many trades or professions, the emigrant who has a capital and a trade or profession, may meet with less difficulty than any of the preceding, if he act with caution. Much in this case depends on making a judicious choice in determining where to establish his business. In most trades, the country beyond the Alleghany Mountains, say Ohio, Kentucky, or Tennessee, holds out greater advantages than the rest of the Union, the profits in business being greater, and the expense of living much less: the climate also is more suitable to European constitutions, as the extreme betwixt the heat of summer and the cold of winter is much less than in the Atlantic States. In some trades he may be expected to keep journeymen, per-

haps Americans, from whom he is advised not to exact
that servility of deportment expected from subordinates
in other countries. He may be faithfully served without it. He loses nothing by this, as those who are his
employers or customers will make no such exactions
from him.

There are several objects in America that present
themselves to the capitalist, in which he may vest his
property with perfect security, and if he act [332]
judiciously, he will have no reason to complain of his
profits. The most prominent object that offers itself
is land. Of this, immense tracts may always be had,
and in particular from the government of the United
States. The price is two dollars per acre; one fourth
of the money to be paid down, and the rest by instal-
ments in five years. The degree of advantage to be
derived from land purchases, depends in a great measure on the judgment and foresight of the speculator,
to whom the country west of the Alleghanies offers the
best field. A very great majority of the emigrants to
that part have only farming in view, and the establishment of towns does not keep pace with the increase
of interspersed population. There are a great many
places, which, from the nature of things, must become
the scites of towns: a person of judgment and observation would easily point them out. The formation of
a number of proximate settlements has an invariable
tendency to raise the price of land in their vicinity: for
this reason, a rich man, who purchases a large tract of
land on speculation, consults his best interests by a
liberal policy towards those who first settle on his
property. Let it be supposed that he purchases four

miles square; this is sixteen square miles or sections, or ten thousand, two hundred and forty acres, which for cash costs sixteen thousand, eight hundred and ninety-six dollars, or £3801 12s. English money.   On this [333] property he ought to possess a scite convenient for a village, and he should also have a waterfall.   If he lays the whole out in quarter sections, he will have sixty-four of one hundred and sixty acres each. Let him lay out the village, and sell, in the first instance, only the intermediate subdivisions, on moderate terms and liberal credit: the reserved subdivisions, together with the village lots, will in a short time rise to a very great value.   The next object of importance is coal, and although the investment of capital in that way may not so speedily produce profit as in land, yet it holds out great advantages.   It has already been stated that coal is abundant in the western country, and that a considerable portion of that region is prairie: it has also been observed, that the existence of a bed of coal scarcely enhances the price of the land under which it lies.   In most parts of the Atlantic States, fifty years ago, one acre of cleared land was worth five of woodland.   Since that time innumerable towns and villages have been established, and the old cities and villages have increased.   Every city or town may be considered as the centre of a circle, within the area of which one acre of woodland is now of much more value than the same extent of the finest meadow. These areas are continually increasing, and consequently the aggregate value of timber.   At a period not very remote the larger cities must resort to the use of coal, and nothing is [334] more certain than that a time will come when that article will be as valuable to America as it is now to England.

The emigrant who goes to America with the intention of applying himself to farming, should take with him some seed wheat of the best kinds, and if he can procure it, perhaps the Syrian wheat (*triticum compositum*) might be worth a trial. It has a much better chance of answering in America than in England, and particularly south of forty degrees of latitude; also a small quantity of lucerne, saintfoin, and vetches: either the seeds or the roots of the two former, but the roots would be preferable. It might also be adviseable to take a small bag of hay seeds from some of the best meadows. Farming implements can be had in any part of the United States, well adapted to the different purposes for which they are wanted. In determining a situation, he has the choice of any climate from latitude twenty-nine to forty-four degrees, comprehending the regions suitable for the culture of sugar, cotton, and grain. If his views are governed by the determination to adopt any particular culture, he will of course settle in the region suitable. If sugar, he will go south of $31\frac{1}{2}°$; if cotton, south of $36°$: for corn, the most agreeable is from $36°$ to $41°$, as further north the severity and length of the winters render the climate [335] less desirable. A farmer, on settling in America, ought not rashly to set up his opinions or former practices against those of the old settlers. Many things which may appear to him at first to be wrong or unnecessary, will be found, on farther experience, both right and expedient; but if he cultivates the good will of his neighbours, and follows their advice, he will not go wrong. He will soon find the succession of crops and the mode of culture vary much from what he has experienced in England, and that a differently modified climate, and a sun more nearly vertical, greatly change the order of the things to which he has been accustomed. He will find his rye harvest to commence in June, and that of his wheat soon after: the oats follow next, and afterwards, if he have a meadow, his grass will be ready for the scythe; then come his potatoes, and lastly his Indian corn. If the emigrant purchases and settles upon what is called wild land, one of his first cares ought to be to plant a peach and apple orchard, and he ought to plant the two sorts alternate, say one peach betwixt two apple trees, and not plant the apple trees less than thirty feet asunder. The peach trees soon come to maturity, and are short lived: they will become of little value by the time the apple trees are in want of room. In the woody region, the axe is for some time the chief implement in the hands of the settler, and he feels a considerable degree of [336] repugnance at the destruction of so much fine timber; but this soon subsides. If he has the courage to proceed as far west as the Illinois, the North-west Territories, or to the west of the Mississippi, the prairies afford him the means of settling without much trouble.

In the early part of the settlement of the rich countries beyond the Alleghanies, agues were very prevalent, and it will perhaps be found, that all countries in a state of nature are liable to this disease in the proportion of their fertility, which has a tendency to produce it, from the vast quantity of vegetable matter which goes to decay in Autumn. As this applies generally in those regions, the new settler has no means of avoiding the consequence but by precautions and preventives: but as it has also a local influence, he may, by a judicious choice of a situation, render himself and family less liable to its attacks. The first settlers having the choice of the whole country, it is very natural that they should adopt the alluvion of the rivers, both on account of the superior fertility of the soil, and the facilities it gives to the transportation of produce; and many in so doing sacrifice their health to their apparent interest. It must be admitted, that some of the valleys in which the rivers flow are as healthy as the uplands; but this depends on whether the river overflows its banks or not, or on [337] the existence or nonexistence of stagnant water in the neighbourhood. As to precautions, the emigrant is apprised that in these countries the dew is very copious, and begins to fall even before sunset. Let him avoid as much as possible exposure either to this or rain; or if unavoidably exposed, he must take off his wet clothes as soon as possible; and if he has flannel shirts, in order to change after copious perspiration, he will find benefit in using them. An important consideration to a family is the quality of the water they use; of course, the purer this is the better. If the settler is not able to analyze it, he may discover the presence of sulphur, iron, an acid, or an alkali, by tests always in his power to procure. Sulphur may be detected by laying a piece of bright silver in the water, which turns black if that substance is held in solution. A little of the inner bark of any of the oaks, infused in a glassful of water, turns it black, if iron is present. Paper, stained blue by the petals of almost any flower of that colour being rubbed upon it, turns green by being dipped in water impregnated with alkali, or red if an acid.

The settler who is accustomed to malt liquor may, with very little trouble, brew his own ale. Barley is cultivated west of the Alleghanies, and hops grow wild in abundance:— the use of this [338] beverage is supposed to be a preventive to the ague. Almost every family has a supposed cure for this complaint; and every one who visits or sees those affected has a favourite remedy, all differing from each other; but the physicians in the Western Country treat it with bark and laudanum: of these the emigrant ought to lay in a sufficiency to administer to his family in case of need.

It has already been observed, that the emigrants to this country are almost of every nation in Europe, but it is a remarkable and striking fact, that the Germans, Dutch, and Swiss succeed much better than those from any other country. This is not so much owing to greater industry or economy, as to the more judicious mode they adopt in settling. In general, before these people emigrate they form associations, lay down their plans, and send an agent over in whom they can confide. He purchases for them a suitable extent of land, and prepares the way: when their arrangements are made, they move over in one body. This system has always been followed by these people, and the consequences are visible in almost every part of the United States, but more particularly in the states of New York, New Jersey, and Pennsylvania, in all parts of which they are in possession of the best lands. The appearance of comfort, ease, and independence exhibited by one of these little colonies [339] is so visible, that the traveller who does not perceive it at first sight, must be very deficient in discernment. Some of the colonies of this kind, besides the tie of common interest, have another bond of union, which is a similarity of sentiment and belief in their religious opinions; this, in some instances, has operated as a cause for regulating their system of colonization: but perhaps that which has most generally influenced them is the circumstance of their language not being the general language of the United States, an inconvenience much less felt by a colony than by an isolated family; but let the cause be what it may, the effect is very manifest, and may be easily accounted for. In the early settlement of any particular district of *new country*,[162] its progress in improvements is slow, until a grist and a saw mill are erected, after which the change is very rapid. Every planter in the vicinity, by the aid of a saw mill, is able to erect a handsome frame house. The grist mill enables him to convert his wheat into flour fit for a market, and he boldly engages and employs hands to assist him in converting the forest into fields, yielding luxuriant crops. These two kinds of mills are the most necessary objects in a new colony; but there are many others, such as roads, bridges, &c. all of which are much sooner effected by a colony having a union of interest, and of course a union of action.

[340] The rapidity with which these colonies acquire

---

[162] The term *new country* signifies one newly settled.— BRADBURY.

wealth or property will appear by a comparison of their present state with their situation when they first sat down; and for the sake of example, one of those societies shall be selected, and a review taken of its progress. This is the Harmonist Society, situated about twenty miles from Pittsburg. They came from Wirtemburg in Germany, where finding themselves oppressed and persecuted by a church and state union, they determined to flee to a land where no human authority would dare to insult the Deity, by arrogating to itself the right of dictating how He shall be worshipped, and where they are too wise or too honest to suppose they can force belief. This country is America, to which in the year 1803 they sent George Rapp and others, as deputies, who fixed on a situation about twenty miles from Pittsburg.[163]

In 1804, the society embarked at Amsterdam in three ships, two of which arrived at Philadelphia, and the other at Baltimore. In the November of that year forty families removed with Mr. Rapp, and before winter they built nine log-houses. In the Spring of 1805, they were followed by fifty more families, making in all ninety. The whole of their property was about twenty thousand dollars: this sum they laid out in the purchase of nine thousand acres of land, which, together with their [341] mental and physical powers, in the Spring of 1805 formed the whole of their possessions. In the summer of this year they built forty-six

---

[163] Bradbury has given here a detailed and accurate account of the founding of Rapp's communistic society. For its later history, see Hinds, *American Communities* (rev. ed., Chicago, 1902). In 1900 there remained but nine members of the society at their town of Economy, in Beaver County, Pennsylvania.— ED.

log-houses, a large barn, a grist mill, and cleared two hundred and five acres of land.

"In 1806 a large inn was built, partly of stone; a frame-barn, a hundred feet long; a blue dyer's shop; an oil-mill; and they established a tannery. Three hundred and fifty-eight acres of land were cleared.

"In 1807 they erected a number of buildings; amongst which was a saw-mill and a brewery. Four hundred acres of land were cleared, and four acres of vines were planted.

"In 1808 they built a meeting-house of brick, together with dwelling-houses and stables, and a bridge over the Conaquenesing creek, two hundred and twenty feet long. A considerable quantity of land was cleared.

"In the year 1809 they erected a fulling-mill, an oil-mill, a mill for breaking hemp, a grist-mill, and a large brick warehouse, with a wine cellar beneath, arched over. The produce of this year was — four thousand five hundred bushels of rye, four thousand five hundred bushels of wheat, six [342] thousand bushels of Indian corn, ten thousand bushels of potatoes, five thousand bushels of oats, four thousand pounds of flax and hemp, one hundred bushels of barley brewed into beer, and fifty gallons of sweet oil from the white poppy.

"In 1810 they began the manufacture of *broadcloth*, from the wool of their Merino sheep; fixed up a carding machine, two spinning Jennies, and built a factory for twenty looms.

"In the year 1811 the property of the society was estimated as follows:—

	Dollars.
Nine thousand acres of land, with improvements .	90,000
Stock of provisions for one year for eight hundred persons	25,000
Stock of goods, spirits, manufactures, leather, implements of husbandry, &c.	50,000
Dwelling-houses	18,000
Mills, machinery, and public buildings . . .	21,000
Horses, cattle, hogs, and poultry	10,000
A thousand sheep, one-third of them Merinoes, of which one ram cost a thousand . . .	6,000
	220,000

The progress made by a small colony of Swiss, who settled in the Indiana Territory about the same time as the society at Harmony, is not less rapid. It consisted of eleven families, who united in forming a vineyard, from which, in 1811, they made more than two thousand gallons of wine.[164]

---

[164] This was the company of Swiss led by John James Du Four, who in 1802 secured a tract from Congress, on favorable terms, in order to experiment with the culture of the vine. Their two thousand five hundred acres on the Ohio River was later organized into the county of Switzerland, where Vevay, the county seat, was laid out in 1813. See account of Vevay in Thwaites, *On the Storied Ohio.*— ED.

No. VII [*i.e.*, VI]

CATALOGUE

OF SOME OF

THE MORE RARE OR VALUABLE PLANTS

Discovered in the Neighbourhood of St. Louis and on the Missouri

Leersia Lenticularis, Woods, American Bottom, St. Louis.
Aristida Pallens, Hills on the Merrimac.
Stipa Juncea, Prairies, Aricaras to the Mandans.
—— *Membranacea*, Fort Mandan.   *Probably not a Stipa.*
Aira Brevifolia, Great Prairie.
Festuca Spicata, common on the Missouri.
Cynosurus secundus, Mississippi Bluffs.
Hordeum Jubatum, valleys near the Aricaras.
Allionia Ovata,[165] banks of the Missouri, above the Big Bend.
—— *Linearis*, ⎫
—— *Hirsuta*, ⎬ bluffs near the Aricara village.
Plantago Lagopus, alluvion of the Missouri, common.
———— *Elongata*, near the Maha village.
Eleagnus Argentea, bluffs near the Mandan nation.
Hippophae Argentea, Mahas, Platte, Ottoes, Missouri.
Pulmonaria Sibirica, high up the Merrimac river.
———— *Lanceolata*, opposite the Aricara village.
[344] *Batschia Canescens*, prairie about St. Louis.
———— *Gmelini*, American Bottom, Illinois.
———— *Longiflora*, first occurs near the mouth of the Platte, on
  ascending the Missouri.
Onosmodium Molle, about St. Louis.
Dodecatheon Meadia, prairie behind St. Louis.

---

[165] These three species of *Allionia* together with the two species of *Bartonia*, have the singular property of flowering in the night: the flowers burst forth just at sun-set, and perish at its rising.— BRADBURY.

Phacelia Fimbriata, at Point L'Abbadie, on the Missouri, *with white flowers*.

Cynoglossum Glomeratum, Big Bend, Missouri.

Solanum Heterandrum, about the Aricara village.

Ribes Aureum, Little Cedar Island, Missouri.

Salsola Depressa, on the Missouri, near the mouth of Knife River.

Hydrocotyle Ambigua, rocks on the Mississippi, near Herculaneum.

Selinum acaule, on the alluvion of the Missouri, from the river Naduet to the Mahas.

Seseli Divaricatum, Missouri Bluffs, at the mouth of the L'eau qui Court.

Linum Lewisii, on Cannon-ball river.

———— *Rigidum*, on the Missouri bluffs, common.

Yucca Angustifolia, Missouri bluffs, opposite the mouth of Papillon Creek.

Lilium Catesbœia, prairie about St. Louis.

———— *Umbellatum*, bluffs near the Mandan village.

Rumex Venosus, Big Bend, Missouri.

Gaura Coccinea,
Oenothera Albicaulis, } bluffs Aricara village.

———— *Macrocarpa*, near St. Louis.

Eriogonum Pauciflorum, } near the Minateree villages on the
———————— *Sericeum,* } Missouri, both growing together.

Cactus Viviparus, Missouri bluffs, above the Poncar village.

Bartonia Ornata, } on the bluffs above Knife River.
———— *Nuda,* }

Geum Triflorum, head waters Blackbird Creek.

[345] *Potentilla Arguta*, bluffs above the Aricara village.

Ranunculus Multifidus, in stagnant pools near the Sepulchre bluffs.

Stachys Fœniculum, Missouri bluffs.

Capraria Multifida, American Bottom, Illinois.

Martynia Proboscidea, St. Louis.

Penstemon Erianthera, common on the bluffs from the Big Bend to the Aricara village.

———————— *Angustifolia*, near the Minataree village.

———— *Glabra*, alluvion of the Missouri, above the Big Bend.
Castilleja Sessilliflora, Upper Louisiana.
Myagrum Argenteum, on limestone rocks, Missouri.

Erysimum Lanceolatum, ⎫ *a connecting link between Erysimum*
    or,   ⎬ *and Cheiranthus, used as medi-*
Cheiranthus Erysimoides, ⎭ *cine by the Aricaras.*

Cleome Pinnata, on the prairies between the Aricaras and Man-
    dans.
Cristaria Coccinea, on the bluffs of the Missouri, above the
    L'eau qui Court.

Hebiscus Militaris, ⎫ American Bottom, Illinois.
———— *Manihot*, ⎭

Ervum Multiflorum, opposite the Sepulchre bluffs, Missouri.
Viccia Stipulacca, Upper Louisiana.
Lathyrus Decaphyllus, sand alluvion of the Missouri, above the
    Big Bend.
Lupinus Pusillus, bluffs near Little Cedar Island.
Amorpha Fruticosa, common on the Missouri and Mississippi.
———— *Mycrophylla*, abundant near the Aricara village.
———— *Canescens*, on the prairie four miles west of St. Louis.

Astragalus Racemosus, ⎫ on the bluffs opposite the mouth of
———— *Tryphyllus*, ⎬ Papillon Creek, and at the Aricara
———— *Carnosus*, ⎭ villages.

Dalea Aurea, on the prairies six miles below the L'eau qui Court.
————*Laxiflora*, Aricara village.
[346] *Psoralea Cuspidata*, on the bluffs near the Chienne river.
———— *Longifolia*, near the Sepulchre bluffs. *Probably not a
    Psoralea.*
———— *Elliptica*, sand hills near the Big Bend.
———— *Esculenta*, bluffs near the mouth of Negro Fork, Mer-
    rimac river.
———— *Tenuiflora*, sand hills, Big Bend.
Cytisus Rhombifolius, at the mouth of Chienne river, and on arid
    places near the Aricara village.
Sonchus Pulchellus, banks of the Missouri, common.
Troximum Cuspidatum, common on the prairies between the
    Mahas and Mandans.

Eupatorium Altissimum, Missouri and Mississippi, common.

Oxytropis Lambertii, on the bluffs from the Maha village to the Poncars.

Artemisia Dracunculus,
———— *Cana*,
———— *Campestris*,   } common on the Missouri.
———— *Santonica*,

Arnica fulgens, prairie from the Aricaras to the Mandans.

Cineraria Integrifolia, common on the Missouri.

Erigeron Hirsutum, Aricara village.

———— *Divaricatum*, common on the Missouri.

Senecio Pauperculus, prairie below the L'eau qui Court.

Aster Argenteus, prairie behind St. Louis, abundant.

Amellus Villosus,
———— *Spinulosus*,   } common on the bluffs of the Missouri.

Galardia Acaulis, on the Missouri near the Aricara village. *Probably a Chaptalia.*

Rudbeckia Columnaris, bluffs above the Aricara village. *Most probably not a Rudbeckia, and ought to form a new genus.*

Iva Axillaris, about Chienne river.

Chelianthes Dealbata and *Vestita*, Manitou rocks on the Missouri.